RURAL CREDIT
Access, Use and Repayment

K. Ravichandran
M. Revathi Bala

ABHIJEET PUBLICATIONS
DELHI 110 094

ABHIJEET PUBLICATIONS
2/46 Tukhmeerpur Extension
Delhi-110 094
Phone: 011-22960492, 65698474
E-mail: abhijeetpublication@gmail.com

RURAL CREDIT: ACCESS, USE AND REPAYMENT

First Published 2008

ISBN 978-81-89886-34-9

PRINTED IN INDIA

Published by J.K. Singh for Abhijeet Publications, Delhi-110 094, Lasertypeset by Gaurav Graphices, New Delhi and Printed at Himanshu Printers, Delhi.

RURAL CREDIT
Access, Use and Repayment

Preface

Rural credit encompasses the range of financial services offered in rural areas by Institutional and Non-Institutional Agencies to the people of all income levels. In India the institutionalization of rural credit started with the enactment of the first Cooperative Credit Societies Act in 1904. From then cooperative banks served as important providers of financial services but they have often faced greater crises of financial instability. The nationalization of 14 major commercial banks and the formation of RRBs and NABARD have developed multi-agency approach to rural credit. Now all these Institutional Agencies have covered cent per cent of the Indian villages and significantly contributed for white revolution and green revolution.

However, certain segments of rural population are always away from the services of Institutional Agencies. Agriculture and allied sector is more capital and credit intensive. Institutional Agencies should be more accessible to this sector so as to meet the demand for credit. The World Bank-NCAER Rural Financial Access Survey of 2003 clearly confirmed that access to the formal financial institutions remained severely constrained in rural areas, particularly for the poorest of the households, with informal lending still remaining substantial. Hence, financial inclusion of the poor has become new slogan among the planners. If access to credit is made easy when it is required, half of the problems in the rural credit market could be solved. But the problems pertaining to the access remains complex and deeper than what is generally perceived and understood.

The present study is an attempt to study the access, use and repayment of institutional credit by borrowers in rural Tamilnadu. The study unearthed certain micro level realities and confirmed that the institutional credit available could not mitigate the problem of rural indebtedness in the study area. The study concluded that the proper way-out is not only enhancing the quantum of credit but also making the Institutional Agencies more borrowers' friendly. In this direction a Business Partnership Model is suggested. We take this opportunity to thank the authorities of the Gandhigram Rural University, Dr. P. Sivaprakasam Professor and Head, Dr. B. Subburaj, Professor and other faculty members in the Department of Cooperation, and other friends in Gandhigram Rural University, Gandhigram, for their encouragements and cooperation in every stage of our academic endeavor. We record our sincere thanks to Mr. Singh and his team in Abijit Publications, New Delhi, who have been constantly motivating us and publishing this book very neatly.

Dr. K.Ravichandran
Dr. M. Revathibala

Abbreviations

AAP	-	Annual Action Plan
ACD	-	Agricultural Credit Department
ACP	-	Annual Credit Plan
AIDIS	-	All India Debt and Investment Survey
AIRCSC	-	All India Rural Credit Survey Committee
AIRCRC	-	All India Rural Credit Review Committee
ARDB	-	Agriculture and Rural Development Banks
ARDC	-	Agricultural Refinance and Development Corporation
ARDRS	-	Agricultural Rural Debt and Relief Scheme
CB	-	Commercial Bank
CCDS	-	Cooperative Credit Delivery System
CD Ratio	-	Credit Deposit Ratio

CSO	-	Civil Society Organization
CRAFICARD	-	Committee to Review the Arrangements of Institutional Credit for Agriculture and Rural Development
DAP	-	Development Action Plan
DCCB	-	District Central Cooperative Bank
DCP	-	District Credit Plan
DRDA	-	District Rural Development Agency
GDP	-	Gross Domestic Product
GLC	-	Ground Level Credit
GOI	-	Government of India
HYV	-	High Yield Variety
IA	-	Institutional Agency
IFAD	-	International Fund for Agricultural Development
IFS	-	Informal Sector
IRDP	-	Integrated Rural Development Programme
KCC	-	Kissan Credit Card
LDB	-	Land Development Bank
LMB	-	Land Mortgage Bank
MoU	-	Memorandum of Understanding
NABARD	-	National Bank for Agriculture and Rural Development
NAFSCOB	-	National Federation of State Cooperative Banks
NGO	-	Non-Governmental Organization

NIA	-	Non-Institutional Agency
NPA	-	Non-Performing Assets
NYK	-	Nehru Yuva Kendras
PACB	-	Primary Agricultural Cooperative Bank
PACS	-	Primary Agricultural Cooperative Societies
PCARDB	-	Primary Cooperative Agriculture and Rural Development Bank
PLP	-	Potential Linked Plan
RBI	-	Reserve Bank of India
RCM	-	Rural Credit Marketing
RFI	-	Rural Financing Institution
RPCC	-	Rural Planning and Credit Cell
RRB	-	Regional Rural Bank
SAA	-	Service Area Approach
SAP	-	Service Area Plan
SCARDB	-	State Cooperative Agriculture and Rural Development Bank
SCB	-	State Cooperative Bank
SGSY	-	Swarnajayanthi Gram Swarozgar Yojana
SHG	-	Self–Help Group
TNCDW	-	Tamil Nadu Corporation for Development of Women Ltd.
VVV	-	Vikas Volunteer Vahini

Contents

1

Rural Credit Market in India

Introduction

Indian economy is a rural economy. The growth and development of the economy depends on the smooth flow of rural credit. Credit becomes crucial factor to production if not available at the right time, quantity needed and in the required institutional forms (Upendra Kunwar: 1987, p. 152). The success of credit oriented development project is significantly depended upon the soundness of the credit institution and the credit system. It is not a panacea but one tool, albeit an important one, in the whole process of rural development (Sinha, S.K.: 1992, p. 9).

In India the Rural Credit Market (RCM) is a diversified and complex subject. All the agencies in the supply side in the RCM can be grouped into: 1) Non-Institutional Agencies (NIAs); and 2) Institutional Agencies (IAs). The informal sector i.e., Non-Institutional Agencies, is age old and has no formal rules and regulations. On the other hand the formal sector i.e., Institutional Agencies is a century old and institutional; it is formally monitored, controlled and regulated by legislations. Since the introduction of the first Cooperative Credit Societies Act in 1904, the formal credit market had undergone several changes based on the recommendations of various Commissions and Committees appointed for this purpose. Even then, the NIAs dominate in the RCM. The coexistence of both formal and informal sources of credit makes the subject more complex.

Nature and Functioning of Non-Institutional Agencies

The NIAs are coming under the broad category of informal sector (IFS). Hart in a study of Ghana in 1971 first coined the term 'informal sector' (Hart, Keith: 1971, p. 2). The first official appearance of the term IFS was in the Report of the International Labour Office's (ILO's) Comprehensive Employment Mission to Kenya during 1972. IFS is that segment of labour market in the developing countries that has absorbed significant numbers of job seekers, mostly in a pattern of self-employment. Most of their activities are termed as 'micro enterprises' and are of small, part-time, mostly businesses that are highly labour-intensive in nature. Their activities depend to a large extent on the local and regional demand (Ravichandran, K. and Revathi Bala, M.: 2004, p. 3). To Bouman, the term IFS covers the activities of a great number of intermediaries such as professional and non-professional moneylenders, pawn shops, merchants and petty traders, landlords, shop keepers, indigenous bankers and finance corporations. The present study confined itself with the professional and non-professional moneylenders, who were traditionally called as the NIAs (Martin Patrick: 1999, p. 3).

The NIAs is also termed as unregulated or unorganized market or informal finance or indigenous financial market. The NIAs is largely beyond the official formalities. Its operations are on a small scale and are localized; the transactions remain outside the official statistics. The NIAs, however, is quite efficient because it: (i) provides at any time, doorstep service, (ii) accepts deposits of any amount, (iii) extends credit of any amount for any purpose, and (iv) does not demand complex formalities. They have large capital and greater risk absorbing capacity with them. The NIAs operates in a localized market, and has the full information about its clients (Raja Ram Gupta: 2005, p. 1229).

The NIAs is heterogeneous by nature. It is associated with number of intermediaries such as pawnshops, merchants, petty traders, landlords, indigenous bankers and other private borrowing and lending arrangements. The All-India Debt and Investment Survey (AIDIS) 1951-52 to 2001-02 discussed 6-lender types of players in this market viz., agricultural moneylenders, professional moneylenders, landlords, traders, friends and relatives and others.

Moneylenders

Moneylenders occupy a predominant position among the NIAs in providing rural finance because the household needs of rural people are not confined only to production credit.

Banking is essentially borrowing and lending. The moneylenders do not accept deposits, but they simply lend money and therefore, their business lacks an important element of banking business namely borrowing (Bhagirath Singh: 2004, p. 90). They charge higher rate of interest. There are two kinds of moneylenders in the villages:

- Professional Moneylenders whose main occupation is money lending;
- Non-professional moneylenders or agricultural money lenders whose subsidiary occupation is money lending.

Both these moneylenders are accessible to farmers whenever they need. They have thorough knowledge of the borrowers so that they lend against land promissory note for higher rate of interest. For these groups moneylending is the best known sources of investment. The All India Rural Credit Survey Committee commented that moneylenders not only have an opportunity of amassing wealth mainly through the snowballing of compound interest charges, but also get innumerable pecuniary benefits by acquiring a thorough grip over the peasant's life (RBI: 1954, p. 167).

Landlords and Others

The small farmers have the practice of borrowing money from their landlords. The landlords offer credit based on the landholdings of farmers. They act as a non-professional moneylender. They occupy the lands of farmer—borrowers who do not settle the amount. Consequently the landless labourers are forced to become bonded slaves.

Trader and Commission Agents

Traders and commission agents provide credit to the farmers based on the condition that the farmers should sell their produces at low prices to them. They deduct commission and other charges towards the repayment of loan amount.

Friends and Relatives

Friends and relatives are the most popular sources of rural credit market. They lend money to fulfill the urgent requirements to the selected persons with or without consideration. But moneylending is not a profession for them.

Others

It refers to any other non-institutional credit agency functioning in villages. Chit funds are also fulfilling the financial needs of the rural households in the unorganized sector of RCM. The persons dealing with Chit fund contribute certain amount periodically on an installment basis. Generally, the first installment contribution was availed by the promoter as remuneration. The subsequent contributions will be distributed to the members as loan either by orderly rotation or by lots system.

Market Share of the NIAs

Among the NIAs, Professional Moneylenders are in the top position. Though the relative share of these groups vary over the years their grip over the RCM has not been loosened.

Table 1.1: Share of Institutional and Non-institutional Agencies in Rural Credit

Agency	*1951-52@*	*1961-62#*	*1971-72**	*1981-82**	*1991-92**	*2001-02*
Government	3.3	2.6	7.1	3.9	5.7	5.3
Cooperatives	3.1	15.5	22.0	29.9	23.6	27.3
Commercial banks	0.9	0.6	2.4	28.9	35.2	24.5
Others	-	-	0.2	0.5	0.7	-
All Institutional Agencies	7.3	18.7	31.7	63.2	66.3	57.1
Landlords	1.5	0.6	8.1	3.6	3.7	2.2
Agricultural moneylenders	24.9	36.0	23.0	8.3	6.8	8.1
Professional moneylenders	44.8	13.2	13.1	7.8	10.7	21.5
Traders & Commission Agents	5.5	8.8	8.4	3.2	2.2	3.2
Relatives & Friends	16.2	8.8	13.1	8.7	4.6	6.7
Others	1.8	13.9	2.6	5.2	2.6	1.2
Non-Institutional Agencies	92.7	81.3	68.3	36.8	30.6	42.9
All Agencies	100.0	100.0	100.0	100.0	100.0	100

Sources: 1. @ Report of the All-India Rural Credit Survey Committee, Abridged Ed., (1954), p. 6

2. # All India Debt and Investment Survey 1961, Quoted by Tandon P. L., A Profile of Rural Indebtedness, Social Scientist, Vol.1 6(4), 1988.

3. *GOI (1998), Debt and Investment Survey, Report 420, p. 26.

4. Compiled from various publications of NSSO (1998a, 1998b and 2005).

Table 1.2: Agency-wise Ground Level Credit Flow for Agriculture and Allied Activities at all India Level in Crores)

Agency	*1992-93*	*1993-94*	*1994-95*	*1995-96*	*1996-97*	*1997-98*	*1998-99*	*1999-00*	*2000-01*	*2001-02*	*2002-03*	*2003-04*	*2004-05*	*2005-06*
Coops	9378 (62)	10117 (61)	9406s (50)	10479 (48)	11944 (45)	13975 (43)	15870 (43)	18260 (40)	20718 (38)	23524 (37)	23716 (34)	26959 (31)	31424 (25)	39403 (22)
CBs	4960 (33)	5400 (33)	8255 (44)	10172 (46)	12783 (49)	15831 (50)	18443 (50)	24733 (54)	27807 (53)	33587 (54)	39774 (57)	52440 (60)	81481 (65)	125859 (70)
RRBs	831 (5)	977 (6)	1083 (6)	1381 (6)	1684 (6)	2040 (6)	2460 (6)	3172 (6)	4219 (8)	4854 (8)	6070 (9)	7581 (9)	12404 (10)	15223 (8)
Others	-	-	-	-	-	110 (1)	87 (1)	103 (1)	83 (1)	80 (1)	-	-	-	-
Grand Total	15169	16494	18744	22032	26411	31956	36860	46268	52827	62045	69560	86980	125309	180485
Growth rate	-	8.73	13.64	17.54	19.88	20.99	15.34	25.52	14.17	17.45	12.11	25.04	44.07	44.07

Source: 1. RBI (2004), Task force on revival of Cooperative Credit Institutions.

2. *www.indiabudget.nic.in*

According to the All India Rural Credit Survey Committee (1954), The share of the NIAs in the total rural credit was 92.7 percent in 1951-52. The percentage has come down to 81.3 in 1961-62 and to 68.3 in 1971-72 (Table-1.1). The Cooperative Banks didn't make much progress before independence in reducing the role of NIAs in the RCM. The nationalization of the CBs and the emergence of RRBs widened the branch network in rural areas thereby reducing the market share of NIAs's from 36.8 per cent in 1981-82 to 30.6 per cent in 1991-92 in the RCM. But again, the share of NIAs has increased up to 42.9 percent in the year 2001 – 02. The dominance of NIAs in the RCM has remained as a factor to reckon with.

Nature and Functioning of the Institutional Agencies

The existence of a strong and efficient credit institution is more than half the battle won especially for the developing countries and the success of credit–oriented development project is significantly dependent upon the soundness of the credit structure i.e., of the credit institution and the credit system. It is not a panacea but one tool, albeit an important one in the whole process of rural development (Sinha, S.K.: 1992, p. 9). Credit should be easily accessible, cheap, and safe as well as productive one. Credit becomes a bottleneck to production if it is not available at the right time, in quantity needed and in the required institutional forms (Upendra Kunwar: 1987, p. 152).

The Government of India first entered into the RCM with a scheme of 'Taccavi Loans' under the Land Improvement Loans Act of 1883 and the Agriculturists Loans Act of 1884. This was the first step taken by the Government to frame an agricultural credit policy in the country. The taccavi loans were very small size of loans disbursed during famine and other conditions of distress, at lower rates of interest. These loans were generally inadequate and tied-up with procedures and formalities and were gradually phased out.

The enactment of the Cooperative Credit Societies Act 1904 was the first effort made by the Government in the country to institutionalize agricultural credit by promoting the cooperatives in a corporate form (Ravichandran, K.: 2000, p. 15). The social control in 1967 and consequent nationalization of Commercial Banks (CBs) in 1969 brought the CBs into the forefront of agricultural credit. The emergence of Regional Rural Banks in 1976 (RRBs) and consequent multi-agency approach widened the institutional network for agricultural credit. The National Bank for Agricultural and Rural Development (NABARD) as a national level-refinancing agency has been streamlining the institutional arrangements for finance for agriculture and Rural Development in this country since 1982. The SHGs have become new institutional framework for rural credit after 1990's. The basic objective behind all these arrangements have been to develop a system of institutional credit that is positive, productive and thrift enhancing and to check the menace of usurious practices in rural credit.

Cooperative Credit Delivery System

By the beginning of the 20th Century, the colonial government realized the Indian farmers' dependence on usurious moneylenders as a major cause of their indebtedness and poverty. At that time the cooperative movement had become well established in Europe and achieved remarkable success there. Convinced that the Cooperative movement could offer the best means of liberating the Indian farmers from the crushing burden of debt and the tyranny of moneylenders, the Indian rulers began to take active interest in promoting credit cooperatives in the country (Task Force on Revival of Cooperative Credit Institutions, 2004, p. 8). Based on the recommendations of Edward Law Committee 1901, The Cooperative Credit Societies Act was enacted on 25th March 1904 with the objective of relieving the poor farmers from the clutches of moneylenders and providing cheap and facile means of credit. This was a laudable measure and hailed as a turning point in the economic and social history of India by Henry Wolf. This Act permitted only the formation of the PACS, which laid more emphasis on the promotion of agricultural credit. The Cooperative Societies Act, 1912 was enacted to form non-credit societies also. Based on the recommendations of the Reforms Commission 1919, the subject Cooperation was transferred to Provincial Governments. Though the Royal Commission on Agriculture 1928 opined that if Cooperation failed, the best hope of rural India would fail, the growth of cooperatives in pre-independent India did not make any break-through due to inherent reasons.

The planned development of Cooperatives, in general, and cooperative banks in particular, started with the recommendations of AIRCSC 1954. The Committee observed that 'Cooperation has failed but it must succeed' and recommended State Partnership for the development of cooperatives in the country. As a result of these recommendations, the cooperative banks received substantial support from the RBI, GOI and Sate Governments. Over the period, a number of Committees and Commissions were appointed and the recommendations of these Committees and Commissions were used to tune the functioning of the cooperative banks. The important such Committees were:

- All India Rural Credit Review Committee, 1969,
- Study Team on Overdue, 1974,
- Committee to Review the Arrangements for Institutional Finance for Agriculture and Rural Development, 1980,
- Agricultural Credit Review Committee, 1989,
- Task Force to Study the Cooperative Credit System and Suggest Measures for its Strengthening, 2002 and
- Task Force on Revival of Cooperative Credit Institutions, 2004.

After all these recommendations, the cooperative banks has been developed as an important institutional support for agriculture and rural development in India.

The Structure of Cooperative Credit in India in general consists of two main wings viz., (i) agricultural credit and (ii) non-agricultural credit. In the case of agricultural credit, two separate structures exist—one for short-term and medium term credit and the other for long-term credit—referred here as Cooperative Credit Structure or Cooperative Credit Delivery System (CCDS). The Cooperative Credit Structure for short and medium-term credit is a three tier and federal one with a State Cooperative Bank at the apex level in each State, the Central Cooperative Bank at the

District level and Primary Agricultural Credit Societies/ Primary Agricultural Cooperative Banks/Large Sized Agricultural Multi-Purpose Societies/Farmers Service Societies at the base level. However, the system is not uniform across the country (Annexure-1).

A separate institutional structure for providing long-term credit in the cooperative sector owes its origin to the report of the Meclagan Committee (1915). The first Land Mortgage Bank (LMB) was established at Jhang (in the then Punjab) in 1920. Before nationalization of commercial banks in 1969, the LMBs were the only institutional agency in disbursing long-term agricultural credit. With the establishment of Agricultural Refinance and Development Corporation (ARDC) and subsequently NABARD, these banks also undertook the schematic lending. They also started to provide loan for non-farm activities. The nomenclature of the banks changed from LMBs to Land Development Banks (LDBs) and later to Agriculture and Rural Development Banks (ARDBs). The structure for long-term credit in some States is unitary; in others, constituting the majority, the structure comprises two-tiers viz., the PCARDBs at primary level and SCARDBs at State level (Annexure-1).

At the All India level, all the State Apex Cooperative Banks have their own national federation namely National Federation of State Cooperative Banks from. the year 1967 at Mumbai. Likewise all the State Agriculture and Rural Development Banks have formed their own National Federation of State Agriculture and Rural Development Banks functioning from 1967 at Mumbai. These two federations are not undertaking any banking and financial activities but only coordination and promotional activities.

The CCDS was designed to serve the rural population primarily for agriculture and rural development. The area of operation and functions at each level of the structure were pre-defined. Service was the main concern and not the returns/profitability to the contributors of the capital funds. At present the system consists of 95670 PACS, 3621 LAMPs, and 2477 FSS at primary level, 367 DCCBs and 30 SCBs in the short-term credit structure. There are 1785 PCARDBs and 20 SCARDBs functioning in the long-term credit structure during the year 2002-03 (NCUI: 2004, p. 17-25). This network covered cent percent of Indian villages and more than 70 percent of the rural households (Annexure-2).

Commercial Banks and Rural Credit: The Dawn of Multi-agency Approach in Rural Credit

Commercial Banks in India are organized as joint stock companies and known as banking companies. These banks are primarily classified into scheduled banks and non-scheduled banks, which include Nationalized Banks, State Bank of India and its subsidiaries, Private Sector banks and Foreign Banks. A bank in order to be designated as a scheduled bank should have a paid up capital and reserves as prescribed by the BR Act. The required amount is Rs. 5 lakh. Nationalized banks include the 14 banks nationalized on 19th July 1969 and the 6 banks nationalized in 15th April 1980. Non-scheduled banks are those which are not included in the 2nd Schedule to RBI Act. They are not entitled to get facilities like refinance and rediscounting of bills etc., from RBI.

Nationalization of Commercial Banks

In 1967, the Government considered to bring in far-reaching changes in the concept and working of banking in the country. The Banking Laws (Amendment) Act was passed in 1968 and brought about social control over banks. The main reason for introducing these changes was that the banks should financially assist agriculture, small–scale industries and export more effectively, as these sectors of the country's economy had been neglected so far.

As social control over banks, which was brought into effect form 1st February 1969, was having little impact on the banking system on 19th July 1969, the Government of India nationalized 14 major Indian Banks, having deposits of more than Rs. 50 crore each. The management of these 14 banks was taken over by 14 new corporate bodies, established under the Banking Companies (Acquisition and Transfer of Undertakings) Act, 1970.

On 15th April 1980, six more banks having demand and time liabilities of not less than Rs. 200 crores were nationalized. At present, there are 27 nationalized banks. Apart from SBI and its 7 subsidiaries, there are 19 nationalised banks, owned and wholly managed by GOI through their respective Board of Directors. They are:

1. Bank of Baroda
2. Punjab National Bank
3. Bank of India
4. Canara Bank
5. Central Bank of India
6. Union Bank of India
7. Indian Bank
8. Indian Overseas Bank
9. Syndicate Bank
10. UCO Bank
11. Allahabad Bank
12. United Bank of India

13. Oriental Bank of Commerce
14. Corporation Bank
15. Vijaya Bank
16. Dena Bank
17. Bank of Maharashtra
18. Andhra Bank
19. Punjab and Sind Bank

Role of Commercial Banks in Providing Rural Credit

The Gadgil Study Group on Organizational Framework for the Implementation of Social Objectives in 1967 found that only 5000 villages out of about 6 lakhs could secure very limited credit facilities from CBs (Shukla Mohanthy: 1991, p. 72). About 39 percent of the total credit requirement of agriculture were met by IAs, of which, CBs' share was a meager 1 percent and the rest being that of the cooperatives registering 38 percent (Satish, P.:1998, p. 321). Evidently, the CBs played a limited role in RCM prior to 1969. The role of commercial bank in rural credit had become noteworthy after the year 1969. The integrated rural credit suggested by AIRCSC 1954, the dawn of the green revolution era against the backdrop of the weaknesses in the structure and functioning of cooperative credit institutions brought to light the essential supplementary role of commercial banking in RCM.

The recommendations of the Gadgil Study Group (1969), which provided the base for launching the Lead Bank Scheme, the implications of the recommendations of All India Rural Credit Review Committee (1969) which stressed the need for multi-agency approach in rural credit, the nationalization of 14 major CBs in 1969 and the recommendations of the Nariman Committee on Branch Expansion Programmes in 1969, cumulatively paved the way for a gradual increase in the role of CBs in rural credit. The co-existence of Cooperative Banks and CBs in RCM was hailed as 'Multi-agency Approach'.

Lead Bank

The idea of 'Area Approach' for the deployment of credit and expansion of banking facilities was given concrete shape by the recommendations of Gadgil group during 1969 through the formulation of the Lead Bank scheme. The Lead Bank acts as a leader to coordinate the efforts of all credit agencies in a district. It helps to undertake branch expansions and to meet the credit requirements of the rural economy. They formulate suitable schemes for implementation in their districts.

Lead Banks prepared the first set of District Credit Plans (DCPs) and launched them in July 1978. The RBI issued fresh guidelines for the preparation of DCP during 1979. The DCP covers various fields viz., service sector, storage, distribution of fertilizers, veterinary services, dairy, poultry, sheep breeding etc. All credit institutions functioning in a particular district such as RRBs, CBs, Cooperative Banks, State Finance Corporation and others participated and the schemes are finalized by the Lead Bank. For effective implementation of DCPs, Annual Action Plans (AAP) was prepared as a separate document. A system of preparing AAPs under DCP was first launched in January 1980. The DCPs were formulated and implemented through AAPs as per the guidelines of RBI.

Regional Rural Banks

It was felt that the benefits of the cooperative banking system were not reaching all the farmers in rural areas. A need was felt for an institution in rural and semi-urban areas which combine local knowledge and familiarity with the problems being faced by cooperative banks with the high degree of organizational ability and resource mobilization capacity of Commercial Banks. The Government of India promulgated the RRBs Ordinance on 26th November 1975, which was subsequently abolished with the enactment of RRBs Act 1976 to provide for the incorporation, regulation and winding up of RRBs.

The RRBs were recognized as the special category of CBs. The main objectives of RRBs was to provide credit for the purpose of development of agriculture, trade, commerce, industry and other productive activities in rural areas, particularly to the small and marginal farmers, agricultural laborers, artisans and small entrepreneurs. RRBs provide banking facilities in remote and unbanked areas. At the request of any bank to be called 'sponsor bank', the Central Government may establish in any State or Union Territory one or more Regional Banks, with a minimum issued capital of Rs. 25 lakh, which may be increased later.

- 50% of this issued capital will be subscribed by the Central Government
- 15% by the State Government and
- The balance 35% by the sponsor bank
- The management of the banks will vest in Board of Directors

- The Area of operations of RRBs will be limited to the specified region in any State or Union Territory.

National Bank for Agriculture and Rural Development (NABARD) (1982)

RBI appointed a Committee to Review the Arrangements for Institutional Credit for Agricultural and Rural Development (CRAFICARD) in March 1979. It reviewed the existing institutional arrangement for agricultural and rural credit under the chairmanship of Mr. B. Sivaraman. The Committee submitted its report in January 1981. Based on the recommendations of CRAFICARD, the NABARD came into existence on 12th July 1982 by an Act of Parliament. NABARD took over the functions of erstwhile Agricultural Credit Department (ACD) and Rural Planning and credit cell of RBI (RPCC) and Agricultural Refinance and Development Corporation (ARDC).

NABARD aimed to promote sustainable and equitable agriculture and rural prosperity through effective credit support, institutional development and other innovative initiatives. It undertakes credit functions, development functions and supervisory functions.

Potential Linked Credit Plan

NABARD has been preparing Potential Linked Credit Plans (PLCPs) from the Seventh Five Year Plan onwards. The PLCP was made available to all banks and developmental functionaries in the district well in advance. It provides realistic ground level information to estimate the credit needs of bank branches in their respective service area at bank level, block level and district level, so that the Lead Bank Manager can finalize the Annual Credit Plan (ACP) of the particular year in time.

Service Area Approach

The RBI* adopted the Service Area Approach (SAA) after considering the recommendations of the Ojha Committee set-up on 29th March 1988. The scheme came into operation from April 1989. This approach plugs the loopholes in the Lead Bank Scheme. The SAA envisages bottom-up approach whereas the Lead Bank Officer opts for the top-down approach. The SAA involves five stages in its operational dynamic (Shukla & Mohanthy: 1991, p. 73):

1) Identification of service area for each branch;
2) Survey of the service area and identification of potential for lending;
3) Preparation of realistic credit plans on annual basis;
4) Coordination between credit institutions and field level development agencies on an ongoing basis; and
5) Continuous system of monitoring the progress of implementation of credit plan, recovery etc.

This new system had some distinct advantages:

1) Branch Managers would be able to focus attention to the development of designated service area;

2) Duplication of efforts by several banks in the same area could be avoided;
3) As the lending would be concentrated, the post disbursement supervision of credit will be more organized and systematic; and
4) The Branch Manger would develop a sense of involvement and commitment on the success of these plans, as he is responsible for its conception and implementation.

After the introduction of the SAA, the credit plans were formulated at bottom level to top. The credit plan was prepared for each of the villages in the service area. After the finalization of village plans, they were aggregated into Service Area Plans at branch level. The Block level credit plans includes the SAPs of all agencies as well as non-service areas within the block.

Development Action Plan

The majority of the cooperative banks in RCM were not strong units and suffered from many deficiencies such as inadequate capital, high level of overdue, political interferences, lack of autonomy and independence etc. In order to make the weak cooperatives viable, the NABARD introduced Development Action Plans in 1994-95 in which viability of the units were examined. The Apex Bank and the State Government have signed Memorandum of Understanding (MoU) with NABARD assuring successful implementation of the DAP.

Self Help Groups and Rural Credit

Poor households need access to a basket of financial

services than just micro credit. Appropriate savings and insurance, as well as loans for emergency expenditure or basic expenses such as education, medical and family could contribute to social and economic security as against the poverty cycle not least among the poorer but more among the vulnerable households. The IAs that ought to cater to the rural credit needs, public or private, have shunned the rural areas for various reasons, which include opportunity cost and low financial creditability. Inadequacies in access to formal finance and the extortionate terms of informal finance demand innovative approaches to serve the financial needs of India's rural poor. Over the last decade Government, financial institutions, and the NGOs made efforts, often in partnership, to develop new financial delivery approaches combining the safety and reliability of formal finance with the convenience and flexibility that are typically associated with informal finance (Priya Basu, Pradeep Srivastava: 2005, p. 1747).

Concept of Self–help Groups

Self–Help Group (SHG) is a small economically homogeneous and affinity group of people, voluntarily formed to save and contribute to a common fund to be lent among its members as per the group decisions and for working together for social and economic uplift of their families and community.

The concept of SHG becomes a viable organized set up to disburse micro credit to the rural women and encourage them to enter into entrepreneurial activities. The socio-economic constraints, which prevented the women's potential for development, have been pushed back through the formation of SHGs.

The group savings in SHGs serve a wide range of objectives other than immediate investments. The following are the objectives of SHGs.

1) To serve as an alternative credit agency for people who do not have easy access to formal banking system.
2) To develop skills for mobilizing savings and credit.
3) To lend within the group on rotational or need basis.
4) To enable banking to poor by ensuring cent percent recovery
5) To promote team spirit among the members in involving economic activities from available resources.
6) To enhance the standard of living of group members and ensure sustainability.
7) To bring an egalitarian society irrespective of caste, creed, race or religion.
8) To enable the poor to live with dignity and self-discipline.
9) To develop harmony, group cohesiveness and neighborliness among the people.

The Working Pattern of SHGs

Generally, the workings of SHGs are confined to mobilization of deposits and lending of loans.

1) Collecting deposits from their members and lending to the needy members for production and consumption purposes.

2) Borrowing loans from banks or voluntary agencies or SHPIs (Self Help Promoting Institutions) in the name of group to meet the credit needs of the members.

3) Convening the group meetings periodically and maintaining records for the transactions.

4) Motivating group members to undertake micro enterprises using locally available resources.

5) Contributing to the socio-economic and cultural development of the village.

Operational Characteristics of SHGs

The following are some of the functional/operational characteristics of SHGs:

1) Groups generate a common fund where each member contributes equally his/her savings on regular basis. The amount of money for regular savings in fixed by the group.

2) Groups meet periodically to discuss their transactions. Attendance is compulsory.

3) Amount of loan, rate of interest and the borrowers are decided by consensus among members.

4) Loans cover a variety of purposes, which includes consumption purposes.

5) Loan amount is small and repayable within short duration

6) Loan procedure is very simple and flexible

7) Defaults are unnoticed phenomenon

8) Rate of recovery generally more than cent

percent, i.e., group members used to repay the installments in advance.

SHG–Bank Linkage Models

In order to facilitate smoother and meaningful banking with the poor, a modest pilot project for providing micro credit by linking SHGs with banks was launched by NABARD in 1991-92. Now, the formal banking system could reach the doorsteps of 116 lakh poor households, providing micro-credit to them through 7.17 lakh SHGs. NABARD's mission under SHG-Bank linkage programme aimed at the economic empowerment of the rural poor by improving their access to the formal credit system through various credit innovations in a cost effective and sustainable manner.

Further, women had poor access to credit with formal agencies. Formation of SHGs would ensure best satisfaction of the poor in a credit programme by providing self-employment and economic empowerment to the rural women who lack access to formal credit institutions (Human Development Centre: 2004, p. 89). Formations of these groups successfully mobilize and manage thrift and savings, cater credit needs and enforce financial self-discipline among the rural women. Hence, the UN declared the year 2005 as the 'International Year of Micro credit'.

There have come into existence three types of SHG-Bank linkage models across the country.

Model I–SHGs Formed and Financed by the Banks

Under this model, the banks themselves act as Self Help Promoting Institutions (SHPIs) i.e., the banks themselves form the groups, open savings account and provides loans to SHG.

Model II–SHGs Formed by NGOs But Directly Financed by Banks

In this model NGOs in the field of micro finance act as facilitators. NGOs form the groups and train them in thrift and credit management. Banks, in due course, link these groups by directly providing loans to them. A major number of SHGs have come under this model.

Model III: SHGs Financed by Banks using NGOs as Financial Intermediaries

In this model, NGOs take on the dual role of facilitators and financial intermediaries. They help in the formation of the SHGs, train them in thrift and credit management. Eventually, the NGOs approach banks for bulk loan assistance for on lending to these SHGs.

At the all India level, therefore, the Cooperative Banks, CBs, RRBs and SHGs have become RFIs and their loan operations are being streamlined by the NABARD.

Market Share of Institutional Agencies

The share of IAs in the RCM increased from mere 7.3 per cent in 1951-52 to 66.3 percent in 1991-92 (Refer Table - 1.1). It stood 57.1 percent in the year 2001 – 02.However, still more than 30 per cent of the rural credit has to be sourced from NIAs and as a result the performance of IAs in RCM has attracted lot of criticism from the planners, academicians and researchers. Further, the grip of NIAs over the RCM could be witnessed through the reported farmer suicides (Refer chapter 3, Box 2).

The growth of employment and reduction in poverty are both infinitely linked to growth performance, especially in agriculture, which employs about 60 percent of the labour force. A systematic approach is needed to enhance agricultural productivity. It means all the inputs must be made available to the farmers in right time and in right quantity. But the deplorable condition of agriculture could be seen from the fact that the number of agricultural holdings has been about 115 million, of which, over three fourth were marginal and small. Their average size was a bare 0.40 hectares for the marginal and 1.44 hectares for the small farmers. The handicap of size of holdings was compounded by the fact that a vast majority of them, about 86 per cent, have been condemned to high cost credit from moneylenders; and supply of credit has not been accompanied by technical advice (*The Hindu*: 2005, p. 11).

Paradoxically enough, India which has been a pioneer in evolving its own brand of institutional framework for rural credit should today find its entire rural credit system in a moribund state. This holds true for all the three wings of the rural credit delivery system—rural branches of CBs, cooperative credit institutions and RRBs. The deterioration in the status of the rural credit system has not been by default but by design (Majumdar, N.A.: 2002, p. 264).

The multi agency approach adopted for rural credit in India is the reflection of the need for different players in this field. When the social control was imposed on

CBs in 1967, it was felt that CBs could also play a major role in the agricultural credit. The trend in the rural banking over the period found that no one agency could succeed in their respective role. The GLC flows as the major indicator of growth showed that the total amount pumped to agriculture and allied activities by the IAs was around Rs. 962 crores during the year 1970-71.

Though agriculture was stated to be a State subject, this sector was considered to be the bedrock of economy during all Central Plans. This resulted in increase in the flow of agricultural credit at ground level from Rs. 15169 crores in 1992-93 to Rs. 62045 crores during the year 2001-02. At the end of 2005–06, it stood Rs. 180485 crores (Table 1.2).

Notwithstanding the shortfalls in meeting Annual Plan Targets, the credit flow to agriculture has steadily increased in both absolute and relative terms. However, there were some trends that were inimical to agricultural lending as noted by the Advisory Committee that looked into the flow of credit to agriculture and allied activities.

Table 1.3: Ratio of Agricultural Credit to Agricultural GDP and Total Credit

Period	*Agricultural Credit as % of Total Credit*	*Agricultural Credit as % of Agricultural GDP*
1970s	5.4	20.5
1980s	8.3	20.1
1990s	7.4	14.4
2001-02	8.7	10.5

Source: Handbook of Statistics on Indian Economy, 2002-03, RBI.

The decline in the share of agricultural credit in total credit from 20.5 percent to 10.5 percent between the 1970s and 2001-02 (despite an increase in the ratio of agricultural credit to agricultural GDP from 5.4 percent to 8.7 percent) suggests a decline in the capital and credit intensity of the sector. Agriculture is both capital and credit intensive sector (Table – 1.3).

Regional disparities in the disbursement of credit with the Southern States claiming nearly 43 percent indicates a near perpetuation of the existing inequitable distribution of development benefits across regions. The predominance of large farmers in total credit disbursement is yet another disturbing trend (Tara S Nair: 2005, p. 1697 and RBI: 2004, p. 36). At the same time according to the Debt and Investment Survey 1991, the incidence of debt was high in Andhra Pradesh and Tamil Nadu and exceptionally high proportion of the households were indebted to NIAs.

The agency-wise analysis showed that the cooperative banks were supposed to be the dominant agency in the formal credit systems before the nationalization of CBs. This condition continued even during the Eighth Plan. However, their relative share to the total GLC flow came down to 37 percent during the year 2001-02 and 21.83 per cent in the year 2005 -06. Though the amount of loan provided by the cooperative banks was low compared to that of CBs and RRBs, the number of loan accounts was high as they were mainly dealt with the small, marginal and tenant farmers (NABARD: 2001-02, p. 15). However, the entire CCDS suffered owing to high levels of loan delinquency, erosion of capital base, paucity of funds for fresh deployment, high level of dependence on higher tiers for funds, lack of professionalism in management, inadequate internal controls and governance structure and non-adherence to norms and regulations. Often this has resulted in, the borrowers, taking the eligible amount from the Cooperative Banks and, maintaining regular account with the commission agents/traders for additional requirements. Money being fungible, often the borrowing from the Cooperative Bank was diverted for meeting other emergent requirements. In the absence of an effective arrangement to meet the total credit requirements of the farmer, the cooperatives generally failed to develop relationship banking with clients and in the process, the private moneylenders maintained a closer relationship with the farmers and also acquired priority in getting repayments. Overtime, these handicaps have become more pronounced and the cooperative banks are being viewed as mere lending institutions rather than providers of a full range of financial services. Various operational restrictions have also been introduced by the multiple supervisors making their working largely dominated by supply side consideration rather than demand side needs (Balasaheb Vikhe Patil: 2005, p. 1225).

The various Committees that examined the problems of agricultural credit, while recognizing the role of CBs, have concluded that in the Indian conditions, there remains no alternative to the cooperatives at the village level for the provision of agricultural credit. The Rural Credit Survey Committee (1954) had made the historical statement that "the cooperatives have failed, but cooperation must succeed" (Balasaheb Vikhe Patil: 2005, p. 1224). The Agricultural Credit Review Committee (1989, p. 188) stated that Indian agriculture had a vital stake in the success of cooperatives because one should believe that there is no better or more responsive and cost effective credit system than the cooperatives to serve the ever growing and diversifying needs of agriculture. Expectation from the nationalized banks/CBs towards agricultural lending after nationalization in 1969 has not yielded any significant contribution (Subrahmanyam: 2003, p. 13). Evidently, credit per bank in rural areas have increased from only Rs. 88.44 crores in 1995-96 to Rs.201.95 crores in 2001-02 and Rs. 614 crores in 2005 -06, which is only 20 percent to total credit. Also the CD ratio came down from 46.9 per cent in 1995-96 to 56 .3 percent in 2005-06 (Table 1.4).

Table 1.4: Credit per Bank and CD Ratio in Rural Areas

Years	*Credit per bank (Rs. in lakh)*	*CD Ratio*
	All India	*All India*
1995-96	88.44	46.9
1996-97	98.08	44.1
1997-98	172.83	64.8
1998-99	125.29	40.0
1999-00	148.01	39.7
2000-01	173.77	40.1
2001-02	201.95	41.1
2002 - 03	272.32	42.2
2003-04	323.58	43.7
2004 -05	416.02	43.7
2005 -06	548.43	56.3

Source: 1. RBI (2006), Banking Statistics, Quarterly Hand out, March Mumbai.

In the case of the SHG credit linkages, the CBs have played a pivotal role that has linked 50 per cent of the groups. Only 12 per cent of the groups have credit linkage with the cooperatives and they disbursed loans also to the extent of only 10 per cent in this connection (Table 1.5). At the end of the year 2005 – 06,. there were 1079091 SHGs which have disbursed loan up to Rs. 39042.08 crores.

Table 1.5: Progress of SHG-Bank Linkage in India (As on 31st March 2005–06)

(Figures in numbers)

Agency	SHGs		Bank Loan	
	Number	%	*Number*	%
Commercial Bank	538422	50	22548.29	58
RRBs	405998	38	12782.58	32
Cooperatives	134671	12	3711.21	10

Source: NABARD (2003), Progress of SHG–Bank Linkage in India, quoted by Mishra, J.K & Thani, R.K. (2004), *Kurukshetra*, Vol. 52(4), p. 15.

The bank loan disbursed was Rs.57 crores in 1999, which increased to Rs.11397.55 crores during the year 2005-06. The refinance from NABARD also multiplied from 52.09 crores in 1999 to 4153.63 crores in 2006 (Table 1.6). Around 90 percent of the SHGs linked were exclusively women SHGs. This level of success was because of the close cooperation and coordination between different field level partners in micro finance, viz., banks, NGOs and the Government agencies. The policy support extended by GOI and RBI and various initiatives taken by the NABARD, including capacity building of partner agencies, contributed to the success of the programme. It is expected that nearly 100 million rural people would get services through 1 million SHGs during the year 2008 (NABARD: 2002-03, p. 4).

A recent study on the impact of Micro Finance on the living standards of SHG members conducted by NABARD has shown extremely positive results. The studies compared the socio-economic conditions in pre and post SHG situations (spanning an average period of 3 years) of the 560 members of 223 SHGs located in 11 states across 5 regions. The findings are given in table 1.7.

Table 1.6: SHG-Bank Linkage Programme–At All India level

(As on 31st March)

Year	*SHGs Financed (No.)*	*Bank Loans Disbursed (Rs. Crore)*	*SHGs Refinanced (No.)*	*Refinance Disbursed (Rs. Crore)*
1999	32,995	57.07	32,995	52.09
2000	1,14,775	192.98	94,645	150.13
2001	2,63,825	480.87	2,13,213	400.74
2002	4,61,478	1,026.34	3,40,131	796.47
2003	7,17,360	2,048.67	4,93,634	1418.80
2004	1079091	3904.21	573824	2718.15
205	1618456	6898.46	642337	3085.91
2006	2238565	11397.55	787021	4153.63

Source: 1. NABARD (2002-03), Annual Report, p. 123.

2. *www.indiabudget.nic.in*

Nature and Functioning of Institutional Agencies in Tamil Nadu

A prelude on the topographic conditions of the State will help to understand the operational dynamics of the RCM in this state. Tamilnadu is located in North Latitude between 8° 5′ and 13° 35′, and East Longitude between 76° 15′ and 80° 20′. It lies on the Southern tip of the country with Kerala State on West, Andhra Pradesh and Karnataka on the North, Bay of Bengal on the East and Indian Ocean down the South. For administrative convenience the State was divided into 30 districts including the State capital Chennai and further into 206 Taluks. Total geographical area of the State is 12.99 million ha. This is around 4.4 per cent of the total geographical area of the country. The entire Eastern part of the State has coastline—having length of around 1000 kms. The climate is mainly tropical with temperatures ranging between 43°C and 18°C. The State receives moderate rainfall, the major share (around 48 per cent) of which is received through North East monsoon during the months of October and December. Total population in the State was 62.11 million as per 2000-01 census. The State has more than 6 percent of the country's population and it holds sixth position in terms of size of population at 2.99 million among the States and Union Territories.

Table 1.7: Impact of Micro Finance on the Living Standard of SHG Members

		Findings	
S. No.	*Parameters*	*Pre SHG situation*	*Post SHG situation*
1.	Member households		• Landless agricultural labourers: 31% • Marginal farmers: 23% • Small farmers: 29% • Others: 17%

2.	Average value of assets	Rs. 6843	Rs. 11,793
3.	Increase in assets	-58%	+58%
4.	Housing conditions	Kucha	Pucca
5.	Savings habit	23%	100%
6.	Average annual savings	Rs. 460	Rs. 1444 per household
7.	Average borrowings	Rs. 4282	Rs. 8341
8.	Average net income	Rs. 20177	Rs. 26889
9.	Sources of income generation		NFS – 43%, Farm – 28% Off-farm – 21%
10.	Percentage of income earned below 22,500	74%	57%
11.	Employment increased	318 man days	375 man days (18% increase)
12.	Consumption loans	50%	25%
13.	Overall loan repayments to banks	84%	94%
14.	Annual interest rates on loans from SHGs to members		12% to 24% range
15.	Incidence of family violence	High	Low
16.	Self-worth and communication with others	Moderate	Well improved

Source: NABARD (2001-02), State Level Seminar, State Focus Paper, p. 62.

Tamil Nadu is predominantly an agrarian state. Agriculture provides livelihood to 65 percent of the State's population and contributes to 62 percent of employment generated in the State. Its contribution to Net Domestic Product declined from 25 per cent (1980-81) to 17 per cent (1999-2000) (NABARD (2004-05, p. 14). The State had 8.23 million farm holdings and 73 percent of them were marginal farmers having area less than one ha. and they operated 29 percent of the total area. The small farmers (owning 1 ha. to 2 ha.) had a share of 16 percent in number and 23 percent of the operated area. Semi-medium and medium farmers accounted for 10 percent in number and 40 percent in the operated area. Large farmers with more than 10 ha. had negligible number of operational holdings and the area operated remained at 8 percent. The average size of holdings in the State was 0.91ha. Of the total gross cropped area of 6.52 m.ha. in the State more than 71 percent (4.66 m.ha.) was under food crops cultivation during 1999-2000. Major food crops in the State include paddy, maize, ginger millet and pulses like black gram, greengram, etc., Non food crops like cotton, groundnut, gingelly, coconut and fodder crops covered 29 per of gross cropped area. High Yielding Varieties (HYV) covered more than 91 percent of the total area under cereals cultivation in the State. Notably around 96 per cent area under paddy cultivation was covered by HYV.

In Tamilnadu also the Cooperative Banks, CBs, RRBs and the SHGs are the IAs in rural credit. The performance of this system at macro level has its profound impact at State and District level also. The State is well linked with the CCDS and the CBs. The State has its credit with many laurels in the rural credit. They are discussed hereunder.

Functioning of Cooperative Credit Delivery System in Tamilnadu

It was then the Government of Madras which appointed one of its Senior Officers, Sir Frederick Nicholson, as early as 1892, to study the methods of land and agricultural banks of Europe, and to report how best such institutional models could be adapted to suit Indian conditions, especially in the Madras Presidency,

Table 1.8: Growth of PACS at All India, Tamil Nadu and District Level

(Rs in Crores)

Parameters	1990-91			1991-92			1992-93			1993-94			1994-95		
	India	TN	DGL	India	TN	DGL	India	TN	DGL	India	TN	DGL	India	TN	DGL
No. of societies (in numbers)	82905	4614	273	82560	4644	273	90025	4568	196	91592	4583	196	91110	4589	197
Membership	8.01	0.069	NA	8.68	0.71	NA	9.06	0.72	NA	8.89	0.74	NA	9.06	0.77	NA
Deposits	1348.97	160.85	28.43	1605.00	171.85	32.30	1943.24	312.72	55.43	2102.35	465.10	62.90	2961.77	598.59	67.97
Loans & Advances	4678.85	282.49	44.08	4973.31	342.49	58.67	6980.76	789.46	74.25	7510.70	1165.93	83.38	10794.71	1556.22	89.42
Percentage of O/D to Demand	45.5	N.A	N.A	39.15	N.A	N.A	45.95	N.A	N.A	42.81	27.5	N.A	33.94	24.8	29.5

Parameters	1995-96			1996-97			1997-98			1998-99			1999-2000		
	India	TN	DGL	India	TN	DGL	India	TN	DGL	India	TN	DGL	India	TN	DGL
No. of societies (in numbers)	92327	4589	197	91588	4589	197	92838	4559	197	95156	4418	197	101545	4589	197
Membership	9.05	0.79	NA	8.03	0.78	NA	8.02	0.79	NA	8.96	0.79	-	10.84	0.84	NA
Deposits	3789.85	1100.23	88.80	5108.09	838.44	131.70	5279.19	1642.34	138.90	7061.70	2136.76	147.90	12283.61	3227.58	159.80
Loans & Advances	12732.09	2454.43	103.76	13605.89	1774.43	151.45	13723.99	2691.89	156.82	17767.80	2997.50	174.40	23297.97	3805.08	79.80
Percentage of O/D to Demand	34.69	29.8	N.A.	35.27	28.8	NA	34.95	32.4	NA	35.45	32.32	NA	35.22	29.12	NA

Table 1.8: *(Contd...)*

Parameters	2000-2001			2001-2002			2002-2003			2003-2004			2004-2005			2005-2006		
	India	TN	DGL	India	TN	DGL	India	TN	DGL	India	TN	DGL	India	TN	DGL	India	TN	DGL
No. of societies (in numbers)	100604	4589	197	95670	4586	197	98000	4573	197	112000	4516	197	106000	4497	197	105735	4482	197
Membership	10.98	0.89	NA	10.28	0.89	NA	10.21	0.91	NA	12.36	0.89	NA	13.54	0.92	NA	15.82	0.96	NA
Deposits	10996.16	3687.87	217.54	13135.32	4327.83	192.36	14846	8906.06	208.33	19120	2813.23	232.16	18143	2605.47	230.86	18142.53	2458.3	242.71
Loans & Advances	24738.57	6520.64	62.28	2936.44	4154.04	2.87	30770	4247	43.32	33996	3433	49.83	35177	4447	61.18	37142.28	4112.73	58.72
Percentage of O/D to Demand	34.27	29	NA	34.83	59.90	NA	41.22	53.24	NA	39.28	54.32	NA	36.18	49.86	NA	37.26	47.18	NA

Sources: 1. NAFSCOB (1999-2000), Performance of Primary Agricultural Credit Societies, p. 1.

2.NCUI (2004), Indian Cooperative Movement–A Profile, p. 17 & 18.3.GOI (1993), Cooperative Movement in India–A Statistical Profile.

3. Compiled from the Annual Reports of NABARD for various years.

4. NABARD (2006–07), Tamil Nadu State Focus Paper, p. 19.

Note: N.A.—Not Available

Table 1.9: Position of PCARDBs at All India, State and District Level

(Rs in Crores)

Parameters	*1990-91*			*1991-92*			*1992-93*			*1993-94*		
	India	*TN*	*DGL*	*India*	*TN*	*DGL*	*India*	*TN*	*DGL*	*India*	*TN*	*DGL*
No. of PCARDBs	709	181	6	709	181	6	709	181	6	727	181	6
Deposits	15.80	4.76	1.79	18.85	7.63	2.82	22.28	9.89	3.86	54.69	24.18	11.73
Loans & Advances	375.46	31.32	9.82	393.08	98.34	23.74	447.22	116.77	31.07	513.21	139.25	33.81
Percentage of O/D to Demand	48	45.2	N.A	47	35.7	N.A	45	40	N.A	45	28	N.A

Parameters	*1994-95*			*1996-97*			*1997-98*			*1998-99*		
	India	*TN*	*DGL*	*India*	*TN*	*DGL*	*India*	*TN*	*DGL*	*India*	*TN*	*DGL*
No. of PCARDBs	732	181	6	738	181	6	745	181	6	755	181	6
Deposits	63.46	32.83	12.88	94.77	49.96	16.71	99	58.29	16.79	166	70.43	17.72
Loans & Advances	936	249.17	34.36	1477	297.03	38.60	1594	244.19	37.30	1735	211.33	43.50
Percentage of O/D to Demand	57	18	N.A	46	57	65.9	39.8	56.5	65.9	41.3	53	60.9

Table 1.9: *(Contd...)*

Parameters	*2000-2001*			*2001-2002*			*2002-03*			*2003-04*			*2004-05*			*2005-06*		
	India	*TN*	*DGL*	*India*	*TN*	*DGL*	*98000*	*4573*	*197*	*112000*	*4516*	*197*	*106000*	*4497*	*197*	*105735*	*482*	*197*
No. of PCARDBs	732	181	6	755	181	6	10.21	0.91	NA	12.36	0.89	NA	13.54	0.92	NA	15.82	0.96	NA
Deposits	235	64.24	18.82	322	63.83	13.37	14846	2906.06	28.33	19120	2813.23	232.16	18143	2605.47	230.86	18145.53	2458.30	242.71
Loans & Advances	1865	231.68	54.83	1943	153.12	57.79	30770	4247	43.32	33996	3433	49.83	35177	4447	61.18	37142.28	4112.73	58.72
Percentage of O/D to Demand	45	57.2	72.4	50.8	56.5	78.2	41.22	53.24	NA	39.28	54.32	NA	36.18	49.86	NA	37.26	47.18	NA

Sources: (1) NABARD (1993-94), PLP for DGL District (with detailed projections), p. 12.

(2) NABARD (1994-95 to 2001-02), PLP for DGL District.

(3) NABARD (1997-98 to 2001-02), PLP for DGL District (with detailed projections), p. 9.

(4) NABARD (2002-2007), PLP for DGL District, p. 11.

(5) GOI (1993), Cooperative Movement in India–Statistical Profile, p. 24.

(6) NCUI (1993), Indian Cooperative Movement–A Profile, p. 13.

(7) NABARD (1993-1994), Important items of data related to credit and non-credit cooperative societies, p. 88.

(8) NABARD (1999), Dossier on Cooperatives - State wise

(9) Status of the Cooperative Credit structure, March, p. III, p. 221.

(10) GOI (1999), Cooperative Movement in India–A Statistical Profile, 1998, p. 34. (12) NCUI (2004), Indian

(11) Cooperative Movement–A Profile, p. 26 & 27.

Note: N A.- Not Available

Table 1.10: Model-wise Position of SHGs Linked with Banks (at the End of March 2006)

(Rs. in crores)

S. No	*Model*	*No. of SHGs*	*Bank Loan*	*Refinance*
i)	SHGs financed by banks without intervention of any NGO	26483.76	251.69	142.46
		(12)	(15)	(16)
ii)	SHGs formed by NGOs and financed directly by banks	176558.4	1325.54	685.58
		(80)	(79)	(77)
iii)	SHGs financed by banks through NGOs	17655.84	100.67	62.32
		(8)	(6)	(7)
	Total	220698	1677.90	890.36

Source: 1. NABARD (2004-05), State Level Credit Seminar—State Focus Paper,Tamil Nadu, p. 167.

2. NABARD (2006-07), State Level Credit Seminar—State Focus Paper,Tamil Nadu, p. 191.

Note: Figures in brackets are percentage to total.

Table 1.11: Agency-wise Ground Level Credit Flow for Agriculture and Allied Activities at Tamil Nadu Level

(Rs in Crores)

Agency	1992-93	1993-94	1994-95	1995-96	1996-97	1997-98	1998-99	1999-00	2000-01	2001-02	2002-03	2003-04	2004-05	2005-06
Co-ops.	596	901	913	1015	1130	1307	1714	2011	2170	2319	2623	2727	3189	4205
	(26)	(31)	(26)	(23)	(21)	(20)	(24)	(23)	(21)	(20)	(20)	(18)	(17)	
CBs	1437	1750	2264	3097	3810	4464	4999	6175	7070	8437	9449	11200	14858	16780
	(62)	(61)	(65)	(66)	(70)	(70)	(70)	(71)	(72)	(74)	(74)	(76)	(78)	(76)
RRBs	48	45	65	78	116	146	152	202	252	290	382	552	692	779
	(2)	(2)	(2)	(2)	(2)	(2)	(2)	(2)	(3)	(2)	(3)	(4)	(4)	(4)
Others	238	196	238	436	359	477	269	357	386	386	370	306	261	272
	(10)	(6)	(7)	(9)	(7)	(8)	(4)	(4)	(4)	(4)	(3)	(2)	(1)	(1)
Grand Total	2319	2892	3480	4726	5415	6394	7134	8745	9878	11432	12825	14785	19000	22036
	(100)	(100)	(100)	(100)	(100)	(100)	(100)	(100)	(100)	(100)	(100)	(100)	(100)	(100)
Growth Rate		24.7	20.3	35.8	14.6	18.1	11.6	22.6	12.9	15.73	12.19	15.28	28.51	15.97

Source: Complied from State Level Credit Seminar, Stare Focus Paper, NABARD, Chennai for various years.

Table 1.12: Agency wise Ground Level Credit Flow for Agriculture and Allied Activities at Tamil Nadu level (Target and Achievement)

(Rs in Crores)

Agency	1998-1999			1999-2000			2000-2001			2001-2002		
	Target	Achieve Ment	% of Achieve Ment	Target	Achieve Ment	% of Achieve Ment	Target	Achieve Ment	% of Achieve Ment	Target	Achieve Ment	% of Achieve Ment
Coops.	1893.36	1713.56	90.50	2140.33	2010.47	93.93	2457.85	2170.01	88.29	2500	2320.06	92.80
CBs	5039.28	4998.24	99.19	5878.95	6174.75	105.03	6818.45	7071.45	103.71	7670.00	8436.16	109.99
RRBs	117.57	152.25	129.50	140.12	201.91	144.10	157.17	251.28	159.88	196.76	290.24	147.51
Others	354.17	270.08	76.26	295.26	357.49	121.07	307.67	385.29	125.23	688.88	385.68	55.99
Total	7404.38	7134.13	96.35	8454.66	8744.62	103.43	9741.14	9878.03	101.41	11055.64	11432.14	103.41

Table 1.12: *(Contd...)*

Agency	2002-03			2003-04			2004-05			2005-06
	Target	*Achievement*	*% of Achieve Ment*	*Target*	*Achievement*	*% of Achieve Ment*	*Target*	*Achievement*	*% of Achieve Ment*	*Target*
Coops.	2991.96	2623.43	87.68	3167.4	2726.9	86.09	3698.4	3189.26	86.23	4204.9
CBs	8823.11	9448.75	107.09	9970.5	11200.8	112.34	13377.6	14858.13	111.71	16780.5
RRBs	222.13	382.38	172.15	270.7	551.1	203.59	590.8	691.95	136.22	778.6
Others	312.88	370.81	173.54	308.2	306.3	99.38	275.8	261.56	144.15	271.6
Total	12350.08	12825.37	103.85	13716.8	14785.1	107.79	17942.6	19000.9	105.90	22035.6

Source: Complied from State Level Credit Seminar, Stare Focus Paper, NABARD, Chennai for various years.

Table 1.13: Credit Gap at State Level

(Amount in Rs. in crores)

Year	State Level			District Level		
	PLP	GLC	Credit gap	PLP	GLC	Credit gap
1998-99	7404	7134	270	235	232	2.72
1999-00	10997	8745	2252	300	243	57
2000-01	12480	9878	2602	343	303	40
2001-02	11379	11622	243	453	406	47
2002-03	12510	12825	315	452	405.91	46.09
2003-04	14499	14785	286	421	487.07	66.07
2004-05	18708	19000	292	531	603.18	72.18
2006-06	21763	22036	273	773	822.10	49.1

Source: Compiled from NABARD—State Focus Paper and PLP for Dindigul District for various years.

in order to relieve the poor people from indebtedness. Thiru Sir D. Rajagopalachariar, the first Registrar of Cooperative Societies, registered the first Cooperative Society in India at Thirur village in the present Thiruvalluvar District of Tamil Nadu on 30.08.1904 under the 1904 Act. After the enactment of 1919 Act, the cooperatives became State subject and the Madras State Cooperative Societies Act was introduced in 1932. Like this, there were many laurels to the Cooperative Movement of Tamil Nadu. The Act, which is now in force in Tamil Nadu, is the Tamil Nadu Cooperative Societies Act, 1983, and Tamil Nadu Cooperative Societies Rules 1988. In the case of Short–term Cooperative Credit Structure, there have been 4482 PACBs and 24 DCCBs (with 755 branches) and the Tamil Nadu State Apex Cooperative Bank has been functioning with 41 branches. In the case of Long-term Cooperative Credit Structure, there have been 181 PCARDBs and the Tamil Nadu State Agriculture and Rural Development Bank head quartered at Chennai has been functioning with 20 Regional Offices.

However, the present state and status of cooperative movement in Tamil Nadu does not tally with its historical pride. The policies of the successive State Governments have almost turned the cooperatives as quasi-governmental bodies and the members use the cooperatives as shareholders and not as stakeholders. Majority of the PACBs, PCARDBs, CCBs, urban banks, spinning mills, sugar mills, consumer cooperatives, marketing cooperatives, industrial cooperatives and weaver's cooperatives have been in doldrums. Some of the cooperatives had been closed. But there have been successful cooperatives too with motivated membership base. The growth of PACBs in Tamil Nadu is given in the Table 1.8. The total number of PACB in 1929-30 was 12439. During the year 1946, there was a tremendous growth of PACS in terms of membership and in the position of loan issued. Over the years, due to amalgamation and restructuring process, it has come down to 4482 PACBs. And the current statistics is still lesser than the figure given here due to the winding up of the loss making PACBs. In the Long term Credit Structure, there were 2 LMBs in 1925.The number of LMBs increased to 126 as on 30th June 1950. As on 31st March 1991, the number of PCARDBs increased to 181 and remained the same as on 31st March 2006 (Table 1.9).

Functioning of Commercial Bank in Tamil Nadu

Tamil Nadu has a wide network of CB system. There were 63 CBs (including the nationalized banks, private sector banks and foreign banks) with 4899 branches and 210 branches of RRBs (there were 3 RRBs viz., Pandian Grameen Bank, Adiyaman Grameen Bank and Vallalar Grameen Bank). Further, out of the total branches of CBs, 14 percent were in rural areas while in the case of RRBs, around 70 percent were in rural areas.

Status of SHGs in Tamil Nadu

In Tamil Nadu, the experiment in SHG was done by a few NGOs with the support of the Government of Tamil Nadu in late eighties. This experiment proved success. It was taken as a laboratory model for the State and the country. In the year 1989, with the help of the IFAD, the Tamil Nadu Government mooted SHGs in 75 panchayat unions of 8 districts. Then SHGs came into existence in all parts of Tamil Nadu.

As on March 2006, 80 per cent of the total number of SHGs in Tamil Nadu were formed by NGOs but directly financed by banks (Table 1.10).

Market Share of IAs at State Level

The neglect of the priority sectors at the macro-level was compounded at the micro-level, by the new banking culture which sought to focus the banking business on the three Cs–credit to consumer durables, credit to the corporate elite, and credit to capital market related activities (Majumdar, N.A.: 2002, p. 255). In Tamil Nadu, the total GLC delivered by this network was Rs. 2319 crores in 1992-93. .This has increased over the years and stood at Rs. 11432 crores during the year 2001-02 and Rs. 22036 crores during the year 2005–06. However the rate of growth was uneven (Table 1.11). The fluctuating trend in credit flow could also be found from the Table 2.12, which shows that against the target, the achievement was uneven over the period in terms of the total as well as agency-wise credit delivered. The agency-wise analysis also confirms the trend.

Providing access to institutional credit for small and marginal farmers and other weaker sections to enable them to adopt modern technology and improved agricultural practice has been the major objective of the credit policy of the State (Government of Tamil Nadu: 2001-02, p. 38). Hence, the Government has been awarding top priority to Cooperative Movement. But the movement itself has suffered with lot of problem, of which the absence of democratic management and mismatch between quantum of credit requirements and quantity of credit lent were in the top. Hence, the share of Cooperative Banks in the total credit provided had come down from 26 percent to 20 percent, though the total loan issued had increased from Rs. 596 crores in 1992-93 to Rs. 2319 crores in 2001-02 an Rs. 4204.9 crores in 2005-06. Further, there were shortfalls in the credit flow against the target fixed. For example, the total production and term loan issued by the Cooperative Banks during the year 1998-99 was Rs. 1713.18 crores, which was 90.5 percent against the target. Though the percentage of achievement came down to 96 percent against the target fixed in 2002-03, it had increased upto 105.9 percent in the year 2004–05. (Table 1.12).

In the case of CBs, the total credit delivered by them was Rs. 1437 crores in 1992-93, which was 62 percent of the total GLC flow during that year. This has increased over the years and stood at Rs. 16780.46 crores at the end of the study period, which was 76 percent of the total GLC flow for agricultural and allied activities during that year. In the case of RRBs, though the credit delivered by them increased over the years, their contribution to the total remained the same.

Population served by CB branch is one of the parameters with which we can measure the penetration of banking institution in the rural areas. In the year 2005-06, the population served per bank branch in Tamil Nadu was 13934, which was lower than the All India level of 15478. It shows that the penetration was high in Tamil Nadu. The credit per bank is a crucial index through which one can measure the effectiveness of flow of credit to the needy sectors. Credit per bank for rural areas in Tamil Nadu was Rs. 158.37 crores in 1995-96, which has increased over the years and stood at Rs. 614 crores in 2005-06 i.e., 20 percent to the total credit per bank. Further, the CD ratio displays the efficiency with which the banks mop-up resources from the public and lend it to the borrowers for productive economic activities. The CD ratio was worked out to 85.6 percent in 1995-96, which drastically came down over the years and stood at 53.1 percent during the year 2001-02 in rural area, whereas it was 96.8 percent at urban and metropolitan areas. Further, RBI set norms for advances to priority sector, agriculture, weaker section and advances under DRI. After the year 2001 –02, the CD ratio of the banks has been steadily increasing which stood 86.2 in the year 2005-06.

Analysis on the GLC flow shows that the credit gap at State level was only around Rs. 270 crores in 1998-99, which was increased to Rs. 2602 crores in 2000-01 and came down to Rs. 243 crores (Table 1.13). It stood Rs. 273 crores in 2005 -06. In order to ensure timely availability of credit and repayments and flexibility in drawls, the Kissan Credit Card System was introduced in 1998-99 (Annexure 3). At the all India level, there were 80.12 lakh cards issued to the value of Rs. 25858 crores in the year 2005-06 (www.indiabudget.nic.in). During the year the total cards issued by the DCCBs in the State was 11,12,715. The respective figure for CBs and RRBs were 818,783 and 71056.

With regard to the SHGs a vast number of them had been established in recent years as self-reliant autonomous local financial intermediaries through NGOs, Government Agencies and banks. Of these, 90 per cent members have been women.

During the year 2001-02, there were 30,100 credit linked SHGs. It had increased upto 98568 SHGs in 2005–

06. The bank loan availed by the groups was to the extent of Rs. 102862.38 crores during the year 2005-06 as against 557.50 lakhs in 1998-99 (Table 1.14). Anticipating active participation of the banks in the linking programme and also the entry of the cooperative banks in this sector, NABARD has set an ambitious target of reaching 100 million of India's rural poor with savings and credit linkage by the year 2008 through 1 million SHGs. During the year 2002-03, the banks in Tamil Nadu have credit linkage of 35701 SHGs. In the year 2003-04, the cumulative number of SHGs credit linked in the State of Tamil Nadu was 220698 and the number of refinance linked SHGs accounted for about 89036.66 (NABARD: 2006-07, p. 17).

Table 1.14: SHG–Bank Linkage Programme in Tamil Nadu

(Rs. in lakhs)

Particulars	*No. of SHGs*	*Bank loan*	*Refinance*
1998-99	2618	557.5	557.5
1999-2k	7671	2273.1	1868
2k-2001	16676	5106.5	5049
2001-02	30100	12404	10463.6
2002-03	35701	22284.5	42551.6
2003-04	51851	5059.96	93142.52
2004-05	70437	74647.47	167789.99
2005-06	98568	102862.38	287435.44

Source: 1. NABARD (2003-04), State level credit seminar, State focus paper, Tamil Nadu, January, p. 158.

2. NABARD (2004-05), State level credit seminar, State focus paper, Tamil Nadu, January, p. 166.

3. NABARD (2006-07), State level credit seminar, State focus paper, Tamil Nadu, January, p. 191

Table 1.15: Position of Commercial Banks at All India, State and District Level

(Rs in Crores)

Parameters	1990-91			1991-92			1992-93			1993-94			1994-95		
	India	TN	DGL	India	TN	DGL	India	TN	DGL	India	TN	DGL	India	TN	DGL
No. of societies	82905	4614	273	82560	4644	273	90025	4568	196	91592	4583	196	91110	4589	197
No. of bank offices	58764	4301	136	59397	4343	136	61169	4382	139	61803	4456	140	62367	4516	139
No. of rural branches	32048	1933	NA	33845	1936	34028	35389	1942	NA	35329	1957	NA	33004	1933	NA
Deposits	185063	13351.33	128.38	235685	16233.51	157.49	274938	19313.75	241.88	323632	21960.94	263.27	386859	25568.79	338 01
Advances	116589	13401.55	124.52	136697	15504.95	174.81	154838	16720.03	232.20	166844	18817.61	293.38	211560	24706.10	374.36
CD Ratio	63	100	97	58	96	112	56.3	87	96	52	87	152	55	97	114

Parameters	1995-96			1996-97			1997-98			1998-99			1999-2000		
	India	TN	DGL	India	TN	DGL	India	TN	DGL	India	TN	DGL	India	TN	DGL
No. of bank offices	63026	4587	139	63550	4642	141	64218	4712	141	64939	4715	141	65412	4712	140
No of rural branches	32995	1844	NA	32915	1846	NA	35878	1806	NA	32857	1806	NA	32734	1806	NA
Deposits	429003	29705.99	485.07	499763	33970.56	535.78	598485	36977.03	665.80	714025	46717.38	743.40	851593	54900.56	803.88
Advances	254015	29540.27	276.36	278401	32798.91	519.70	324079	33209.07	652.48	368837	41211.89	624.46	454069	46440.77	570.75
CD Ratio	59	99	57	56	97	97	54	90	98	52	88	84	53	85	71

Table 1.15: *(Contd...)*

Parameters	*2000-2001*			*2001-2002*			*2002-2003*			*2003-2004*			*2004-2005*			*2005-2006*		
	India	*TN*	*DGL*	*India*	*TN*	*DGL*	*India*	*TN*	*DGL*	*India*	*TN*	*DGL*	*India*	*TN*	*DGL*	*India*	*TN*	*DGL*
No. of bank offices	66004	4712	138	66276	4751	138	66436	4727	137	66970	4757	137	68116	4846	137	68681	4899	137
No. of rural branches	32640	1806	NA	32567	1781	NA	32380	1793	80	32303	1793	80	32121	1719	80	32082	1737	80
Deposits	989141	63332.57	842.33	1097049	74642	878.43	1278667	85716	936.27	1517200	98873	1041.95	1753174	110329	1115.34	2093.42	125539	1183.76
Advances	529272	52024.49	589.63	683591	62914	687.26	759210	74157	761.48	890866	88622	839.65	1157807	108605	772.77	1517497	131971	683.19
CD Ratio	54	82	70	NA	77	NA	59.40	86.5	69	58.72	89.63	73	66	98.4	76	72.5	105.1	71

Source: RBI (2001), Basic Statistical Returns of CBs in India, Vol.30, March, p. 1.

GOI (1993-94), Tamil Nadu–An Economic Appraisal, Evaluation and Applied Research Department, p. 468.

GOI (1996-97), Tamil Nadu–An Economic Appraisal, Evaluation and Applied Research Department, p. 367.

NABARD (1998-99), State Level Credit Seminar–State Focus Paper, December, p. 10.

NABARD (1999-2000), State Level Credit Seminar–State Focus Paper, December, p. 5.

NABARD (2002-2003), State Level Credit Seminar–State Focus Paper, December, p. 38.

NABARD (2003-2004), State Level Credit Seminar–State Focus Paper, December, p. 32.

NABARD (1993-94 to 1996-1997), PLP for DGL District (with detailed projections), p. 12.

NABARD (1994-95), (1995-1996), (1996-1997), PLP for DGL District (with detailed projections), p. 8, 5, 3.

NABARD (1997-98) to 2001-2002, with detailed projections, p. 9.

NABARD (2001-2002) and (2002-2001), PLP for DGL District p. 7 & p. 11.

Banking Statistics (2003), Quarterly Hand Out, March RBI, Mumbai, http://www//.tn.goverin/deptst/Tab25_o1.htm.

Table 1.16: Agency-wise Ground Level Credit Flow for Agriculture and Allied Activities at Dindigul District Level

(Rs in Crores)

Agency	*1992-93*	*1993-94*	*1994-95*	*1995-96*	*1996-97*	*1997-98*	*1998-99*	*1999-00*	*2000-01*	*2001-02*	*2002-03*	*2003-04*	*2004-05*	*2005-06*
Coops.	27.7 (41)	32.3 (39)	44.6 (33)	50.5 (31)	55.6 (35)	64.0 (34)	73.6 (32)	65.01 (24)	97.80 (35)	112.07 (31)	130.24 (32)	154.07 (32)	187.9 (31)	216.89 (26)
CBs	38.5 (58)	50.4 (60)	88.9 (65)	102.3 (63)	99.82 (63)	117.6 (62)	155.6 (67)	198.19 (74)	177.98 (63)	247.44 (68)	26954 (66)	324.55 (67)	408.8 (68)	595.68 (73)
Others	0.7 (1)	0.9 (1)	3.3 (2)	8.7 (6)	4.10 (2)	7.7 (4)	2.9 (1)	5.84 (2)	5.47 (2)	5.09 (1)	6.13 (2)	8.45 (1)	6.4 (1)	9.53 (1)
Grand Total	66.9	83.6	136.8	161.5	159.52	189.3	232.0	269.04	281.25	364.60	405.91	487.07	603.1	822.10
Growth Rate	-	24.9	63.4	18.08	-1.19	18.69	22.54	15.95	4.54	29.63	11.33	19.99	23.84	36.29

Source: Complied from PLP for Dindigul District, NABARD for various years

Nature and Functioning of Institutional Agencies in Dindigul District

Dindigul is one of the 30 districts of the Tamil Nadu and has been formed by bifurcating areas of Madurai District on September 15, 1985. It is located 400 kms away from the State Capital Chennai and 65 kms from the temple city Madurai and 100 kms from the rock city–Trichy in South–West part of Tamil Nadu. Dindigul is the head quarter of the district. The district is divided into 7 taluks namely Dindigul, Kodaikanal, Natham, Nilakottai, Oddanchatram, Palani, and Vedasandur. It is further divided into 14 blocks. There are 358 small villages and 304 village panchayats in the district. It is located between 10.05 and 10.9 North latitude and 77.30 and 18.20 East latitude, and is bound by Erode, Coimbatore and Trichy districts on the North, by Sivaganga and Trichy districts on the East, by Madurai district on the South and by Coimbatore district and Kerala State on the west. The district receives average annual rainfall of 936 mm of which 46 percent is received from North East Monsoons and only 30 percent from South West monsoons. The lowest rainfall is recorded at the Guziliamparai block i.e., 630 mm. (NABARD, 2002-07, p. 12).

Dindigul is one of the very few districts which have two distinct agro climatic zones viz., semi-arid tropical climate in the plains and subtropical climate in the hills of western ghats (mainly in Kodaikanal block). A large variety of fruits and vegetables are grown in the varied agro-climatic conditions available in the district. Agriculture and animal husbandry are the predominant economic activities in the district. Industry, business and commerce are also other important activities prevalent in the district. The district is drought prone and has received less than average rainfall during the last two years. Very small land holdings of less than one ha account for 67 per cent of the total holdings but constitute less than 24 per cent area of such holdings. The district is devoid of any major industries or huge resources for irrigation except a few dams, which depend entirely on monsoon rains for water storage. The southwest and northwest monsoons are the major sources of rainfall and they often fail. The major food crops grown in the district are paddy, cholam (sorghum), cumbu (bajra), maize, pulses and oilseeds like groundnut and gingelly. The major commercial crops cultivated are cotton, sugarcane and tobacco. The major fruit crops grown in the district are mango, guava, banana, grapes, sapota, pineapple, plums, pear etc. Different types of flowers such as jasmine, marigold, chrysanthemum, kanakambaram, arali, cockscomb and rose are also grown (NABARD: 2004-05, p. 4 & 5).

The Dindigul District is well covered by a network of bank branches and financial institutions. The 193 PACBs registered an overall growth of 9 percent in deposits by reaching a level of Rs.86 crore during the year 2005-06. The total loans and advances outstanding of all the PACBs stood at Rs.154 crores. Recovery was 54 percent of demand during the year 2005-06. The PACBs had high level of imbalance with Dindigul DCCB.

The 6 PCARDBs and the Dindigul DCCB with its 29 branches and 193 PACBs play an important role in the agricultural financing and rural development. Of the 6 PCARDBs functioning in the district, none could achieve the DAP targets. The overall target for advances to be issued during the year 2006-07 was Rs.677 lakh. The achievement was only 541 lakh, i.e., 88 percent of the target. The combined recovery was only 38 percent of demand.

Market Share of Institutional Agencies at District Level

The total ground level credit flow for agriculture and allied activities was Rs. 66.91 crores in 1992-93, which has increased over the years and stood at Rs. 364.60 crores in 2001-02 and Rs. 822.10 crores in the year 2005-06 (Table 1.16). However, the rate of growth has been uneven. Further, inconsonance with the trend at National and State level, the share of CBs in the total GLC provided for agricultural and allied activities was high during the study period.

There were several factors affecting the loan operations of CBs and Cooperative Banks both at State and District level. Though certain factors were specific to the region, majority of them were common to the State as a whole. They are listed below:

- Bankers, who had negative attitude, viewed rural lending as unprofitable and a risky;
- With some of the bank's procedures were rigid and with less flexibility to cater to the needs of the poor;
- Banks, were not able to lend to the poor practically who required very small amount of money frequently;
- Many bankers insist on collaterals as additional security even from the poor whereas the poor are assetless and the Government has exempted the same upto a specified limit.

- Bank's lending formalities have been time consuming and increasing the transaction cost of the rural borrower viz., cost of repeated visits to the branch, cost for obtaining quotations for purchases out of the loan, cost for getting land ownership certificates from the authorities and so on;
- Timing of credit delivery was not assured and often delayed defeating the very purpose of the loan.
- Interference by middlemen in siphoning off a portion of loan amount from the rural poor exploiting their lack of awareness of procedures;
- Unrealistic target orientation in implementing Government sponsored poverty alleviation programmes;
- Rural credit programmes were just launched with the announcements from the top and without much focus on the felt needs of the poor;
- High operational cost for the rural branch and poor volume of business as lending was not given thrust;
- Manpower shortage in the rural and remote branches resulted in poor monitoring of the loan portfolio and consequent deterioration of asset quality;
- Increase in non-performing assets, requiring higher provisions and thereby affecting the profitability of the rural branches, leading to closure or merger of branches;
- Due to the manual operation of the rural

branches in many banks and because of low value and high volume nature of business, the per employee productivity has been low;

- Double financing by cooperatives banks and other RRBs or nationalized banks, leading to overdues in both institutions;
- Gradual erosion of moral values and repayment ethics as the people had tasted the benefits of loan/interest waiver offers;
- Loopholes in enforcing the legal contracts on the wilful defaulters;
- Poor follow up by the branch, as numbers of small accounts are more (Swain B.K: 2004, p. 165 & 166);
- Low off-take of credit due to recession in industrial sector and slowdown in agricultural production (Government of Tamilnadu: 2001-02 p. 101);
- The continuance of drought in several parts of the State including in Dindigul district affected the agricultural operations resulting in low off-take of credit; and
- The Government Policy towards rural credit affected the loan recovery climate and eroded the financial structure of RFIs.

The factors that affect GLC flow to the disadvantaged group as identified by the Vyas Committee (RBI: 2004, p. 61) are given below:

- Higher transaction costs to both banks and borrowers;
- Client-unfriendly procedures, systems and documentation formalities;

- Borrowers' inability to provide collateral securities;
- Distortion of normal banking principles caused by linking credit with capital/interest subsidies under various poverty alieviation programmes;
- Announcements or expectations of interest/loan waivers affecting recovery climate;
- Legal difficulties in foreclosure of loans;
- Non-availability of tenancy agreements/updated land records;
- Inadequate risk mitigation mechanism available to the small borrowers in the event of micro enterprise failure and to the banks in the event of loan failure; and
- The mindset that banking with the poor is not profitable.

Conclusion

In the Indian context, the RCM is a more complex subject not only because of the characteristics of the suppliers of credit but also the peculiar nature of demand for credit itself. The institutional framework that has been developed over the years to provide supervised credit to the agriculture and allied sector has generated adequate infrastructure, which helped for both the green and white revolutions. However, the credit requirements of this sector has not been fully realized and met by the IAs, resulting in the proliferation of the NIAs. The regional imbalances in GLC flow, large scale failure of rural banking, widespread poverty, continuance of usurious practices of NIAs, and reported farmers' suicides altogether resulted in the proposed enhancement of GLC during Tenth Plan. For example, at all India level, the total credit flow to agriculture in the Ninth Plan (1997-2002) amounted to Rs. 2,29,956 crores. A substantial jump in the credit flow to agriculture is envisaged in the Tenth Plan (2002-07) which is projected at Rs. 7,36,570 crores, almost three times the Ninth Plan Achievement. Although there was a substantial increase in the agricultural credit in the first two years of the Tenth Plan, the increase was not commensurate with the plan projections (www.indiabudget.nic.in, p. 159). On the other hand, though the SHGs–Bank Linkage programmes have helped certain sections of the community to have access to the financial products of IAs, still major segment of the rural population depend on the NIAs. This was proved from the World Bank-NCAER study Scaling–up Access to Finance for India's Rural Poor. Agriculture and allied sector is more capital and credit intensive. IAs should be accessible to this sector so as to meet the demand for credit. The proper way-out is not only enhancing the quantum of credit but also making the IA's infrastructure more borrowers friendly.

REFERENCES

1. Balasaheb Vikhe Patil (2005), Rural Banking–Problems of Localized Banking Institutions, *Economic and Political Weekly*, Vol. XL (12), March 19-25, p. 1225.
2. Bhagirath Singh (2001), *Rural Finance*, RBSA Publishers, Jaipur, p. 66.
3. Government of Tamil Nadu (2001-02), *Tamil Nadu–An Economic Appraisal*, p. 38.

4. Government of Tamil Nadu (2001-02), *Tamil Nadu—An Economic Appraisal*, p. 101.
5. Hart, Keith (1971), Informal Income Opportunities and Urban Employment in Ghana; quoted in: *Self-Employment and Successful entrepreneurship* by Martin Patrick (1999), Kanishka Publishers, New Delhi, p. 2.
6. *Human Development in South Asia* (2002), Mahabub ul haq Human Development Centre, Oxford, p. 89.
7. Majumdar N.A. (2002), *Financial Sector Reforms and India's Economic Development*, Vol. 2, Academic Foundation, Ghaziabad, p. 255 & 264.
8. Martin Patrick (1999), *Self-Employment and Successful Entrepreneurship,* Kanishka Publishers, New Delhi, p. 3.
9. NABARD (2001-02), *Annual Report*, p. 15.
10. NABARD (2002-03), *State Focus Paper*, p. 4.
11. NABARD (2002-07), *Potential Credit Plan for Dindigul District*, p. 12 & 81.
12. NABARD (2002), *Two decades of dedicated service to the Nation,* (1992–2002), p. 1
13. NABARD (2004-05), *Potential Linked Credit Plan for Dindigul District*, p. 4 & 5.
14. NABARD (2004-05), *Sate Focus Paper*, p. 14
15. NCUI (2004), *Indian Cooperative Movement–A Profile*, pp. 17-25.
16. Priya Basu, Pradeep Srivastava: (2005), Exploring Possibilities—Micro Finance and Rural Credit Access for the Poor in India, *Economic and Political Weekly*, Vol. XL(17), April, p. 1747.

17. Raja Ram Gupta (2005), Micro Finance in India– Empirical Evidence, Alternative Models and Policy Imperatives, *Economic and Political Weekly*, Vol. XL (12), March 19-25, p. 1229.

18. Ravichandran, K. & Revathi Bala, M. (2004), *'Challenges Faced by Entrepreneurs in Informal Sector Enterprises in Dindigul District—A Study'*, the paper presented in UGC sponsored national seminar on Challenges before Indian Entrepreneurs in the 21st century held on 10th April 2004 organized by Adirampattinam Khadir Mohideen College, Adirampattinam, April 2004, p. 3.

19. Ravichandran, K. (2000), *Crop Loan System and Overdues,* Spell Bound Publications, Rohtak, p. 15.

20. RBI (1989), *The Agricultural Credit Review Committee*, p. 188.

21. RBI (2004), *Report of the Advisory Committee on Flow of credit to Agriculture and Related Activities*, p. 36.

22. RBI (2004), *Report of the Advisory Committee on Flow of Credit to Agriculture and Related Activities*, Mumbai, June 2004, p. 61.

23. RBI (2004), *Task Force on Revival of Cooperative Credit Institutions*, p. 8.

24. Satish, P. (1998), *Advanced Rural Banking–Rural Financial Institutions,* Module D., Indian Institute of Bankers, p. 321.

25. Shukla & Mohanthy (1991), *Rural Credit in India*, Syndicate Publications, Patna, p. 72 & 73.

26. Sinha, S.K. (1992), *Recovery of Loans from Farmers*, Deep & Deep Publications, New Delhi, p. 9.

27. Subrahmanyam, B. (2003), Lending Agricultural Credit at Nine Percent a view point of Agricultural Cooperative Credit Institutions, *NAFSCOB Bulletin*, Vol. 20(3), NAFSCOB, July-September, p. 13.

28. Swain, B.K. (2004), Indian Banks in 2010: Emerging Scenario, *IBA Bulletin*, Vol. 26 (1), January, p. 165 & 166.

29. Tara S. Nair (2005), The Transforming World of Indian Micro Finance, *Economic and Political Weekly*, Vol.XL (17), April, p. 1697.

30. *The Hindu* (2005), Monday, May 23, p. 11.

31. TNCDW (2002), *Project Officer's Review Meeting*, Dindigul, Agenda 2 held on 29.11.2002 & 30.11.2002, p. 3.

32. Upendra Kunwar (1987), *Banking and Agricultural Growth–A Study of Land Development Bank*, Deep & Deep Publications, New Delhi, p. 152.

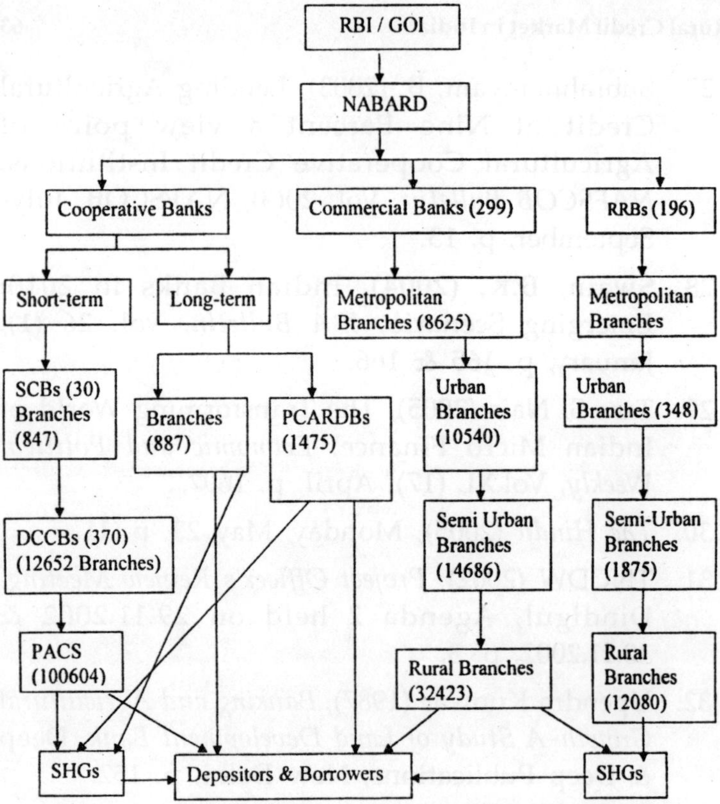

Chart 1.1: Institutional Arrangements for Agriculture and Rural Credit in India

2

The Design and Execution of the Study

Introduction

India is an agrarian economy. Even though the relative importance of agriculture in the Indian economy declined, its significance has not diminished[1]. The total population of India is 102.7 crores as per 2001 census, of which 72.2 per cent of the population constitute the rural. (www.indiapost.org). The majority of them depend on agriculture and allied activities as cultivators and agricultural labourers. As agriculture depends on monsoon, a major segment of this population does not have sufficient income even to meet their daily expenses and for them the possibilities of savings and investment are almost stagnant. They require credit in their day-to-day life, to purchase agricultural inputs and adopt modern technology. Thus, timely and adequate quantum of credit is critical for the socio-economic development of the rural households.

The basic approach to rural credit in India has been the dispensation of loans at a concessional rate through government apparatus targeting the rural people engaged either in agricultural and non-agricultural activities. The enactment of the Cooperative Credit Societies Act, 1904 and the subsequent formation of the Primary Agricultural Cooperative Societies (PACS)[2] was the first effort made by the Government in the country to institutionalize the agricultural credit. After independence, the Government of India and the State Governments took keen interest in organizing and managing the Cooperative Credit Institutions, Commercial Banks (CBs) and Regional Rural Banks (RRBs) so as to enable the rural people to avail credit at concessional rate.

The era of globalization has brought another institutional approach for rural credit i.e., Self-Help Groups (SHGs). Both Government and Non-Governmental Organizations took keen interest in organizing and registering the SHGs among small group of members. It has been stated that the SHGs have reduced the transaction cost, serving as a link between the borrowers and banks and ensured proper recovery. At present, the Institutional Agencies (IAs) for rural credit consists of the Cooperative Banks, CBs, RRBs and SHGs at ground level and NABARD as a refinancing agency at national level.

Statement of the Problem

The structural readjustment programme and WTO regime affected agriculture at several points. Indian agriculture has been at crossroads. A great deal of attention has been paid to studying the nature and functioning of Rural Credit Markets (RCM), for they have become so complex during this period. In the pre-economic reform period, the Government wanted to provide rural credit at concessional rate through the Cooperative Banks and CBs. The NABARD was established with the sole objective of integrating the efforts of the various agencies in this context. The post-economic reform period has created adverse climate for rural credit by scaling down the institutional credit available for the priority sector (Majumdar: 1999, p. 1 and Puhazhendi & Jayaraman, B.: 1999, p. 16). This prioritization of rural credit has created panic in the minds of the rural borrowers, dragged them to the doorsteps of the moneylenders, and ultimately increased their indebtedness. Contrary to this, some of the studies showed that access to formal credit has increased the indebtedness of the borrowers (Gautham Purkhayastha: 2001, p. 4).

On the other hand, the informal agencies i.e., Non-institutional Agencies (NIAs), have been dominating the rural credit market with no rules and regulations. The problems like inadequate availability (Somorendro Singh: 2001), unequal distribution of formal credit (Balishter & Pankajkumar: 1995, p. 16), lack of access to formal credit to rural borrowers (N.V. Namboodiri: 2001, p. 402) and absence of supervision over the end use of loans (Jaya S. Anand: 1995, p. 33) etc., in IAs widened the gap between the IA and the rural borrowers. Further, the viability of rural credit business for the IAs has been a debatable issue due to increasing overdue (K. Ravichandran: 2000, p. 76), high transaction cost (K.G. Karmakar: 1997, p. 481 and Sankar Bhowmick: 2002, p. 2), time consuming procedures, delay in payment (Lokanadhan et.al: 1991, p. 111) and absence of involvement of borrowers in the planning process (Daman Prakash: 2001, p. 5). This has gradually strengthened the role of the NIAs in the RCM.

Each of the above aspects has drawn considerable research attention during the past, but no broad generalization could be formed regarding the actual nature and functioning of the RCM. This has raised many questions, such as: How the formal and informal loans have been distributed in rural areas? What has been the nature of participation of various categories of rural households in RCM? Who are the NIAs and who borrowed from whom in RCM? What determines the rural households' access to formal loan? Whether the access to institutional credit has reduced the indebtedness of the borrowers? What is the utilization pattern of loan? Is there any significant relationship between the access, utilization and repayment of institutional credit? Which institutional repayment do the rural borrowers delay? What are the factors responsible for non-repayment of loan? By addressing all these questions the present research seeks to build a knowledge base about the structure and actual nature of operation of RCM in Tamilnadu.

Review of Literature

Credit provided by the IAs has attracted considerable research attention during the past. The research studies conducted by the Government of India, RBI, NABARD, State Governments and individual researchers have covered various dimensions of the nature and operations of this credit. Some of these studies are reviewed here, under three broad categories viz., access, use and repayment of institutional credit.

Access to Credit

Access to institutional credit is influenced by many factors. If institutional credit is made easily accessible to rural households, it will develop a check over the growth of the NIAs, but very few studies have been conducted on access to credit.

The first comprehensive study conducted during the post-independence era was the survey done by the All India Rural Credit Survey (AIRCS) Committee (1954). The survey revealed that 92.7 percent of the cultivators depended on the NIAs for borrowing. The studies conducted by Subbi Reddy, T. and Ramamuni Reddy (1980, p. 32), Tiwari, S.N. and Sharma, P. K. (1986, p. 30), Basavaraj Banakar and Suryaprakash, S. (1987, p. 78) and Satyasai, K.J.S. et al. (1987, p. 54) confirmed the continuance of poor access to formal sources of credit even during the eighties.

A study conducted by Pratap Singh (1988, p. 286) confirmed that although the IAs were providing credit to cultivators, the farmers of all categories had to depend on the moneylenders. The ignorance and conventionality, non-fulfillment of productive needs from the Cooperatives, inflexible and untimely Cooperative finance, high intimate knowledge on the part of moneylenders regarding local production potentialities, the innate and age old link of the borrowers with moneylenders and poor access to formal capital because of the failure on the part of the farmers to repay the Cooperative dues—all these reasons have underlined the survival of the moneylenders as a source of finance.

Viswa Prasad and Parthasarathy, P. B. (1993, p.

336) found that moneylenders formed the most important source of credit to small farmers as compared to other sources and that the large farmers utilized more from Commercial Banks and Cooperatives signaling the alarm that the small farmer's credit requirements were mostly met by the private lenders to the tune of 50 percent. According to Rajput, A.M. et al. (1993, p. 55) security formalities, inadequate credit and unplanned disbursements were the serious problems of the farmers in obtaining credit from the institutional agencies. The study conducted by Modi, M.K. and Rai, K.N. (1993, p. 252) found that the NIAs i.e., the commission agents formed the major proportion of total crop production credit advanced to small and medium farmers.

According to Ramachandra Reddy, D. and Bagavan Reddy (1994, p. 58), though the difference in formal borrowing was noticeable between the borrowers and non-borrowers in the delta and non-delta regions, the grip of the moneylenders was not loosened. Lakshmi Narasaiah, M. and Venkata Naidu G. (1999, p. 255) who studied the difficulty in access to formal credit observed that considerable number of beneficiaries had to waste their time and money due to the repeated visits to the banks and DRDA office. Bureaucratic hurdles, delay in releasing subsidy, dependence of middlemen in securing loans, and inadequate provision of financial assistance were the problems faced by the beneficiaries.

The Agro-Economic Research Centre, Ministry of Agriculture, GOI (2002, p. 533) estimated that out of the total loan amount, over 21 percent was borrowed from the private traders who charged exorbitant rates of interest as they were the ultimate sources of credit.

The small and marginal farmers, particularly from socially backward caste groups, had generally been perceptual debtors to private moneylenders.

Studies were also conducted on the extent of indebtedness along with the access to credit. The study conducted by Sankar Bhowmick (2002, p. 2) revealed that the rate of participation of the rural households in the RCM had been extremely high. More than 90 percent of all households have turned out to be the borrowing households, which reflected the acute need for credit. However, the rural households did not confine themselves to the formal credit sources alone. Informal credit operates simultaneously and indeed more strongly alongside the formal credit in rural West Bengal. The reason for more access to informal sources was revealed by the study conducted by Satyasai, K.J.S. and Viswanathan, K.U. (2003, p. 21). The rural households needed consumption credit; this was not supplied by the IAs but by the NIAs. Lower level of awareness of the households about the credit avenues available as well as the systems and procedures to be followed might be another factor which led to the continued dependency on the NIAs. Sukhdev Singh, So NIAs Goyal and Mandeep Mahal (2004, p. 90) identified the reasons for the preference of the NIAs. The major ones were easy availability of loans and no time limit for repayment.

The above studies showed that informal credit were easily accessible to the rural households perpetrating the dominance of the moneylenders in the RCM. The discrimination in access to formal credit was also showed by the other studies.

Balasundaram, S.K. (1991, p. 39) inferred that the amount of credit obtained from the credit institution did not match with the requirements of the farmers. As a result, they resorted to private sources of credit wherein the extent of borrowings was high, especially in the case of medium farmers. Singh, A.K., Bajpai, D.K. et al. (1993, p. 401) reported that around 70 percent of the indebted households obtained loans from the institutional sources. Further, the access of institutional credit to small farmers was greater as compared to that of the marginal farmers and land allottees who had to depend on private sources to a much greater extent.

Atibudi, H.N. and Singh, J.P. (1995, p. 3) inferred that farm characteristics influenced the flow of credit to different categories of farmers and it was discriminatory against small and marginal farmers. Balishter and Pankaj Kumar (1995, p. 16) pointed out that the Cooperative institutions were dominated and still continued to be dominated by the medium and large farmers. A study conducted by Ramachandra Reddy, D. and Ramakrishna Reddy, M. (1995, p. 10) revealed that high asset possession and the large income generated there from, enabled the medium and large farmers to have better access to the RCM.

The institution wise analysis also found the continuance of this trend. Though institutional credit was accessible to the rural borrowers to some extent, discrimination among the category of borrowers was found by the other studies. Srivastava, A.P. (1991, p. 190) found out that still big cultivators were having the lion's share in the Cooperative finance. Jugale, V.B. (1992, p. 84) reported that irrespective of various sizes of holdings of the farmers, the proportion of borrowing from other than Cooperative sources was significantly larger than the proportion from the

Cooperative sources. Further, as a farmer can borrow loan in accordance with the size of his land holdings, the share of small farmers in total borrowing was relatively less.

Sinha, S.K. (1992, p. 210) found that the Cooperatives seemed to have served more to the upper income groups of the society whereas its establishment was specifically made for promoting the development of the weaker sections of the society. Contrary to this, the studies conducted by Siddappa, B. (1997, p. 107) revealed that the sample households belonging to the IRDP and non-IRDP categories were capable of reducing their borrowings or stopped their borrowings from the NIAs after the RRB came into operation.

Dinesh Singh Yadav (1999, p. 78) reported that despite the availability of several financial institutions in the study area, the farmers had positive opinion to become members of the Cooperative Credit Societies as their membership in the societies was increasing over time which in turn caused an increase in the deposits and amount of loan sanctioned simultaneously. Sarthak Chowdhury and Prabuddha Ray (2001, p. 163) found that women were not given equal opportunity in availing credit from the Cooperative Banks. The Rural Access to Finance Survey (2003, www.worldbank.org) conducted by the World Bank – National Council of Applied Economic Research revealed that only 19.4 per cent and 24 per cent of the rural households have had access to credit with the formal sources in the states of UP and AP respectively as against 44.1 per cent and 32.6 per cent of the households depending on non-formal sources in the respective states. The RBI (2004, www.rbi.org) observed that the dividing line between production and consumption needs remained very thin for the poor. It recommended that the banks should provide a separate flexible revolving credit limit to the small borrowers of production and investment loans for meeting their temporary short falls in family cash flow.

From the above analyses, it could be inferred that the poor access to credit from the IAs to the rural households helped for the sustenance of the NIAs in the RCM.

Utilization of Credit

The next major area in the institutional credit is utilization of credit. When the credit is utilized for the purpose for which it is provided, it could ensure proper repayment. There are number of factors influencing the utilization pattern of institutional credit.

The study conducted by Kalyankar (1983, p. 102) found that low utilization of loan for productive purposes led to the non-repayment of the loan. Reddy C.R. (1988) revealed that all the farmers in the small and medium farmer groups had diverted the loan inevitably due to inadequacy of credit whereas the big farmers diverted it purposively due to availability of cheap credit. Majority of the small farmers have used the maximum loan for the redemption of old debts.

Kulwant Pathania and Yoginder Varma (1991, p. 155) identified that no significant relationship existed between different family size of farmers and credit utilization for unproductive purposes. Further, misutilisation of credit was found to be significantly more among the farmers who borrowed low amount of credit. Social and religious ceremonies were found to be the most unproductive purposes among all categories of farmers borrowing different amount of credit. Vaikunthe, L.D. (1991, p. 42) and Jaya S. Anand (1995, p. 33) found that small farmers were more in the practice of diverting the loan for other unproductive purposes than the big farmers.

Goyal, S.K. et al., (1993, p. 296) observed that the defaulter borrowers utilized a relatively large proportion of their total earnings on consumption purposes thereby leaving less for investment in production process. This resulted in low repaying capacity of the loan on the part of the defaulter borrowers. Mukesh Singh Rathore (1994, p. 16) observed that the availability of easy credit from the moneylenders, Cooperative Societies or the government allures them to abandon their attitude towards savings and encourages them to be somewhat extravagant with borrowed money.

Venugopala Reddy and Ratnakar (1996, p. 34) found that the factors such as land holding, education, and agency contact were found to be the most influential factors on the credit utilization pattern of the farmers. Pathania, K.S. (1998, p. 219) reported that 38.3 percent of the respondents only fully utilized the loan. Among the unproductive purposes, social ceremonies and purchase of essential commodities were found to be the first two major purposes among all the farmers with varying family size. Mazumdar, D.K. and Baruah (1999, p. 5) revealed that the proportion of misutilisation did not vary much among the size group.

Namasivayam, D. and Ramachandraiah, G. (2000, p. 419) pointed out that the defaulter group families were composed of large size family and they had to meet out their foreseeable and unforeseeable expenditure of their daily life, which tended to divert the loan to unproductive use. A study conducted on institutional finance and rural development by Benson Kunjukunju & Mohanan S. (2002, p. 168) found that the utilization of loans was better among the borrowers of the CBs and PCARDBs than the PACS.

Ravichandran, K. and Revathi Bala, M. (2003, p. 86) found that misutilisation or diversion of loans for other purposes for which the loan was not provided was a common phenomenon among all class of farmers. Both the members and employees of the Cooperatives accepted the prevalence of this trend and pointed out that the following were the causes for this problem: (i) loan was not available when it was required; (ii) the scale of finance fixed for all types of loans were based on arbitratory procedures and no relevance to the field level realities; and (iii) advance money required to subscribe the shares for getting crop and medium term loan was not available. Further, when the loan was available, the Cauvery water was not adequate for cultivation. Farmers, instead of investing in lands, diverted the loan amount for some other purposes. Well-to-do farmers borrowed from the PACBs for money-lending business, which was a common phenomenon. Lalitha, N. and Dayanandan, R. (2005, p. 244) assessed that 47 percent of the borrowers misutilized the borrowed amount for family commitments including social obligations followed by consumption expenses and pre-settlement of old debts.

From the above studies, it is inferred that non-economic factors, official procedures, inadequacy of credit, availability of cheap credit, redemption of old debts, social ceremonies, consumption needs, land holding, level of education, contact with change agents etc., have been the factors that influenced the utilization behaviour of the borrowers.

Repayment

The titles repayment, overdue and willful defaulters have attracted considerable studies during the recent past as they directly influenced the business of the IAs. Some of the important studies conducted on these areas are reviewed hereunder.

The All India Rural Credit Survey Committee (RBI: 1954, p. 62) found that defective lending policies were the causes for poor repayment and consequent overdue at institutional level. The All India Rural Credit Review Committee (RBI: 1969, p. 56) which studied the progress of the Cooperative credit after 1954, stated that overdue were a common problem both in developed and under developed areas and found that the bulk of overdues were caused by the big farmers. The Study Team on Overdues 1974 identified that, among the cultivators, lack of will and the discipline to repay was the principal factor responsible for the prevalence of overdue in the Cooperatives.

Dadhich (1977, p. 234) found that there was no association between landholdings and repayment performance, literacy and repayment and the quantum of amount borrowed and repayment;. the deciding factors in repayment, however, were irrigation and caste of the borrowers since all variables (fertilizers, crops, occupation) centered around irrigation and caste.

The CRAFICARD (1980, p. 87) while endorsing the findings of the Study Team on Overdues found that failure to tie-up lending with development programmes and want of a sense of discipline and responsibility among the borrowers in regard to prompt repayment of debts were the important causes among others for the overdue.

Chinnappa Reddy et.al., (1987, p. 5) found that overdue among the farmers largely depended on net farm income, debt and assets position, capital investments and non-farm income among the marginal farmers. Munikrishna Reddy et al. (1987, p. 26) indicated that majority of the regular credit users repaid the loan amount in time in order to get further loans. Rest of the regular credit users repaid as they wanted to be honest and due to good market price for their produce. Arul Anandam, M.A. and Namasivayam, N. (1988, p. 296) found that there was no relationship between caste, landholdings, amount borrowed and repayment of overdue. On the other hand, strong relationship was found to prevail between education, age, irrigation and occupation of the borrowers and repayment of dues.

The ACRC (RBI: 1989, p. 533), which dealt with the issue of overdue in a separate chapter called 'Overdue Syndrome', stated that there was significant relationship between agro-climatic conditions, literacy rate, major crops grown and overdue. However the phenomenon of overdue was generally neutral to the category of borrowers financed and the variations in recoveries between different classes of borrowers were only marginal. The Committee deduced that the general climate in rural areas was becoming increasingly hostile to recoveries due to increasing politicization of agricultural credit.

Renga Reddy, A. (1990, p. 124) assessed that two-thirds of the defaulters have had agriculture as their main occupation. Social consumption and crop failure were the major factors affecting the delinquency of unwilful defaulters. Bhupal Singh Negi (1990, p. 227) concluded that apart from willful defaults, misutilisation or underutilization of the Cooperative Credit in Pauri–Garhwal district, Uttar Pradesh was one of the major factors responsible for the overdue. Rambabu, P. et al. (1991, p. 160) indicated that repayment of other debts was the main reason for the majority i.e, 50 percent, of the borrowers for their partial repayment behaviour. Absence of other sources of income and unsuitable repayment schedule were the factors responsible for the partial repayment behaviour of the respondents. Balishter et al. (1991, p. 38) reported that the farmers who did not repay the LDB loans had repayment capacity quite in excess to the loan repayable. However, they repaid in part the loans availed from the private agencies due to the pressure from the lenders with higher rate of interest payable on such loans and thus kept open the source for the future supply of credit. Vaikunthe L.D. (1991, p. 42) identified that the percentage of repayment was more among the farmers of the non-irrigated area compared to the farmers of the irrigated area.

Reddy, C.R. (1993, p. 110) reported that as much as 40 percent of the borrowers had the attitude that their loan would be wiped off. Balishter et al. (1994, p. 382) identified that the majority of the defaulters did not repay the loans due to the persuasion by the political parties and their manipulative local influence. Ramachandra Reddy, D. (1995, p. 67) reported that, in case of the wilful defaulters, the variables viz., landholding, proportion of cash crops, political influence, education and proportion of dependent members to total members showed positive relationship to loan overdues.

Sharma, A.K. and Kharmowphlang, M. (1995, p. 123) found that none of the farmers in the study area were having overdue against the non-institutional agencies. Poor supervision of loans by the institutional agencies was one among the many causes of institutional overdue in the study area. Reddy, B.R. and Laxminarayana (1996, p. 20) indicated that the proportion of interest in the total repayment of old debts was much higher than the repayment of fresh loans. Kalia, S.K. (1997, p. 31) identified that apart from the defective loan policies and procedures, the other factors such as infructuous investments, non-realisation of anticipated level of return, willful defaults, defective legal framework, government interferences etc. have also contributed to the mounting overdue.

Joy Joseph Puthussery (1999, p. 10) found that all socio-economic factors affected the nature of default. Further, wilful default was high in the case of defaulters having big size of landholding, higher education, alternative occupation, lower age group, high amount of loan, high family expenditure and high family income. Sudarshan Reddy, A. and Venkatesh Rao (1999, p. 83) reported that the depletion of ground water and drought conditions were mainly responsible for the economic deterioration and consequent inability to repay the loans among 90 percent of the defaulters. The Task Force to Study Cooperative Credit System and Suggest Measures for its Strengthening (RBI: 1999) highlighted that defective loan policies and procedures, poor quality of lending, inadequate and ineffective supervision over the end–use of credit, overemphasis on target achievement and faulty selection of beneficiaries were some of the factors adversely affecting the recoveries of the Cooperative Banks.

Ravi Varma and Bhagavan Reddy (2000, p. 233) stated that diversion of credit, failure of crops, unremunerative prices, inadequate income, natural calamities and politics have been identified to be the major factors contributing to poor recovery. Ravichandran K. (2000, p. 167) observed that the reliance on Cooperative Credit by wilful defaulters often revealed the tendency to resort to this source of finance as it was cheap and could easily be evaded repayment. The factors like literacy and political affiliations remained so interwoven that they caused wilful default.

Viswanath, A.R. (2001, p. 58) identified that defective agrarian structure, misutilisation of loans, natural calamities and wilful defaults were the external factors that made unfavourable climate for the recovery. Moniruzzaman (2002, p. 78) observed that a majority of the members had repaid the loan in time owing to the fear of additional interest and penalties, on pressure by the group members and also driven by the temptation for having loan in future, which was due for both the societies and groups.

The Agro-Economic Research Centre, Ministry of Agriculture, GOI (2002, p. 56) estimated that the recovery of loans with the private traders was timely and cent percent. The study conducted on the NFS loans (Ravichandran, K.: 2003, p. 17) found that the problem of overdue and NPA was neutral to banks. Because of this, there was probability of every new loan for agricultural purposes becoming overdue and every new borrower becomes defaulter to banks. The Report of the Task Force on Revival of Cooperative

Credit Institutions (RBI: 2004, p. 54) pointed out that the low recovery of loans obviously affected the profitability of the institutions and poor loan recovery had resulted in a peculiar phenomenon, often referred to as imbalances. It also viewed that the institutions at ground level viz., the PACS were mainly conducting their business through borrowed funds.

From the above studies it is found that certain socio-economic and political factors influenced the repayment behaviour of borrowers of IAs and the general climate has turned inimical to recoveries. Further, as in access to credit, in the recovery also, the NIAs dominate in the RCM. The failure on the part of the IAs in ensuring easy access, proper utilization and recovery of loan could be derived from the above studies.

The studies on SHGs highlighted the success and salient features of the growing rural credit delivery mechanism.

Ramana Rao, D.V.V. (2001, p. 16) found that the SHG members became self-confident and had social solidarity, habit of regular savings followed by economic independence. Further, a majority of the members of the SHG groups could own assets, were free from debt and could engage in economic activities. Girija, S. and Satish, P. (2001, p. 636) found that lending through the SHGs and NGOs bore the least cost to the lenders when compared to other types of bank lending. It was also observed that the linkage between the banks and the SHGs worked to the advantage of both the bank and the borrower.

Ranjit Karmakar and Bholanath Ghosh (2002, p. 649) could observe that the loan recovery position was highly satisfactory among the SHG members. The inculcation of savings habit, group habit and taking responsibility of the group to disburse loans, led to lesser possibility of wastage of money by the borrowers. Malcolm Harper (2002, p. 30) found that most of the SHGs promoted by the banks and by individuals achieved nearly 100 percent internal repayment rates. Further, all members of the SHGs had borrowed at least once and the amount borrowed was reasonably equitable. According to Pattarnarakha, K. (2003, p. 265), age, length of membership and attitude towards the group were positively correlated with group participation. Nirmala V., Sham Bhat K. and Bhuvaneswari, P. (2004, p. 204) observed that increased participation in social service and organized action, the access to new skills and training and better access to credit facilities were the benefits of the SHGs.

Ravichandran, K. and Revathi Bala, M. (2004, p. 16) found that the dominance of the moneylenders could still be found in satisfying the credit needs of the members of the PACBs. Even though the SHGs, as an alternative institutional credit sub-system, have overcome this problem, more than 50 percent of the SHG members approached their friends and relatives for their additional credit needs. Also, they were not totally free from debt since they got new loan immediately after repaying the old loan.

Though these studies concentrated to identify the causes for the problem of access to the particular source of credit, utilization and repayment of credit by borrowers, the studies rarely highlight the relationship between the access, use and repayment of credit by borrowers. Most of the studies proved that non-institutional credit was more accessible to the rural households than the institutional source. The various factors such as pressure of old debts, unforeseen and household expenses, and willful defaults, pushed the borrowers again and again into the trap of the moneylenders. The studies also highlighted on the various factors responsible for poor repayment and consequent increase in overdue at institutional level. But they failed to measure:

i. How many borrowing families in a particular region were in debt trap?

ii. What was the extent of institutional coverage?

iii. What was the actual magnitude of institutional borrowers in the study area? and

iv. Which factor decided the accessibility of particular institutional source of credit availed by the borrowers?

These issues have not yet been addressed by the earlier studies. In the pursuit of maintaining consistency, and continuity, there is dire need for regular surveys so that it is possible to outline the existing gaps and the future studies are to be pursued accordingly (Goel, G.B. 1997, p. 89). Bearing this in mind, the researcher attempts to address the above said issues in the study area; hence the present study.

Objectives of the Study

The following are the major objectives of the study:

1. To study the role of the institutional agencies in providing rural credit

2. To study the nature, extent and causes for rural indebtedness
3. To examine the access and use of institutional credit by the borrowers
4. To study the repayment behaviour of the borrowers
5. To suggest measures for strengthening the institutional credit structure and reducing the credit gap.

Hypothesis

The hypotheses of the study are as follows:

1. Institutional credit is not able to mitigate the problem of indebtedness of the rural borrowers;
2. Accessibility to institutional credit has profound influence on the utilization and repayment practices and patterns;
3. Productive utilization leads to proper repayment;
4. Diversion of loan arrests the repayment capacity of the borrowers; and
5. Repayment practice is much better in wet areas than in dry areas.

Definitions of Concepts

Access to credit

The means or sources that are accessible to or approached by the borrowers to satisfy their credit needs, which may either, be formal or non-formal, institutional or non-institutional.

Credit

Credit is defined as a temporary transfer of funds, which forms a contract for the future repayment of money by the borrower to the lender.

Credit Gap

Gap between the loan borrowed by the borrower from IAs and his total credit requirement.

Crore

Indian unit of number indicating one followed by seven zeros.

Lakh

Indian unit of number indicating one followed by five zeros.

Lead Bank

The bank that usually having maximum number of branches in the district has been given the responsibility for credit planning and operates as an informal leader of bankers at district level for developmental planning with the help of credit.

Long-Term Credit

Long-term credit is generally granted for periods longer than 5 years and extending up to 15 years. Such credit is granted for making permanent improvements on land like reclamation, sinking of wells, construction of farm houses, cattle seeds, purchase of land and farm machineries, etc.

Marginal Farmers

The study considers farmers whose landholdings are less than 2.5 acres of dry land or less than 1.25 acres of wet land as marginal farmers.

Medium Term Credit

The period of medium credit generally ranges from 3 to 5 years and they are issued for purposes such as land improvements, purchase of implements, machinery, livestock etc.

Micro Finance

Micro Finance is a financial service of small quantity provided by financial institutions to the poor. These financial services may include savings, credit, insurance, leasing, money transfer, equity transactions etc.

Misutilisation

When the loan is not used for the purpose for which it was granted, it is termed as misutilisation or diversion.

Non–Institutional Agencies (NIAs)

Moneylenders, Friends, Relatives, Commission Agent, Village Trader and Chit Funds are considered as NIAs or Informal Agencies.

Overdue

The loan amount which is not repaid within due date is called as overdue.

Priority Sector

All those sectors of the economy and sections of the society which are considered as crucial for the development of the nation.

Rural Area

Villages, towns or other localities, the population of which does not exceed 10000.

Rural Financial Institutions or Institutional Agencies

The term Rural Financial Institutions (RFIs) or formal credit agencies or Institutional Agencies (IAs) refers to institutions like Commercial Banks (CBs), Regional Rural Banks (RRBs), Primary Agricultural Cooperative Banks (PACBs), Primary Cooperative Agriculture and Rural Development Banks (PCARDBs) and Self–Help Groups (SHGs).

Self-help Groups

Self-help group is a small economically homogeneous and affinity group of rural/urban poor, voluntarily formed to save and contribute to a common fund to be lent to its members as per the groups decision and for working together for social and economic uplift of their families and community.

Service Area

Service area refers to the command area of a branch of a bank for the purpose of lending and recovery.

Short-Term Credit

Short-term credit is granted for periods ranging from 6 to18 months and is primarily meant to meet seasonal requirements of agriculture such as seeds, fertilizer, insecticides, hiring of labour etc. These credits are also known as seasonal credit or production credit or crop loans. Jewel Mortgage Loans are also called as short–term credit.

Small Farmers

A small farmer is one who possesses a landholding of 0.25 acres to 2.5 acres of irrigated land or 2.5 to 5 acres of dry land.

Utilization of Credit

Utilization of credit refers to the use of credit for the purpose for which it is granted.

Weaker Sections

All those sections of the population, who are living below the poverty line and drawing an income of Rs.11000 per annum in rural areas and Rs. 11850 per annum in semi-urban areas, are considered as weaker sections. Presently, the norms vary between Rs.13000 to Rs. 19650 among different States.

Methodology

The Survey Method was followed for this study. Both primary and secondary sources of data were collected through structured and pre tested interview Schedule. Economic Survey of Government of India, Annual Reports of NABARD, NABARD State Focus Paper, Tamil Nadu–An Economic Appraisal and The Potential Linked Credit Plan of NABARD for Dindigul District were referred to elicit data regarding the extent of flow of institutional credit at ground level, credit gap and nature and extent of indebtedness. The statistical tools such as Simple Correlation, Regression Analysis and Kendall's Coefficient of Concordance were used to analyze the data.

Sampling Technique

The Non-probability Sampling Procedure was adopted for identifying the study area i.e., Dindigul District, because of its unique characteristics. For identifying the respondents, a Multi-stage Purposive Random Sampling Procedure was used. The sampling plan is given in Chart 2.1. In the first stage, the dry and wet blocks of Dindigul District viz., Athur and Guziliamparai Blocks were selected. In the second stage, Akkarapatty Panchayat in Athur Block and Landhakkottai

Panchayat in Guziliamparai Block were selected for representing wet and dry Blocks. All the 16 villages of these panchayats were chosen for the study. In the third stage, 30 percent of the households were selected randomly and from among them the institutional borrowers were identified and selected for the study. The number of institutional borrowers in wet area

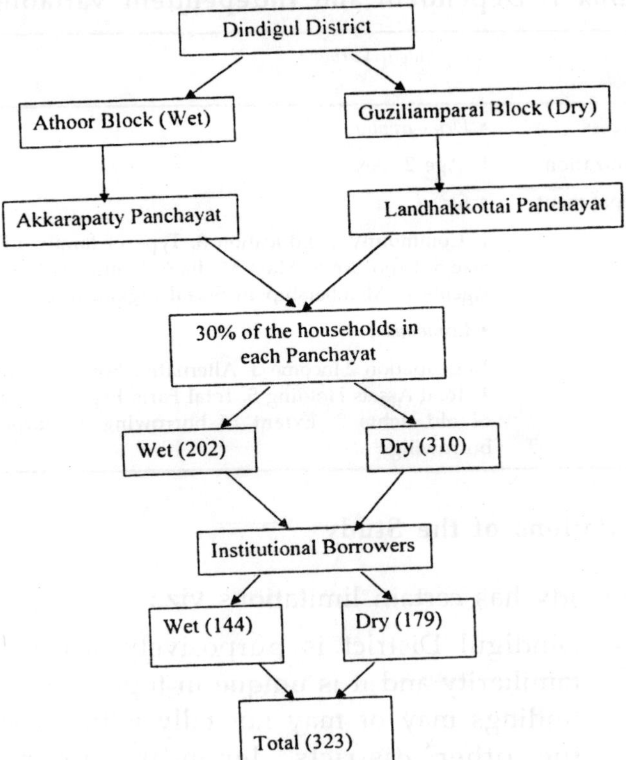

Chart 2.1: Sampling Plan

was 144 and in dry area was 179. Hence the total sample for this study was 323. The names of the selected institutional borrowers were counterchecked with the lists obtained from the concerned IAs.

The dependent and independent variables used for the study are stated below:

Box 1: Dependent and Independent Variables

Dependent Variable	*Independent Variable*
• Access	• *Demography*
• Utilization	1. Age 2. Sex
• Repayment	• *Social*
	1. Community 2. Education 3. Type of family 4.Family Size 5. Exposure to Mass Media 6. Contact with Change Agents 7. Membership in Social organizations
	• *Economical*
	1.Occupation 2.Income 3. Alternative Sources of income 4. Total Assets Holding 5. Total Farm Expenses 6. Extent of old debts 7. Extent of borrowing 8. Purpose of borrowing

Limitations of the Study

The study has certain limitations viz.:

- Dindigul District is purposively selected on familiarity and it is unique in topography. The findings may or may not tally with those for the other districts depending upon the concurrence factors. Uniformity in the secondary sources of data was not maintained intentionally so as to include the latest data available on rural credit.
- The SHGs are treated as one of the agencies of the IA in this study as they are given credit linkage by the banks. The comparison is intended to identify and unearth the factors that might contribute to an alternative to the present state of affairs concerning rural credit. It must be stressed that the SHGs are also given credit rating by the Tamil Nadu Women Development

Corporation and functioning with simplified procedures. This study covered only rated SHGs.

- The study is borrower-centered and hence the institutional performance data are not complete. The GLC at district level has been correlated whenever required.
- Wherever the sampling size was small, the Simple Correlation technique was adopted as against Regression; and
- Rural Credit remains such a deep area that it embraces and transcends all the socio-economic spheres from the rural household to globalization. The problems of rural credit demand solution, which could sprint only from the macro sphere. As such the suggestions offered in this study remain restricted to the micro study of the borrowers' plight alone and might smack of remedies rather than solutions or alternatives. However, these limitations were conscious and were not allowed to affect the purpose of the study and its logical presentation.

Chapter Scheme

The study is presented in five chapters as presented below:

Chapter 1: Rural Credit Market in India

Chapter 2: The Design and Execution of the Study

Chapter 3: Indebtedness and Access to Credit

Chapter 4: Utilization Pattern and Repayment Behaviour of Borrowers

Chapter 5: Findings, Conclusions and Suggestions.

Notes

1. Though agriculture accounts for 22 per cent of the GDP, it provides livelihoods to 58 per cent of the country's population.
2. The Primary Agricultural Cooperative Credit Societies (PACS) are called as Primary Agricultural Cooperative Banks (PACBs) in Tamil Nadu with effect from Government Notification–G.O. Ms. No. 507, COOPERATION (CCI) DEPARTMENT Dated: 1.9.1987 and Letter No.32651/CG.2/87-1, Dated: 13.5.1989. Though this pattern is not uniform across the country, their functions are similar except accepting deposits from members. They are referred to as PACBs here. The Primary Societies which are functioning in the hilly regions are named as LAMPS. The Primary Societies, which are functioning in plains and involved in multi-activities, are named as FSS.
3. In India, The first effort to organize The Land Mortgage Banks was made at Jhang, Punjab as early as 1920. Based on the recommendations of AIRCSC 1954 and AIRCRC 1969 the nomenclature of these banks were changed as Primary Land Development Banks. Again during late 1990s, they were named as Primary Agriculture and Rural Development Banks. As far as Tamil Nadu is concerned, these banks are functioning with new nomenclature since 15.12.1999 based on the 50th Act of 1999 Published in the Special G.O. of Tamil Nadu Government Ms. No. 943.

REFERENCES

1. Arul Anandam, M.A. & Namasivayam, N. (1988), 'Cooperative Overdues—The Influence of Socio-Economic Factors of Borrowers—A Case Study, *Indian Cooperative Review*, Vol. 25 (3), January, p. 296.

2. Atibudhi, H.N. & Singh, J.P. (1995), Flow of Credit to Different Categories of Farmer—A Study in Cuttack District, Orissa, *Land Bank Journal*, Vol. 34 (2), p. 3.

3. Balasundaram, S.K. (1997), Facts of Rural Credit: An Analytical Survey, In: *Cooperative Credit and Banking—Strategies for Development* (Ed. by) Garg M.C. & Joshi N.N., Deep & Deep Publication, New Delhi, p. 39.

4. Balishter and Pankaj Kumar (1995), A Study of Institutional Finance in Agriculture, *Land Bank Journal*, Vol. 34(1), September, p. 16.

5. Balishter, Roshan Singh and Singh, A.K. (1991), 'Overdues of Loans in Land Development Banks in Agra District of Uttar Pradesh', *Cooperative Perspective*, Vol. 26 (1), April-June, p. 38.

6. Balishter, Singh, A.K. and Vishwajit (1994), A Study of Overdues of Loans in Agriculture, *Indian Cooperative Review*, Vol. 31 (4), April, p. 382.

7. Basavaraj Banakar, Suryaprakash (1981) Borrowing and Utilization of Crop Production Credit in Karnataka: A Case Study, *Prajnan*, Vol. 16(1), January–March 1987, p. 78.

8. Benson Kunjukunju & Mohanan, S. (2002), *Institutional Finance and Rural Development*, New Century Publications, Delhi, p. 168.

9. Bhupal Singh Negi (1990), *Cooperative Credit and Regional Development*, Deep & Deep Publications, New Delhi, p. 227.
10. Chinnappa Reddy, B.V., Venkataram, K.V. and Keshava Reddy, T.R. (1987), 'An Economic Analysis of Overdues among Farmers in Srinivaspur Taluk, Kolar District', *Land Bank Journal*, Vol. 26(2), December, p. 5.
11. Dadhich, C.L. (1977), *Overdues in Farm Cooperative Credit—A Case Study of Rajasthan*, Popular Prakashan Private Ltd., p. 234.
12. Daman Prakash (2001), Challenges and Development Issues before the Agricultural Cooperatives and Farmer's Organizations in Asia, *Cooperative Perspective*, Vol. 35 (4), Jan-March, p. 5.
13. Dinesh Singh Yadav (1999), 'Performance and Prospects of Agricultural Cooperative Credit Societies in Block Bilhapur District, Kanpur Dehat (U.P), *Indian Cooperative Review*, Vol. 37(2), October, p. 78.
14. Gautham Purkhayastha (2001), Rural Indebtedness in Assam, www.epw.org, p. 4
15. Girija Srinivasan and Satish, P. (2001), Networking for Micro Credit Delivery, *Journal of Rural Development*, Vol. 20(4), October-December, p. 636.
16. GOI (2002), *The Role of Cooperative Credit in the Development of Different Size Groups of Farmers in Gujarat*, Agro-Economic Research Centre, Ministry of Agriculture, Gujarat, p. 533.
17. GOI (2003-04), *Annual Report*, Department of

Agriculture and Cooperation, Ministry of Agriculture, p. 56

18. Goyal S.K., Pandey R.N. and Modi M.K. (1993), Repayment Capacity of Defaults and Defaulter Borrowers of Cooperative Societies in Haryana, *Indian Cooperative Review*, Vol. 30(3), January, p. 296.

19. Goyel, G.B. (1997), Cooperative Research: Identification of Priority Gaps, *Indian Cooperative Review*, Vol. 34(5), p. 89.

20. Jaya S. Anand (1995), 'Utilisation of Long-Term Credit: A Case Study', *Land Bank Journal*, Vol. 34(2), December, p. 33.

21. Joy Joseph Puthussery (1999), 'Socio-Economic Characteristics and Nature of Default—A Study of Primary Agricultural and Rural Development Banks in Kerala, *Land Bank Journal*, Vol. 38(3), December, p. 10.

22. Jugale, V.B. (1992), *Cooperative Credit in Indian Agriculture—Its Socio-Economic and Technological Impact*, Mittal Publications, New Delhi, p. 84 & 85.

23. Kalia, S.K. (1997), Cooperative Rural Credit Institutions: Process of Reforms; In: *Cooperative Movement in India* (A Case Study of An Indian State) (ed.,) Baidyanath Misra, A.P.H. Publishing corporation, New Delhi, p. 31.

24. Kalyankar, S.P. (1983), *Crop Loan Overdues of Cooperative Finance*, Rainbow Publications, Coimbatore, p. 102.

25. Karmakar, K.G. (1997), Supplementary Rural Credit Delivery System—Some Asian Models,

Journal of Rural Development, Vol. 16, July-September, p. 481.

26. Kulwant Pathania & Yoginder Verma (1991), Impact of Size of Loan and Types of Farmers on Cooperative Credit Utilisation, Indian Cooperative Review, Vol. 29(2), October, p. 155.
27. Lakshmi, Narasaiah M. & Venkata Naidu, G. (1999), *Role of Banking in Rural Development*, Discovery Publishing House, New Delhi, p. 255.
28. Lalitha, N. & Dayanandam, R. (2005), *NABARD and Rural Transformation*, Dominant Publishers and Distributors, New Delhi, p. 244.
29. Lokanadhan, K. & Varadharajan, S. (1991), A Study on the Recovery of Crop Loans in Primary Cooperative Banks of North Arcot District, *Indian Cooperative Review*, Vol. 29(2), October, p. 111.
30. Majumdar (1999), *Reviving Rural Credit*, June 19, www.epw.org, p. 1.
31. Malcolm Harper (2002), *Promotion of Self-Help groups under the Bank SHG-Bank Linkage Programme in India*, paper presented at the seminar SHG-Bank Linkage Programme organized by NABARD in collaboration with the SDC, GTZ and IFAD at New Delhi, on 25th and 26th November, p. 30.
32. Mazumdar, D.K. and Baruah, H.K. (1999), Repayment Performance of Institutional Finance on Allied Agricultural Activities—A Case Study, *Indian Cooperative Review*, Vol. 37(1), July, p. 5
33. Modi, M.K. and Rai, K.N. (1993), Credit Utilisation Pattern on Different Categories of Farms in

District Kurukshetra, *Indian Cooperative Review,* Vol.30(3), January, p. 252.

34. Moniruzzaman (2002), Loan Utilization Pattern of Bangaladesh Rural Development Board Women Cooperatives and Grammen Bank Groups: A Comparative Analysis, *Journal of Rural Development,* Vol. 21(1), Jan-March, p. 78.
35. Mukesh Singh Rathore (1994), *Role of Institutional Finance in Development of Agriculture in India,* Mohit Publication, New Delhi, p. 16.
36. Munikrishna Reddy (1987), Repayment Performance of agricultural credit users, *Land Bank Journal,* Vol. 25(4), June, p. 23.
37. Munikrishna Reddy, M., Ramesh Kumar Reddy and Reddy, G.P.V. (1987), 'Repayment Performance of Agricultural Credit Users', *Land Bank Journal,* Vol. 25(4), June, p. 26.
38. NABARD (2002-03), *Annual Report,* p. 123
39. NAFSCOB (2005 –06), *National Conference on Rural Cooperative Credit and Banking Institutions–Observations & Recommendations,* November, p. 33.
40. Namasivayam, D. & Ramachandraiah, G. (2000), End-Use of Credit and Repayment Performance of the Institutional Borrowers: An Integrated Analysis, *Journal of Rural Development,* Vol.19(3), p. 419.
41. Namboodiri, N.V. (2001), Potential Role of SHGs in Rural Financing Deepening, *Indian Journal of Economics,* Vol. 56(3), July-September, p. 402.
42. NCUI (2004), *Indian Cooperative Movement—A Profile,* pp. 17, 22, 23 and 27.

43. Nirmala, V., Sham Bhat, K. & Bhuvaneswari, P. (2004), SHGs for Poverty Alleviation in Pondicherry, *Journal of Rural Development*, Vol. 23(2), April-June, p. 204.
44. Pathania, K.S. (1998) *Management of Cooperative Finance in India*, Anmol Publications Private Ltd., New Delhi, p. 219.
45. Pattaranarakha, K. (2003), Member's Participation in the Activities of a Production Credit Group in Southern Thailand, *Journal of Rural Development*, Vol. 22(2), April-June, p. 265.
46. Prasad J.V.S., Naidu, M.R. and Venkateswaralu U. (1987), 'Credit Overdues–Certain Factors for Default–A Micro Analysis, *Land Bank Journal*, Vol. 25(4), p. 11.
47. Pratap Singh (1988), Causes Underlying the Survival of the Money Lending Business in the Rural Economy of Punjab, *Indian Cooperative Review*, Vol. 25(3), New Delhi, p. 286.
48. Puhazhendi & Jayaraman, B. (1999), Rural Credit Delivery: Performance and Challenges before Banks, Jan. 16-23, www.epw.org
49. Rajput, A.M., & Verma, A.R. (1993), Impact of Farm Loans on Farm Productivity—A Case Study of State Bank of India in Indore District of Madhya Pradesh, *Indian Cooperative Review*, Vol. 31(1), July p. 55.
50. Ram Babu, P. , Daivadeenam, P. & Eswara Prasad (1991), Repayment Pattern of Agricultural Credit–A Study of Andhra Bank in Guntur District, A.P., *Indian Cooperative Review*, Vol. 29(2), October, p. 160

51. Ramachandra Reddy, D. & Bagavan Reddy (1994), Cooperative Credit in Delta and Non-Delta Regions of Cuddappa, *Cooperative Perspective,* Vol. 29(3), October–December, p. 58.

52. Ramachandra Reddy, D. & Ramakrishna Reddy, M. (1995), 'Cooperative Overdues: A Study of a set of PACS and Defaulters in Nellore Distirct: Andhra Pradesh, *Land Bank Journal,* Vol. 34(2), December, p. 10.

53. Ramachandra Reddy, D. (1995), Influence of Socio-Economic Factors of Borrowers in Cooperative Overdues: A Case Study', *Cooperative Perspective,* Vol. 29(4), January–March p. 67.

54. Ramana Rao (2001), *Impact of Institutional Credit on the Socio-Economic Conditions of Rural Women in SHGs: A Case Study in Bidar District of Karnataka,* NIRD, Hyderabad p. 16

55. Ranjith Karmakar and Bholanath Ghosh (2002) Role of Women in SHGs: An Emerging Possibility to Cooperativization at grass root, *Man in India,* Vol. 82(3&4), July–December, p. 449

56. Ravi Varma, S. (1992), Utilisation and Overdues of Cooperative Loans in Andhrapradesh A Case Study of Nagari Block of Chittoor District, *Indian Cooperative Review,* Vol. 29(3), January, p. 233 & p. 234.

57. Ravichandran, K. & Revathi Bala, M. (2003), Challenges before PACBs An Empirical Study in Rural Tamil Nadu, In: *A New World Through Cooperatives,* ed.by., Frank Ratna Kumar, Savarimuthu & Ravichandran K., p. 86.

58. Ravichandran, K. & Revathi Bala, M. (2004), Role of Cooperatives and SHGs in Rural Credit Market,

RBI-CAB Calling, Vol. 28(1), January-March, p. 16.

59. Ravichandran, K. (2000), *Crop Loan System and Overdue*, Spellbound Publications, Rohtak, p. 167.
60. Ravichandran, K. (2003), Non–Farm Sector Loans—Approaches and Challenges Ahead, In: *Innovative Approaches and Challenges in Rural Credit*, (ed.by) James Mathew, Nirmala Academic Research & Publications, Nirmala College, Muvattupuzha, Kerala, p. 17.
61. RBI (1954), *Report of the All India Rural Credit Survey Committee*, Abridge, Ed., p. 62.
62. RBI (1969), *Report of the All India Rural Credit Review Committee*, p. 56
63. RBI (1974), *Report of the Study Team on Overdues of Cooperative Credit Institutions*, p. 73
64. RBI (1980), *Report of the Committee to Review Arrangements for Institutional Credit for Agriculture and Rural Development*, p. 87
65. RBI (1989), *Agricultural Credit Review Committee*, p. 533.
66. RBI (2001), *Basic Statistical Returns of Scheduled Commercial Banks in India*, Vol. 30, March, p. 1
67. RBI (2004), *Report of the Advisory Committee on Flow of Credit to Agriculture and Related Activities*,. Mumbai, June 2004, p. 54.
68. RBI (2004), *Report of the Task force to study the Cooperative Credit System and Suggest Measures for its Strengthening*, www.rbi.org.
69. RBI (2006), *Banking Statitstics-Quarterly Hand out*, Mumbai, March, p. 56.

70. Reddy, B.R. and Laxminarayana (1996), Overdues in Cooperatives: A Case study in Andhra Pradesh, *Cooperative Perspective,* Vol. 31(3), p. 20.

71. Reddy, C.R. (1988) *Cooperative Agricultural Finance,* Chugh Publications, Allahabad, p. 99.

72. Reddy, C.R. (1993), *Overdues Management in Cooperative Banks,* Himalaya Publishing House, Bombay, p. 110.

73. Renga Reddy, A. (1990), *Agricultural Development: Rural Credit and Problems of its Recovery,* Mittal Publications, New Delhi, p. 124.

74. Sankar Bhowmick (2002), 'Structure and Operations of Rural Credit Markets in West Bengal' www.microcredit.com, p. 2

75. Sarma, A.K. & Kharmowphlang, M.D. (1995), An Analysis of Overdues of Agricultural Credit in East Khasi Hill District of Meghalaya State, *Indian Cooperative Review,* Vol. 33(2), October, p. 123.

76. Sarthak Chowdury and Prabuddha Ray (2001), Cooperative Credit in Rural Sector–A Case Study, *Economic Affairs,* Vol.46(3), September, p. 163.

77. Satyasai, K.J.S. & Viswanathan, K.U. (2003), Role of Moneylenders in Rural Credit Markets—A Temporal Comparison based on All-India Debt & Investment Survey, *National Bank News Review,* Vol.19(4), October–December, p. 21.

78. Satyasai, K.J.S., Venkateswarlu, U., Seetharam, S. and Raghu Ram, P. (1987), Structure of Rural Credit in West Godavari District, A.P. *Land Bank Journal,* Vol. 26(2), December, p. 54.

79. Sharma, D.K., Koshta, A.K., Jain, B.C. (1991), Availability and Utilization of Crop Loan in

Central Madhya Pradesh, *Land Bank Journal*, Vol. 30(1), September, p. 18.

80. Siddappa, B. (1997) Impact of RRB Credit on other Credit Institution in Karnataka, In: *Cooperative Credit and Banking—Strategies for Development* (Ed. by) Garg M.C. & Joshi, N.N., Deep & Deep Publications, New Delhi, p. 107.

81. Singh, A.K., Bajpai, D.K. and Gairia, P. S. (1993), Institutional Finance and the Rural Poor: Findings of a Field Study in a Backward Area, *Indian Cooperative Review*, Vol. 30(4), April p. 401.

82. Sinha, S.K. (1992), *Recovery of Loans from Farmers*, Deep & Deep Publications, New Delhi, p. 210.

83. Somorendra singh (2001), Trend in Recovery of Loan in PACS, *The Maharashtra Cooperative Quarterly*, Vol. 34(4), April-June, p. 14.

84. Srivastava, A.P. (1991), Cooperative Credit for Rural Development, *Indian cooperative review*, Vol. 29(2), October, p. 190.

85. Subbi Reddy, T. and Ramamuni Reddy, C. (1980), Utilisation of Loans, *Land Bank Journal*, Vol. 18(3), March, p. 32.

86. Sudarshan Reddy, A. & Venkateshwar Rao (1999), Performance and Challenges of Cooperative Credit in the Context of Sustainable Rural Development–An Experience of MCRB, *Indian Cooperative Review*, Vol. 37(2), October, p. 83.

87. Sukhdev Singh, Sonia Goyal and Mandeep Mahal (2004), Debt of Peasants: Causes and Consequences, *IASSI quarterly*, Vol. 22940, p. 90.

88. Tiwari, S.N. & Sharma, P. K. (1986), Farm Credit

and Rural Savings, *Cooperative Perspective,* Vol. 21(1), April–June, p. 30.

89. TNSCARDB (2005–06), *Annual Report,* p. 11 & 12.

90. UNI Survey (1975) quoted by: Memoria C.B. and Badri Bishal Tripathi, *Agricultural Problems of India,* Kitab Mahal Agencies, Alahabad, 2001, p. 395.

91. Vaikunthe, L.D. (1991), Agricultural Cooperative Credit–Utilisation and Recovery Performance', *Indian Cooperative Review,* Vol. 29(1), July, p. 42.

92. Venugopala Reddy and Rathakar (1996), 'Credit Utilization Pattern of Farmers, *Land Bank Journal,* Vol. 35(1), September, p. 34.

93. Viswa Prasad, P. & Parthasarathy, P. B. (1993), Supply of Short-term Credit and Estimation of Credit Gaps in Medak District (A.P), *Indian Cooperative Review,* Vol. 30(4), April p. 336.

94. Viswanath, A.R. (2001), An Analysis of the Performance of Agricultural Credit Cooperatives and their Overdues Problems in India, *Indian Cooperative Review,* Vol. 39(1), July, p. 58.

95. www.indiapost.org.

96. www.worldbank.org.

97. www.indiabudget.nic.in

3

Indebtedness and Access to Credit

Introduction

The access to credit by the poor in South Asia has been recognized as one of the crucial factors in the alleviation of rural poverty (Human Development in South Asia: 2002, p. 89). In India, since the introduction of the first Cooperative Credit Societies Act, 1904 and the nationalization of CBs in 1969, various schemes and programmes of the Government developed institutional infrastructure which, in turn, resulted in the creation of massive network for rural banking. Green revolution and white revolution would not have been feasible without the support of this institutional infrastructure for credit. Sizeable numbers of rural households are, however, away from the purview of the institutional sources and the dominance of village moneylenders could not be eliminated.

Access to Institutional Credit

Access to institutional credit is a major indicator, which

decides the productivity of rural households. Social scientists have been paying much importance to the problems associated with access to credit in the RCM. It is especially after 1990s, the subject drew wider attention due to following reasons:

1. The introduction of the New Economic Policy of the Government has curtailed the credit flow to agriculture. The growth in short-term credit to agriculture was 11.8 percent during the period 1970-71 and 1981-82 but decelerated to 10 percent during the period 1982-83 and 1991-92 (Desai B.M.: 1996, p. 2).
2. The introduction of the prudential norms and their impact on the balance sheet of the banks abated even the resemblance of the interests of the bankers in rural lending.
3. The recurrent incidence of drought and its severity dragged the borrowers in the debt trap and made them ineligible for the subsequent loan with IAs.
4. The aggregate amount of outstanding debt of rural households has increased from Rs.1956 crores in 1961 to Rs.22211 crores during the year 1991 (GOI: 1991-92, p. 17).
5. The average amount of outstanding of credit by borrower increased from Rs. 17311 in March 1999 to Rs. 28110 in March 2005 (Subba Rao: 2007, p. 358).

Besides the above, the cumbersome procedures, ineligibility of borrowers due to small holdings, delay in disbursement, continuance of traditional method of cultivation, increase in consumption expenses, lack of awareness on Government schemes and programmes etc., also affected the accessibility of institutional credit by the rural borrowers.

The World Bank-NCAER Rural Financial Access Survey of 2003 clearly confirmed that access to the formal financial institutions remained severely constrained in rural areas, particularly for the poorest of the households, with informal lending still remaining substantial (Priya Basu, Pradeep Srivastava: 2005, p. 1747). If access to credit is made easy when it is required, half of the problems in the RCM could be solved. But the problems pertaining to the access remains complex and deeper than what is generally perceived. Both the institutional and individual factors decide the accessibility of institutional credit. The institutional factors are: the Type of the bank, Location, Experience of bank in rural lending, Procedures followed, Transaction Cost involved, Amount of Loan available and its Interest, Perception of the Employees on rural credit etc. The Individual factors are the demographic, social and economic profile of the individuals, their relationship with the bank, perception of individuals on the functioning of the bank etc. The present study primarily aims at unearthing the factors at the borrower level, contributing or otherwise to the access to institutional credit in RCM.

Demographic, Social and Economic Profile of the Respondents

There are two sets of variables, which help an individual to occupy a particular social position. The first set of variables include caste, kinship relationships, family relationships, family occupation, income etc., The other set encompasses the individual attainment through the efforts like education, occupational skills, economic returns etc. In addition to these two sets of variables, the 'life experiences' of an individual also influence his or her attitude and behaviour pattern (Savitha Thakur Joshi: 1999, p. 8). Identifying the demographic characteristics of the respondents as well as their socio-economic background would, in turn, help to fix the borrower households on the social ladder of the area under study. The researcher would then be in a position to establish the relationship between the demographic socio-economic variables and access to credit of the rural households in the RCM. These form the bases for this chapter.

Age

Age as an important demographic variable not only determines an individual's physical and mental maturity but also depicts his or her life experiences. It determines whether one is economically active or dependent upon others. It decides the participation of the individual in the affairs of the rural credit institutions. There is close relationship between age and member's participation in cooperatives (Pattarnaraka, K. 2003, p. 265). While studies have attempted to prove that age influenced the repayment behaviour and ethics of the respondents (Sivaprakasam, P.: 1993, p. 46, and Joy Joseph Puthussery: 1999, p. 9), the other studies proved contra (Chidambaram, K. *et.al.*, 1999, p. 4).

The age wise distribution of respondents shows that in all RFIs, the participation of middle age group has been high except in PACB in both regions. The respondents above 50 years of age were high in PACB in both wet and dry regions (Table-3.1). This may be

Table 3.1: Age-wise Distribution of the Respondents

(Figures in numbers)

Age	PACB		PCARDB		CB		SHG		Total		Grand
	Dry	Wet	Dry	Wet	Dry	Wet	Dry	Wet	Dry	Wet	Total
>35	8 (7)	7 (6)	-	1 (8)	3 (7)	6 (17)	5 (40)	2 (27)	16 (9)	16 (11)	32 (10)
36-50	48 (45)	30 (36)	8 (60)	6 (58)	21 (47)	21 (57)	8 (60)	5 (55)	85 (48)	62 (43)	147 (45)
Above 50	51 (48)	50 (58)	6 (40)	4 (34)	21 (47)	10 (26)	-	2 (18)	78 (43)	66 (46)	144 (45)
Grand Total	107	87	14	11	45	37	13	9	179	144	323

Source: Compiled from respondents schedule

Note: Figures in parenthesis indicates percentage to column total.

due to the fact that this group of respondents had high affinity with their cooperatives due to their long years of membership. Though the impact of age of the respondents in their relationship with their institutions and repayment behaviour have varied across the region and institution, the participation of middle age group has been high; this is a sign of development on both sides.

Sex

One significant universally accepted criterion of development is gender. There is a clear distinction made in development literature between sex and gender. Sex relates to the biological differences between male and female, whereas gender relates to the roles assigned to male and female in the society. Thus, gender is a socio-economic variable involving roles, responsibilities, constraints, opportunities and needs of males and females in an economy (Sharma, K.C. 1988, p. 126). The banking institutions may not formally indulge in sex discrimination against women for the purpose of extending loan, but, there may be a number of formalities, which a loanee has to complete and the rural women, being ignorant, may not have easy access to credit. Secondly, while advancing loans, the banks may also demand surety or guarantee, which in the villages is primarily based on land. As family lands are in the name of the male members, women are further put to disadvantageous position (Human Development in South Asia: 2002, pp. 114-155).

In this study, it was found that women constituted only one third of the total sample population. Only, 25 percent women in wet and 6 percent of them in

Table 3.2: Sex-wise Distribution of the Respondents

(Figures in numbers)

Sex	*PACB*		*PCARDB*		*CB*		*SHG*		*Total*		*Grand*
	Dry	*Wet*	*Dry*	*Wet*	*Dry*	*Wet*	*Dry*	*Wet*	*Dry*	*Wet*	*Total*
Male	107 (100)	68 (78)	14 (100)	9 (83)	45 (100)	33 (88)	-	-	166 (94)	110 (75)	276 (86)
Female	-	19 (22)	-	2 (17)	-	4 (12)	13 (100)	9 (100)	13 (6)	34 (25)	47 (14)
Grand Total	107	87	14	11	45	37	13	9	179	144	323

Source: As in table – 3.1

Note: As in table – 3.1.

dry had access to institutional credit. Among the total respondents, only around 15 percent of women had access to institutional credit. At present, the SHGs play remarkable role in promoting women's participation towards the economic development of the village. The institution-wise analysis showed that in the sample area where only the women SHGs were functioning, more than 46 percent of the total women respondents were having access to credit with their SHG. Another major segment of the women respondents constituting 40 per cent had access to credit with PACB (Table-3.2). This proves that PACBs have not been discriminating members on the basis of sex.

Community

The Indian society remains stratified on caste and this is more true in rural areas. Caste is perceived as an important factor, which determined one's social prestige and social intercourse. The position of a caste in the hierarchy is independent of its status.

The community-wise analysis showed that in dry region, the scheduled caste people had relationship only with the PACB and in both the regions (Table - 3.3) they did not have any relationship with SHGs. It was found that the SHGs formed especially for this community could not continue their operations. The continuous migration of the labour force due to drought and the inability of the NGOs to develop these SHGs as IGPs, were found to be the reasons. However, these reasons have not affected the interests of the NGOs in the study area to form new SHGs especially for this community.

Table 3.3: Community-wise Distribution of the Respondents

(Figures in numbers)

Community	PACB		PCARDB		CB		SHG		Total		Grand
	Dry	*Wet*	*Dry*	*Wet*	*Dry*	*Wet*	*Dry*	*Wet*	*Dry*	*Wet*	*Total*
SC	19 (17)	13 (15)	-	1 (8)	-	16 (43)	-	-	19 (11)	30 (21)	49 (15)
MBC	3 (3)	12 (14)	-	4 (33)	9 (20)	4 (12)	3 (20)	1 (9)	15 (8)	21 (15)	36 (11)
BC	85 (79)	62 (71)	14 (100)	6 (59)	36 (80)	17 (45)	10 (80)	8 (91)	145 (81)	93 (64)	238 (74)
Grand Total	107	87	14	11	45	37	13	9	179	144	323

Source: As in table – 3.1

Note : As in table – 3.1.

Educational Status

Whether literacy is synonymous with education in the developing countries and with reference to the weaker sections is a question confronts the social scientists. Viewed as synonymous, education not only widens the knowledge but also helps a person to make use of rational and scientific approach to solve problems. Education has positive impact on social life and the quality of life; and vice versa with illiteracy; the educated borrowers have a tendency to utilize their loans on productive and specified purpose (Debrata Das: 2002, p. 27). Credit has directly and indirectly affected the education pattern (Jugale; V.B.: 1992, p. 86). Some studies revealed that the borrowers with lesser education had fear consciousness and had respect to the laws of the land (Prasad J.V.S. et.al: 1987, p. 5). Owing to the ignorance and illiteracy, the rural households borrow to secure a minimum subsistence for himself and his family. (Mamoria C.B. and Badri Bishal Tripathi: 2001, p. 397). The shrewd moneylenders use this chance to exploit them. It has been said that the moneylender tempts rural people to borrow, the lawyer to quarrel and the trader to waste (Perumalsamy, P.: 1996, p. 382).

In Tamil Nadu the privatization process accelerated the growth of educational institutions from primary to collegiate level even in rural areas. This process has brought quality and status in education. As far as the study area is concerned, both the regions were having facilities from primary to higher education. The analysis showed that the percentage of respondent with no formal education was slightly higher in the wet region than the dry region. The institution wise

Table 3.4: Educational Status of the Respondents

(Figures in numbers)

Educational Status	PACB		PCARDB		CB		SHG		Total		Grand Total
	Dry	Wet	Dry	Wet	Dry	Wet	Dry	Wet	Dry	Wet	
No Formal Education	17 (16)	19 (22)	3 (20)	2 (17)	6 (13)	5 (14)	3 (20)	3 (36)	29 (16)	31 (22)	60 (19)
Primary	41 (39)	41 (47)	5 (40)	2 (25)	15 (33)	11 (29)	3 (20)	5 (55)	64 (36)	59 (40)	123 (38)
Secondary	28 (26)	14 (16)	3 (20)	4 (33)	21 (47)	13 (36)	7 (60)	1 (9)	59 (33)	32 (22)	91 (28)
Higher Secondary	16 (15)	7 (8)	-	2 (17)	3 (7)	4 (10)	-	-	19 (11)	11 (8)	30 (9)
Degree	5 (5)	6 (7)	3 (20)	1 (8)	-	4 (12)	-	-	8 (4)	11 (8)	19 (6)
Grand Total	107	87	14	11	45	37	13	9	179	144	323

Source: As in table 3.1

Note: As in table 3.1.

analysis showed that the number of respondents with formal education was high in PACB compared to other institutions. Most of the respondents belonging to CBs were at the level of secondary school education. Interestingly, it could be found that the SHGs were targeting the people with no formal education and school drop-outs (Table 3.4).

Marital Status

In Indian society, marriage is supposed to be a religious obligation. In the social context, it is the prelude to the family formation, expansion or even bifurcation. After marriage, there is a transition in the status of men and women with attendant rights and obligations.

Marital status of the respondents showed that respondents in the unmarried category were having access with all institutions except SHGs though they were in small number. The SHGs target only the married and widowed (Table 3.5). The Unmarried women were not accommodated in the SHGs, as the chance of mobility is high after the marriage.

3.9 Type of Family

The family background plays an important role in moulding the behaviour of its members. The family provides the recognition and security for the individuals as also their identity. The living arrangements are very crucial for the socio-economic status of a person.

In the study area, it was found that irrespective of the agency, to which the respondent belonged, majority of them in both regions belonged to nuclear family system (Table 3.6) which reflected the growing tendency

Table 3.5: Marital Status of the Respondents

(Figures in numbers)

Martial Status	*PACB*		*PCARDB*		*CB*		*SHG*		*Total*		*Grand Total*
	Dry	*Wet*	*Dry*	*Wet*	*Dry*	*Wet*	*Dry*	*Wet*	*Dry*	*Wet*	
Unmarried	8 (7)	6 (7)	3 (20)	-	3 (7)	1 (2)	-	-	14 (8)	7 (5)	21 (7)
Married	99 (93)	81 (93)	11 (80)	10 (92)	42 (93)	36 (98)	8 (60)	7 (82)	160 (89)	134 (93)	294 (91)
Widowed	-	-	-	1 (8)	-	-	5 (40)	2 (18)	5 (3)	3 (2)	8 (2)
Grand Total	107	87	14	11	45	37	13	9	179	144	323

Source: As in table – 3.1

Note: As in table – 3.1.

Table 3.6: Type of Family-Wise Distribution of the Respondents

(Figures in numbers)

Type of Family	*PACB*		*PCARDB*		*CB*		*SHG*		*Total*		*Grand Total*
	Dry	*Wet*	*Dry*	*Wet*	*Dry*	*Wet*	*Dry*	*Wet*	*Dry*	*Wet*	
Nuclear	57 (53)	62 (71)	14 (100)	6 (58)	36 (80)	29 (79)	8 (60)	7 (82)	115 (64)	104 (72)	219 (68)
Joint	50 (47)	25 (29)	-	5 (42)	9 (20)	8 (21)	5 (40)	2 (18)	64 (36)	40 (28)	104 (32)
Grand Total	107	87	14	11	45	37	13	9	179	144	323

Source: As in table – 3.1

Note : As in table – 3.1.

among the younger generation to live separately from their parents when they became economically independent (Maninder Kaur et.al: 1997, p. 31). The advantage or otherwise of the joint or nuclear family system remains an area beyond the scope of the researcher. The point to be noted has been that the nuclear family system has boosted the dispensation of rural credit.

Number of Members in the Family

There have been a number of studies showing the relationship between the family size and borrowings. The size of the family of the borrowers determines the scope of consumption and potentialities of production and thereby the solvency of the borrowers (Dadhich, C.L: 1977, p. 53). The family size of the beneficiaries is related to the repayment performance (Chidambaram. K.: 1999, p. 5). The defaulter group families were often found to be of large size and caught in the vicious circle of the mundane realities of life, which might be a reason for their failure to use the loan productively (Namasivayam, D. and Ramachandraiah, G.: 2000, p. 419). However, the relationship between the family size and the nature of default has not found to be quite significant (Joy Joseph Puthuserry: 1999, p. 9).

The present study found that in tune with the nuclear family system, the number of members in the family was four in majority of the respondent families (Table 3.7).

Table 3.7: Total Number of Members in the Family

(Figures in numbers)

Total Number	*PACB*		*PCARDB*		*CB*		*SHG*		*Total*		*Grand*
of Members	*Dry*	*Wet*	*Dry*	*Wet*	*Dry*	*Wet*	*Dry*	*Wet*	*Dry*	*Wet*	*Total*
Below 4	89 (84)	75 (86)	14 (100)	4 (33)	33 (73)	26 (69)	13 (100)	7 (82)	149 (83)	112 (78)	261 (81)
Above 4	18 (16)	12 (14)	-	7 (67)	12 (27)	11 (31)	-	2 (18)	30 (17)	32 (22)	62 (19)
Grand Total	107	87	14	11	45	37	13	9	179	144	323

Source: As in table – 3.1

Note: As in table – 3.1.

Exposure to Mass Media

The information revolution has deeply penetrated into the rural life. The village tea-shops remain the common meeting centres for the rural folk and they offer the Dailies in vernacular language for public reference as also the radio and T.V. services. The State Government has provided T.V. sets to all the panchayats for public information services. The competition between the T.V. channels and radio has loaded information on village life. Transport remains unattractive without the T.V., or FM Radio facilities. The exposure to the mass media enabled the rural people to understand the day-to-day developments regarding the social welfare measures and economic schemes concerning agriculture and rural development.

With a view to rate the exposure of the sample respondents regarding their access to the media and consequent awareness, the data were collected as part of the study and it was found that, in both regions, the Newspapers were the major source of information whereas in the case of the TV and Radio, the majority of the respondents in both the region were found to have regular access due to reasons stated above (Table 3.8).

Contact with Change Agents

The Government and Non-Government Organizations including Cooperatives are considered to be the change agents of the village economy. Through various programmes and schemes, these agents work for the development of the village economy. The contact established by an individual with these agents enhances

Table 3.8: Exposure to Mass Media

(Figures in numbers)

Particulars	*PACB*		*PCARDB*		*CB*		*SHG*		*Total*		*Grand*
	Dry	*Wet*	*Dry*	*Wet*	*Dry*	*Wet*	*Dry*	*Wet*	*Dry*	*Wet*	*Total*
Regularly	70 (65)	70 (80)	8 (60)	7 (67)	12 (27)	19 (52)	8 (60)	6 (64)	98 (55)	102 (71)	200 (62)
Occasionally	37 (35)	12 (14)	6 (40)	2 (17)	27 (60)	15 (41)	5 (40)	2 (27)	75 (41)	31 (22)	106 (32)
Rarely	-	5 (6)	-	1 (8)	6 (13)	2 (4)	-	1 (9)	6 (3)	7 (6)	15 (5)
Never	-	-	-	1 (8)	-	1 (3)	-	-	-	2 (1)	2 (1)
Grand Total	107	87	14	11	45	37	13	9	179	144	323

Source: As in table 3.1

Note: As in table 3.1.

Table 3.9: Contact with Change Agents

(*Figures in numbers*)

Particulars	*PACB*		*PCARDB*		*CB*		*SHG*		*Total*		*Grand*
	Dry	*Wet*	*Dry*	*Wet*	*Dry*	*Wet*	*Dry*	*Wet*	*Dry*	*Wet*	*Total*
No	59	54	3	3	24	14	-	-	86	71	157
	(55)	(62)	(20)	(25)	(53)	(38)			(48)	(49)	(49)
Yes	48	33	11	8	21	23	13	9	93	73	166
	(45)	(38)	(80)	(75)	(47)	(62)	(100)	(100)	(52)	(51)	(51)
Grand Total	107	87	14	11	45	37	13	9	179	144	323

Source: As in table – 3.1

Note: As in table - 3.1.

his or her access to various agricultural programmes, facilitates and their grip over a development process. To measure the contact of the individual with the change agents, the questions such as: Do the Government Officials come to your village to meet the public? Do the Non-Government Officials come to your village to meet the public? Have you met any of them any time? In a month how many times you are meeting them? were freely asked.

It was found that more than 50 percent of the respondents were having contacts with Government and Non-Government Organizations in the study area. Further, it was found that all the respondents belonging to the SHG were having regular contact with the change agents (Table 3.9).

Membership

An institution is a change inducing and change formalizing organization; Its functions and services are related to society's commonly agreed upon requirements as tested by their adaptability to human needs and values; Its internal structures protect the commonly held norms and values of the society; Its achievements include influencing the environment in positive ways through the values it creates (Taimani, K.K.: 1993, p. 240). In very many occasions, the grass-root institutional agencies, viz., Cooperatives, SHGs and Panchayat Raj Institutions serve as platforms for the blossoming of inherent leadership ability of an individual. As far as the CBs were concerned, they were having only customers and not members. In this study, an effort has been made to understand the level of association of the respondents with these agencies.

Table 3.10: Membership in Institutions

(Figures in numbers)

Name of the Institution	*Dry*	*Wet*	*Total*
CB	45 (25)	37 (26)	82 (25)
PACB	107 (60)	79 (54)	186 (57)
PCARDB	14 (8)	11 (8)	25 (8)
SHG	13 (7)	9 (6)	22 (7)
PACB & PCARDB	-	5 (4)	5 (2)
PACB & SHG	-	3 (2)	3 (1)
Grand Total	179	144	323

Source: As in table 3.1

Note: As in table 3.1.

Note 2: As far as respondents associated with CB were concerned they were only customers and members.

It was found that in both the regions, a majority of the respondents (57 percent) were having membership with the PACB (Table 3.10 and chart – 3.1). As far as the PACBs were concerned, the majority of the members in both regions (66 per cent in the dry and 55 per cent in wet) had membership for more than 10 years. Similar findings have also been reported by (Krishna Naik, C.N. & Siddaiah 1990, p. 38). The SHGs, based on membership, were found in both regions during the last 3 years (Table 3.11).

Table 3.11: Duration of Membership

(Figures in numbers)

Particulars	PACB		PCARDB		CB		SHG		Total		Grand
	Dry	Wet	Dry	Wet	Dry	Wet	Dry	Wet	Dry	Wet	Total
Non-member	-	-	-	-	45 (100)	37 (100)	-	-	45 (25)	37 (26)	82 (25)
1-3	5 (5)	-	-	-	-	-	13 (100)	19 (100)	18 (10)	19 (13)	37 (12)
4-6	11 (10)	13 (16)	-	2 (17)	-	-	-	-	11 (6)	15 (10)	26 (8)
7-9	20 (19)	22 (29)	-	2 (25)	-	-	-	-	20 (11)	24 (17)	44 (14)
Above 10	71 (66)	42 (55)	14 (100)	7 (58)	-	-	-	-	85 (48)	49 (34)	134 (41)
Grand Total	107	87	14	11	45	37	13	9	179	144	323

Source: As in table 3.1

Note: As in table 3.1.

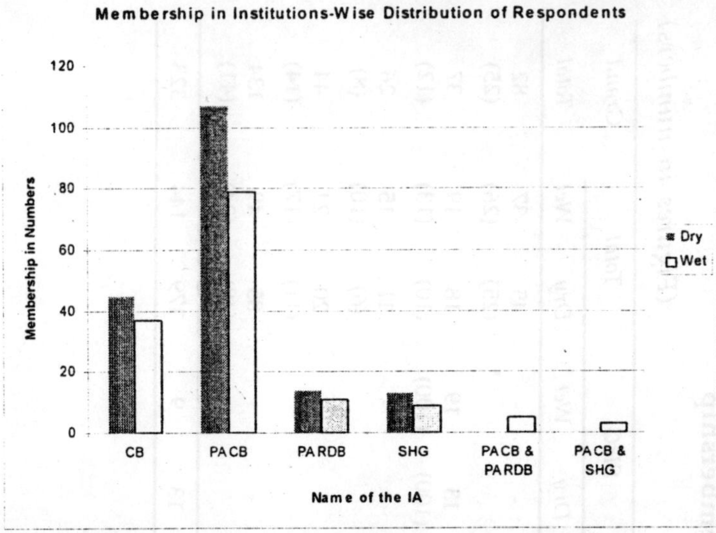

Chart 3.1

Membership of the Family Members in Institutions

During the study, it was found that in a family more than one person was made the member of the PACB, PCARDB or SHG.

Among the various reasons stated by the respondents like additional voting rights arising from new membership, the empowerment of women, increased association between family and the institution etc., the prime reason identified was that the additional membership of the family members enhanced the borrowing capacity of the family. In both regions, it was found that the majority of the family members of the sample respondent families had membership with the PACB (Table 3.12).

Table 3.12: Membership of the Family Members in Institutions

(Figures in numbers)

Particulars	PACB		PCARDB		CB		SHG		Total		Grand
	Dry	Wet	Dry	Wet	Dry	Wet	Dry	Wet	Dry	Wet	Total
PACB	14 (13)	17 (20)	6 (40)	2 (18)	-	5 (5)	5 (40)	1 (18)	25 (14)	22 (15)	47 (14)
PACB & PCARDB	-	-	-	2 (18)	-	-	-	-	-	2 (2)	2 (1)
Sub Total	14	17	6	2	-	5	5	1	25	24	49
No Member Ship	93	70	8	7	45	35	8	8	154	120	274
Grand Total	107	87	14	12	45	37	13	9	179	144	323

Source: As in table 3.1

Note : As in table 3.1.

Membership in Social Organizations

The study found that there was interaction between the respondents and the social organizations, which included caste organizations and political organizations. It was found that political intervention in the dispensation of rural credit and its management had become a necessary evil. Political groups or parties counted their strength in the number of Cooperatives and village Panchayats under the control. Cooperatives and village Panchayats often turned into platforms for village politics and oriented along political lines (Jugale, V.B.: 1992, p. 87). The interference of politics in the Cooperative Movement resulted in the polarization of theory and practice (Jugale, V.B.: 1994, p. 61). Better social and political links resulted higher magnitude of borrowings and consequent overdues (Chinnappa Reddy, B.V. et.al.,: 1987, p. 4). A large number of willful defaulters emerged because of political influences which resulted in poor recovery performance (Rajput, A.M. et.al: 1993, p. 56). In general the existence of the political network enhances the social and political contacts in society (Padmini, C: 2004, p. 28).

It was found that majority of the respondents belonging to the PACB (80 per cent) and PCARDB (above 40 per cent) had membership with the political parties in both the regions. The respondents of CB also had membership with political parties in both the regions (13 per cent in dry and 46 per cent in wet) (Table 3.13).

Table 3.13: Membership in Social Organizations

(Figures in numbers)

Particulars	*PACB*		*PCARDB*		*CB*		*SHG*		*Total*		*Grand*
	Dry	*Wet*	*Dry*	*Wet*	*Dry*	*Wet*	*Dry*	*Wet*	*Dry*	*Wet*	*Total*
Caste organization	11 (15)	10 (21)	3 (21)	4 (57)	-	8 (54)	-	-	14 (15)	23 (32)	37 (22)
Social organization	62 (85)	38 (79)	11 (79)	3 (43)	6 (100)	7 (46)	-	2 (100)	79 (85)	48 (68)	127 (78)
Total	73	48	14	7	6	15	-	-	93	71	164
No membership	34	39	14	4	39	22	13	9	86	73	159
Grand Total	107	87	14	12	45	37	13	9	179	144	323

Source: As in table 3.1.

Note: As in table 3.1.

Occupation

Occupation determines the social standing of a family. This is due to the fact that the different occupations decide the status as also the varying privileges and economic benefits (Savita Thakur Joshi: 1999, p. 42). A study on the occupational pattern in rural areas throws light on the number of people who depend on agriculture and those on non-agriculture and both. Agriculture is a labour-intensive enterprise. Though agriculture provides work for most of the people, non-agricultural activities are important supplementary sources of income for the rural households. A shortage of remunerative work opportunities off the farm during the slack season might increase the poverty of those whose holdings are too small or too unproductive to provide an adequate livelihood (Shakuntala Devi: 1996, p. 8). After 1980s, the level of poverty declined in many states due to the growth in rural non-farm sector.

It was found that agriculture remained the major economic activity of the sample respondents in the study region (51 per cent in dry and 62 per cent in wet). Next to this, in dry region, the borrowers depended on weaving (18 per cent) and self-employment (11 per cent) whereas the second strata of respondents in the wet region were agricultural labourers (12 per cent). A small percentage of respondents were self-employed (6 per cent) in wet region (Table 3.14). As the drought has had direct impact on agriculture, the continuance of drought in this region has led to severe socio-economic and cultural implications on the society. A farm based non-farm sector development would be able to address all these problems, generate employment opportunities and, even

Table 3.14: Primary Occupation

(Figures in numbers)

Name of the	*PACB*		*PCARDB*		*CB*		*SHG*		*Total*		*Grand*
Occupation	*Dry*	*Wet*	*Dry*	*Wet*	*Dry*	*Wet*	*Dry*	*Wet*	*Dry*	*Wet*	*Total*
Agriculture	88 (72)	83 (95)	11 (80)	8 (75)	14 (7)	13 (21)	-	-	113 (63)	105 (73)	218 (56)
Dairy	3 (3)	4 (5)	-	-	-	2 (5)	-	1 (18)	3 (2)	7 (5)	10 (3)
Agri-Labour	-	-	-	2 (17)	-	7 (19)	10 (80)	3 (37)	10 (6)	12 (12)	22 (8)
Non-agri. Labour	-	-	-	-	-	4 (12)	3 (20)	2 (19)	3 (3)	6 (6)	9 (4)
Govt. Employee	-	-	-	-	3 (7)	4 (10)	-	1 (9)	3 (2)	5 (4)	8 (3)
Weaving	16 (15)	-	-	-	18 (40)	-	-	-	34 (18)	-	34 (11)
Self-employed	-	-	3 (20)	1 (8)	10 (22)	7 (19)	-	1 (9)	13 (11)	9 (6)	22 (9)
Grand Total	107	87	14	11	45	37	13	9	179	144	323

Source: As in table 3.1
Note: As in table 3.1.

in the long run, reduce the dependence on agriculture by the village population.

Further, the dependence on agricultural activities by the sample respondents in both the regions could be found from the figures given in the table-3.14. In both regions, very high proportion of the total respondents had depended on dairy, self-employment and weaving as the secondary occupation.

The advantage of having secondary occupation is that the income generated from that occupation could substitute the growing need of the individual family. Generally, Animal Husbandry was found to be the secondary occupation in the rural areas. But the mechanization of agriculture and continuance of drought severely hit this occupation too. On the other hand, the big farmers and landlords have developed dairy farms (30 per cent in dry and 38 per cent in wet). As the available water sources could be sufficient for cultivating fodder for dairy animals, dairy industry would become a natural subsidiary occupation (Maninder Kaur, et.al: 1997, p. 32) in the wet region (38 per cent) whereas in the case of the dry region, in addition to the dairy (30 per cent), self-employment (10 per cent) and weaving (14 per cent) have been the supporting occupations for the rural households (Table 3.15). The institution wise analysis showed that a majority of the SHG respondents were agricultural and non-agricultural labourers.

Type of House

The concept of property in the villages is confined to the size of the land holdings and the type of the house in which the family live. Generally, the concept of

Table 3.15: Secondary Occupation

(Figures in numbers)

Agriculture	*PACB*		*PCARDB*		*CB*		*SHG*		*Total*		*Grand*
	Dry	*Wet*	*Dry*	*Wet*	*Dry*	*Wet*	*Dry*	*Wet*	*Dry*	*Wet*	*Total*
Agriculture	17	10	3	2	6	3	-	-	26	15	41
	(16)	(11)	(20)	(17)	(13)	(7)			(15)	(10)	(18)
Dairy	39	36	6	6	9	10	-	2	54	54	108
	(36)	(42)	(40)	(55)	(20)	(5)		(27)	(30)	(38)	(48)
Weaving	16	-	-	-	6	-	3	-	25	21	46
	(15)				(13)		(20)		(14)	(15)	(20)
Self-employed	10	9	5	-	-	2	3	1	18	12	30
	(8)	(10)	(40)			(5)	(20)	(9)	(10)	(8)	(14)
Grand Total	107	87	14	11	45	37	13	9	179	144	323

Source: As in table 3.1

Note: As in table 3.1.

property has two components i.e., real property, and the movable property. As it is difficult to get information about the movable property of the respondents under study, it was decided to confine the study only to the real property i.e., the size of the land holdings and the house type.

The house is the prestigious asset for the individual family in Indian culture. Every individual wants to have a separate house. This has given boost to the construction industry. But, institutional support available for house construction has not touched the rural population. House asset is not only the main asset for the rural people. It serves the main security for obtaining credit from certain credit agencies.

The study found that majority of the respondents were having tiled houses (89 per cent), and they were followed by those who have the huts and terraced buildings in the wet region (Table 3.16). As the financial institutions have the strong conviction that the rate of default would be high due to the reason that even after the implementation of the liberal financial schemes for housing by the Government, the majority of the rural households had only tiled houses or huts. However, all the sample rural households were living in their own houses only.

Majority of the respondents' value of the house in the dry region was between Rs. 20000 to Rs. 40000 due to mud walls whereas in the wet region, it was between Rs. 40000 to Rs. 60000 due to cement walls (Table 3.17). This was because; most of the respondents in the wet region had constructed their houses by using Government schemes and benefits.

Table 3.16: Type of House

(Figures in numbers)

Particulars	*PACB*		*PCARDB*		*CB*		*SHG*		*Total*		*Grand Total*
	Dry	*Wet*	*Dry*	*Wet*	*Dry*	*Wet*	*Dry*	*Wet*	*Dry*	*Wet*	
Hut	8	6	-	-	-	1	3	2	11	9	20
	(7)	(7)				(2)	(20)	(27)	(6)	(6)	(6)
Tiled	96	73	14	11	45	31	10	7	165	122	287
	(90)	(84)	(100)	(100)	(100)	(83)	(80)	(73)	(92)	(85)	(89)
Terraced	3	8	-	-	-	5	-	-	3	13	16
	(3)	(9)				(15)			(2)	(9)	(5)
Grand Total	107	87	14	11	45	37	13	9	179	144	323

Source: As in table 3.1

Note: As in table 3.1.

Table 3.17: Value of the House

(Figures in numbers)

Home Value	*PACB*		*PCARDB*		*CB*		*SHG*		*Total*		*Grand*
(in Rs.)	*Dry*	*Wet*	*Dry*	*Wet*	*Dry*	*Wet*	*Dry*	*Wet*	*Dry*	*Wet*	*Total*
10001-20000	6 (5)	10 (12)	-	1 (8)	-	4 (10)	3 (20)	4 (46)	9 (5)	19 (13)	28 (9)
20001-40000	51 (48)	32 (37)	8 (60)	3 (25)	21 (48)	7 (19)	3 (20)	2 (27)	83 (46)	44 (31)	127 (39)
40001-60000	34 (32)	29 (33)	3 (20)	7 (64)	15 (33)	15 (41)	7 (60)	2 (18)	59 (33)	53 (37)	112 (35)
60001-1lakh	14 (13)	11 (12)	3 (20)	-	6 (13)	7 (19)	-	1 (9)	23 (13)	19 (13)	42 (13)
Above 1lakh	2 (2)	5 (6)	-	-	3 (7)	4 (11)	-	-	5 (3)	9 (6)	14 (4)
Grand Total	107	87	14	11	45	37	13	9	179	144	323

Source: As in table 3.1

Note: As in table 3.1.

Table 3.18: Land Holdings

(Figures in numbers)

Particulars	*PACB*		*PCARDB*		*CB*		*SHG*		*Total*		*Grand Total*
	Dry	*Wet*	*Dry*	*Wet*	*Dry*	*Wet*	*Dry*	*Wet*	*Dry*	*Wet*	
No	-	-	-	-	18 (40)	24 (64)	13 (100)	9 (100)	31 (13)	33 (23)	64 (20)
Yes	107 (100)	87 (100)	14 (100)	11 (100)	27 (60)	13 (36)	-	-	148 (83)	111 (77)	259 (80)
Grand Total	107	87	14	11	45	37	13	9	179	144	323

Source: As in table 3.1

Note : As in table 3.1.

Land Holdings

Land is the main asset, next to the house for the rural people. House provides shelter whereas land helps the respondents to win their daily bread. Land is not only prestigious but is the place of occupation and the focal point of survival for many. Size of landholding in agriculture is a crucial factor on which the development activity is to be taken into account. A small size of farm is not economical (Reddy, C.R.: 1993, p. 33). As the size of the farm increased, the net profit also increased (Dhimen Namhata *et.al*: 1988, p. 306).

Majority of the respondents belong to CBs (40 per cent in dry and 64 per cent in wet) and all the sample respondents of SHG do not posses any land. Majority of the landowners have availed credit from the Cooperative Banks (Table 3.18).

Land as an asset which is deciding the socio-economic status of the rural people, has profound influence on the access, use and repayment of institutional credit. Hence, the ownership of the land is inherited by the legal heirs often resulting in the fragmentation of landholdings. The fragmentation, loss of land due to debt, continuance of drought, absence of improved methods of agriculture, over dependence on agriculture etc., all have bred the small and marginal farmers. When the intensity of the above said factors are high, even a segment of this farming community becomes landless. In tune to the national trend, the study found that majority of the respondents (48 per cent) were medium farmers in the study area (Table 3.19).

Table 3.19: Total Size of Land Holding

(Figures in numbers)

Particulars	*PACB*		*PCARDB*		*CB*		*SHG*		*Total*		*Grand*
	Dry	*Wet*	*Dry*	*Wet*	*Dry*	*Wet*	*Dry*	*Wet*	*Dry*	*Wet*	*Total*
Below 2.5	11 (10)	6 (7)	3 (21)	1 (9)	12 (44)	2 (15)	-	-	26 (18)	9 (8)	35 (14)
2.5 – 5	56 (52)	38 (44)	-	6 (55)	15 (56)	10 (77)	-	-	71 (48)	54 (49)	125 (48)
Above 5	40 (38)	43 (49)	11 (79)	4 (36)	-	1 (8)	-	-	51 (34)	48 (43)	99 (38)
Total	107	87	14	11	27	13	-	-	148	111	259
Grand Total	107	87	14	11	45	37	13	9	179	144	323

Source: As in table 3.1

Note : As in table 3.1.

Cropping Pattern

Raising crops by inter as well as intra cropping is termed as cropping pattern. The cropping pattern depends on the agronomic nature of the region. The determining factors of the cropping pattern are the rainfall in the current year; prices of agricultural commodities and shift in pattern of crops in the preceding year.

The wet region has a potential for cultivation of chilies and onions. At present, the farmers shift for cultivation of coconut, vegetables, flowers, maize, etc. In dry region, half of the farmers cultivate paddy; the rest of them cultivate maize, coconut, vegetables and fruits (Table 3.20).

Total Assets Value

Land and house were the major assets of the sample respondents. As dairy is accepted as an alternative occupation in the study area, animal assets also occupy a vital place in the total asset holdings of the farmers. Hence, the total asset has been the combination of house, land, household and animal assets.

Majority of the respondents in the study areas (36 per cent in dry and 28 per cent in wet) came under the category of holding assets between Rs. 2 lakhs to 3 lakhs. Majority of the respondents belonging to SHGs held within Rs. 1 lakh. It was also evident that the SHGs gave shelter for the landless and resourceless (Table 3.21), the condemned of the earth.

Table 3.20: Cropping Pattern

(Figures in numbers)

Name of	*PACB*		*PCARDB*		*CB*		*SHG*		*Total*		*Grand*
Crops	*Dry*	*Wet*	*Dry*	*Wet*	*Dry*	*Wet*	*Dry*	*Wet*	*Dry*	*Wet*	*Total*
Paddy	55	-	8	1	12	-	-	-	75	1	76
	(51)		(57)	(9)	(44)				(51)	(1)	(29)
Maize	23	1	-	-	12	-	-	-	35	1	36
	(21)	(1)			(44)				(24)	(1)	(14)
Fruits	5	2	-	1	-	2	-	-	5	5	10
	(5)	(3)		(9)		(15)			(3)	(5)	(4)
Vegetables	5	10	-	1	3	2	-	-	8	13	21
	(5)	(12)		(9)	(12)	(15)			(5)	(11)	(9)
Flowers	-	18	-	-	-	1	-	-	-	19	19
		(21)				(8)				(17)	(7)
Millets	-	2	-	-	-	-	-	-	-	2	2
		(2)								(2)	(1)
Coconut	19	54	6	8	-	8	-	-	25	70	95
	(18)	(62)	(43)	(73)		(62)			(17)	(62)	(36)
Total	107	87	14	11	27	13	-	-	148	111	259
No landholding	-	-	-	-	18	24	13	9	31	33	64
Grand Total	107	87	14	11	45	37	13	9	179	144	323

Source: As in table 3.1

Note: As in table 3.1.

Income from Agriculture

It is a common practice to calculate the repaying capacity of the borrowers by evaluating the size of holdings and other socio-economic factors. As land is the major asset of the rural households, the land holdings are used as the security on which loans are issued. But it is a fact that the land as immovable property, causes more maintenance charges in order to productively utilizes it. The income of the farmers cannot be assessed accurately for agriculture depends on various fluctuating factors like yield and price of the products, storage, marketing facilities and monsoon (Joy Joseph Puthussery: 1999, p. 10).

The present study found that majority of the respondents (53 per cent) got an income from agriculture below Rs. 10000 in both the regions. They belonged to the Cooperative Banks, those for whom agriculture was the primary occupation, earned an annual income from land below Rs. 20000 (more than 32 per cent in dry and 24 per cent in wet). The respondents getting above Rs. 20000 were very few in both the regions (Table 3.22).

Marketing of Agricultural Produces

There lies a close association between the income and the marketing services in agriculture. In the agricultural sector as elsewhere in the Indian context, money and marketing, the 2 Ms, are the basic tenets to improve the economic quality of life. If these two closely cooperate, the risk of overdues is considerably reduced (RBI: 1969, p. 534). The money economy and higher prices ruling in the market tempt the peasants to

Table 3.21: Total Assets Value

(Figures in numbers)

Particulars	*PACB*		*PCARDB*		*CB*		*SHG*		*Total*		*Grand*
	Dry	*Wet*	*Dry*	*Wet*	*Dry*	*Wet*	*Dry*	*Wet*	*Dry*	*Wet*	*Total*
Below 50000	-	-	-	-	3 (7)	6 (16)	2 (15)	2 (22)	5 (3)	8 (5)	13 (4)
50,001-1,00,000	3 (3)	1 (1)	-	-	9 (20)	12 (32)	11 (85)	6 (67)	23 (12)	19 (13)	42 (13)
1,00,001-2,00,000	14 (13)	9 (10)	-	1 (9)	12 (27)	7 (19)	-	1 (11)	26 (15)	18 (13)	44 (14)
2,00,001-3,00,000	45 (42)	28 (32)	2 (14)	6 (55)	18 (40)	6 (16)	-	-	65 (36)	40 (28)	105 (33)
3,00,001-4,00,000	26 (24)	23 (26)	6 (43)	2 (18)	3 (6)	5 (14)	-	-	35 (20)	30 (21)	65 (20)
Above 4,00,000	19 (18)	26 (31)	6 (43)	2 (18)	-	1 (2)	-	-	25 (14)	29 (20)	54 (16)
Grand Total	107	87	14	11	45	37	13	9	179	144	323

Source: As in table 3.1.

Note: As in table 3.1.

Table 3.22: Income from Agriculture

(*Figures in numbers*)

Income	*PACB*		*PCARDB*		*CB*		*SHG*		*Total*		*Grand*
Amount (Rs.)	*Dry*	*Wet*	*Dry*	*Wet*	*Dry*	*Wet*	*Dry*	*Wet*	*Dry*	*Wet*	*Total*
Below 10,000	67	31	6	5	21	8	-	-	94	44	138
	(63)	(36)	(43)	(50)	(18)	(57)			(64)	(40)	(53)
10,001-20,000	34	21	8	2	6	3	-	-	48	26	74
	(32)	(24)	(57)	(20)	(22)	(21)			(32)	(22)	(29)
20,001-50,000	6	30	-	2	-	2	-	-	6	34	40
	(5)	(35)		(20)		(15)			(4)	(31)	(15)
50,000-1,00,000	-	5	-	1	-	-	-	-	-	6	6
		(5)		(10)						(6)	(2)
Above 1,00,000	-	-	-	-	-	-	-	-	-	1	1
										(1)	(1)
Total	107	87	14	11	27	13	-	-	148	111	259
No land	-	-	-	-	18	24	13	9	31	33	64
Grand Total	107	87	14	11	45	37	13	9	179	144	323

Source: As in table 3.1

Note: As in table 3.1.

dispose all of his produce without any reserve and then drive him to buy his food at times of need, that too for a very high price (Mamoria, C.B. & Badri Bishal Tripathi: 2001, p. 400).

The farmers in the study area had access to several informal market linkages viz., the village trader, village trader cum moneylenders and traders at mondi centres. Most of the respondents used to approach the village traders for marketing their produce in order to avoid transport risks, to enjoy the privileges of immediate cash payment and to fall in line with the customary practice of courtesy. Next to them, about 25 percent of the respondents in both regions market their produce in the nearest markets (Table 3.23). These respondents have been very conscious not to loose the marginal difference of income. The village trader cum moneylenders and traders at mondy centre are also approached by more than 20 percent of the respondents, in both the regions, which facilitates the marketing the produce as well as the continuance with the informal credit dealings. No institutional arrangement for marketing was accessible to these respondents.

Annual Income

Income decides the background of a person. It is the yardstick to perceive the standard of living. Poverty line and standard of living of a person are measured by using the income as the prime indicator. However, it is difficult to get accurate information about the income of the family, because the people may not be able to reveal real worth of the goods exactly, which they produce for self-consumption. For them, income means the goods sold in the market, or the money

Table 3.23: Marketing of Agricultural Produces

(Figures in numbers)

Particulars	PACB		PCARDB		CB		SHG		Total		Grand
	Dry	Wet	Dry	Wet	Dry	Wet	Dry	Wet	Dry	Wet	Total
Loss	6 (6)	4 (5)	-	-	5 (18)	-	-	-	11 (8)	4 (5)	15 (5)
Village Trader	42 (39)	28 (32)	6 (43)	4 (37)	14 (52)	4 (29)	-	-	62 (42)	36 (32)	98 (38)
Village Trader Cum Money Lenders	5 (5)	4 (5)	-	1 (9)	-	-	-	-	5 (3)	5 (5)	10 (4)
Trader at Money Centre	20 (18)	20 (23)	2 (14)	3 (27)	5 (19)	6 (50)	-	-	27 (18)	30 (27)	57 (22)
Others	34 (31)	31 (35)	6 (43)	3 (27)	3 (11)	2 (21)	-	-	43 (29)	36 (33)	79 (31)
No land	-	-	-	-	18	24	13	9	31	33	64
Total	107	87	14	11	27	14	-	-	148	112	260
Grand Total	107	87	14	11	45	37	13	9	179	144	323

Source: As in table 3.1

Note: As in table 3.1.

Table 3.24: Annual Income

(Figures in numbers)

Particulars	*PACB*		*PCARDB*		*CB*		*SHG*		*Total*		*Grand*
	Dry	*Wet*	*Dry*	*Wet*	*Dry*	*Wet*	*Dry*	*Wet*	*Dry*	*Wet*	*Total*
Below 11,000	10 (10)	17 (19)	-	2 (16)	-	8 (21)	3 (20)	5 (64)	13 (7)	32 (22)	45 (13)
11,001-25,000	78 (73)	46 (53)	5 (40)	5 (50)	33 (73)	20 (55)	7 (60)	1 (9)	123 (69)	72 (50)	195 (60)
25,001-50,000	16 (14)	24 (28)	9 (60)	4 (34)	12 (27)	8 (22)	3 (20)	1 (9)	40 (22)	37 (25)	77 (24)
50,001-75,000	3 (3)	-	-	-	-	-	-	2 (18)	3 (2)	2 (2)	5 (2)
Above 75,000	-	-	-	-	-	1 (2)	-	-	-	1 (1)	1 (1)
Total	107	87	14	11	45	37	13	9	179	144	323

Source: As in table 3.1

Note : As in table 3.1.

received as salary or wages, but family income does not only mean the economic return from the main occupation; it includes income earned by the family from all the sources. Family income here refers to all the sources through which the respondents have had some returns of their economic activities.

In the study area, it was found that majority of the respondents (60 per cent) were having income between Rs.11000 to Rs. 25000 (Table 3.24). Among the respondents having alternative sources of income, more than 50 per cent of the respondents in both the regions earned an income below Rs.5000 (Table 3.25).

Family Expenses Incurred

Family expenses are the major portions of the expenditure for the rural households. If the expenses incurred are within the level of income earned, the households can augment their savings and investment. If a person is unable to get the expected income from his occupation, his consumption need pushes him to depend on the informal sources, especially the moneylenders. The loss in business or agriculture, interest burden, insufficient income, additional investments in the farm or business out of family income drive the borrower to carry the heavy burden of family expenses.

The study found that majority of the respondents have been in the income level within Rs.25000 and they incurred expenses above Rs.30000 (Table 3.26). Higher expenses over and above the income pushed the rural households to approach more than one credit agency and shoulder heavy burden of debt.

Table 3.25: Alternative Sources of Income

(Figures in numbers)

Particulars	*PACB*		*PCARDB*		*CB*		*SHG*		*Total*		*Grand*
	Dry	*Wet*	*Dry*	*Wet*	*Dry*	*Wet*	*Dry*	*Wet*	*Dry*	*Wet*	*Total*
Below 5000	67 (69)	24 (53)	8 (57)	6 (75)	9 (43)	8 (53)	3 (50)	2 (67)	87 (63)	40 (56)	127 (61)
5001-10000	27 (28)	17 (37)	6 (43)	2 (25)	8 (38)	2 (14)	3 (50)	1 (33)	44 (32)	22 (31)	66 (32)
Above 10000	3 (3)	4 (10)	-	-	4 (19)	5 (33)	-	-	7 (5)	9 (13)	16 (7)
Total	97	45	14	8	21	15	6	3	138	71	209
No alternative Source of income	10	42	-	3	24	22	7	6	41	73	114
Total	107	87	14	11	45	37	13	9	179	144	323

Source: As in table 3.1

Note: As in table 3.1.

Table 3.26: Family Expenses

(Figures in numbers)

Particulars	*PACB*		*PCARDB*		*CB*		*SHG*		*Total*		*Grand*
	Dry	*Wet*	*Dry*	*Wet*	*Dry*	*Wet*	*Dry*	*Wet*	*Dry*	*Wet*	*Total*
10,001-20,000	8 (7)	6 (7)	-	1 (8)	15 (33)	7 (19)	3 (20)	5 (64)	26 (15)	19 (13)	35 (11)
20,001-30,000	36 (34)	19 (22)	-	5 (50)	9 (20)	12 (33)	7 (60)	2 (18)	52 (29)	38 (26)	90 (28)
30,001-40,000	40 (37)	28 (32)	11 (80)	2 (17)	15 (33)	4 (12)	3 (20)	-	69 (39)	34 (14)	103 (32)
40,001-50,000	13 (12)	10 (12)	3 (20)	2 (17)	6 (14)	10 (26)	-	-	22 (12)	22 (15)	44 (14)
Above 50,000	10 (10)	24 (27)	-	1 (8)	-	4 (10)	-	-	10 (5)	29 (20)	39 (12)
Total	107	87	14	11	45	37	13	9	179	144	323

Source: As in table 3.1

Note : As in table 3.1.

Farm Expenses

The farm expenses include those for inputs, labour, technology, irrigation methods, machinery, reclamation of land etc.

The sample respondents incurred heavy farm expenses ranging from Rs. 5000 to above Rs. 50000 according to the size of holdings, extent of irrigational pattern adopted etc., The respondents of PACB in dry areas incurred farm expenses within Rs.20000 whereas in the wet region most of them incurred more than Rs. 20000 (Table 3.27).

Deposit in Institutions

Mobilization of deposits at the institutional level would also help to absorb overdues and keep up the flow of credit in an uninterrupted manner. Mobilization of deposits very much depends upon the degree of confidence which such institutions enjoy in the eyes of their clients, the efficient banking services, interest and enthusiasm of staff and top management and finally the rate of interest (Dadhich, C.L.: 1977, p. 242). But at present, the deposit position of the Cooperative Banks is not satisfactory. It shows that the Cooperative Movement has failed to inculcate the habit of thrift and savings among the members; instead the PACS are working as the agency for advancing the loans of the higher organizations only (Srivastava: 1991, p. 189). However, SHG savings serve a wider range of objectives other than immediate investment; it imposes credit discipline on group members; enhances the self-confidence of the individual; covers the individual risk against normal business risk, normal variations of

Table 3.27: Average Farm Expenses

(Figures in numbers)

Particulars	PACB		PCARDB		CB		SHG		Total		Grand
	Dry	Wet	Dry	Wet	Dry	Wet	Dry	Wet	Dry	Wet	Total
1-5,000	10 (9)	18 (21)	-	1 (11)	-	1 (8)	-	-	10 (7)	20 (18)	30 (12)
5,001-10,000	14 (13)	12 (14)	3 (21)	1 (11)	3 (11)	3 (21)	-	-	20 (14)	16 (15)	36 (14)
10,001-20,000	48 (45)	14 (16)	-	1 (11)	21 (78)	3 (21)	-	-	69 (47)	18 (16)	87 (34)
20,001-30,000	29 (27)	13 (15)	-	1 (11)	3 (11)	3 (21)	-	-	32 (21)	17 (16)	49 (19)
30,001-50,000	6 (6)	20 (23)	11 (79)	3 (33)	-	3 (21)	-	-	17 (11)	26 (24)	43 (17)
Above 50,000	-	10 (11)	-	2 (23)	-	1 (8)	-	-	-	13 (11)	14 (6)
Total	107	87	14	9	27	14	-	-	148	110	259
No land	-	-	-	-	18	24	13	9	31	33	64
Total	107	87	14	9	9	10	13	9	179	144	323

Source: As in table 3.1

Note: As in table 3.1.

income etc.; and demonstrates the strength of unity (Karmakar, K.G.: 1999, p. 211).

It was found that the expenditure pattern of the respondents has been a deterrent to their habit of savings. They were very particular in access to credit with several sources. The study found that 50 percent of the respondents belonging to the CB have had savings whereas it was cent percent in SHGs (Table 3.28).

The SHGs adopt thrift based lending approach and made savings compulsory among the voluntarily associated group members. But majority of the respondents belonging to the Cooperative Banks and 50 percent of the respondents belonging to CB did not have any savings due to the interest burden, failure of agriculture, insufficient income, and attitude to avail loan only. As for the type of deposits, majority of the respondents had Savings or Recurring Deposit accounts (Table 3.29).

Reasons to select the Institution to save the money

Frequent contacts with an institution led the respondents to save the money in that institution. It gives secure feelings and encourages them to select the agency to save the money.

It was found that safety and security were the main reasons for the respondents to select at agency to save the money, which was followed by friendliness of the employees. The SHG borrowers who maintained savings in their institution opined that lesser formalities and availability of adequate loan were the major reasons to maintain savings in SHGs. While safety and security was the major reason for the respo dents belonging

Table 3.28: Deposit in Institutions

(Figures in numbers)

Particulars	PACB		PCARDB		CB		SHG		Total		Grand
	Dry	*Wet*	*Dry*	*Wet*	*Dry*	*Wet*	*Dry*	*Wet*	*Dry*	*Wet*	*Total*
No	74	61	14	8	23	19	-	-	111	88	199
	(69)	(70)	(100)	(73)	(51)	(51)			(62)	(61)	(62)
Yes	33	26	-	3	22	18	13	9	68	56	124
	(31)	(30)		(27)	(49)	(49)	(100)	(100)	(38)	(39)	(38)
Total	107	87	14	11	45	37	13	9	179	144	323

Source: As in table 3.1

Note: As in table 3.1.

Table 3.29: Type of Deposits

(Figures in numbers)

Particulars	*PACB*		*PCARDB*		*CB*		*SHG*		*Total*		*Grand*
	Dry	*Wet*	*Dry*	*Wet*	*Dry*	*Wet*	*Dry*	*Wet*	*Dry*	*Wet*	*Total*
Savings	-	5	-	2	4	4	13	9	17	20	37
		(19)		(67)	(18)	(22)	(100)	(100)	(25)	(36)	(30)
Recurring	20	17	-	-	-	2	-	-	20	19	39
	(61)	(65)				(11)			(29)	(34)	(32)
Current	-	-	-	-	-	1	-	-	-	1	1
						(6)				(2)	(1)
Fixed	-	1	-	1	18	6	-	-	18	8	26
		(4)		(33)	(82)	(33)			(27)	(14)	(21)
LIC	13	3	-	-	-	5	-	-	13	8	21
	(39)	(12)				(28)			(19)	(14)	(17)
Total	33	26	-	3	22	18	13	9	68	56	124
No deposit	74	61	14	8	23	19	13	9	111	88	199
Grand Total	107	87	14	11	45	37	13	9	179	144	323

Source: As in table 3.1

Note: As in table 3.1.

to the PACB, friendliness of employees was the major reason for the respondents of the CBs (Table 3-30.).

Rural Indebtedness

Rural debt and rural credit are the two sides of the same coin. When the rural people borrow from IAs or NIAs for productive purposes, the borrowings result in additional income to the people, out of which loan installments could be repaid regularly. But this is only an ideal situation, which does not exist. The problem becomes serious when people inevitably spend the money for unproductive purposes, which badly affects their repayment capacity and the consequent overdue takes the form of indebtedness (Grewal, P. S.: 1985, p. 95). Ultimately, the farmer lives a life of indebtedness with the burden of unproductive debts remaining an unlimited liability till death. They even leave their debts as legacy for posterity. 'Debts acquired as legacy of inheritance, drive the heirs to calmly pursue the same path. (Charles Malamoud: 1983, p. 154). Instead of the old saying—'the Indian farmer is born in debt, lives in debt and dies in debt, (Royal Commission Report on Agriculture: 1966, p. 280), it is very apt to say that the farmer may die to make his debt burden alive.

The general opinion is that the farmers are mainly interested in the assured and timely availability of credit from the institutional sources and not so much in anticipating cheap credit as they are in any case paying very high rates of interest on borrowing from the informal sources (*The Financial Express:* 1996, p. 7). The interest rates vary from 36 percent to 100 percent. In the backward districts of Andhra Pradesh,

Table 3.30: Reasons to Select the Institution to Save the Money

(Figures in numbers)

Particulars	*PACB*		*PCARDB*		*CB*		*SHG*		*Total*		*Grand*
	Dry	*Wet*	*Dry*	*Wet*	*Dry*	*Wet*	*Dry*	*Wet*	*Dry*	*Wet*	*Total*
Safety and Security	14 (43)	8 (31)	-	-	6 (27)	2 (11)	5 (39)	1 (12)	25 (37)	11 (20)	36 (28)
Attractive rate of Interest	4 (12)	7 (27)	-	-	3 (14)	-	-	-	7 (10)	7 (13)	14 (11)
Lesser Formalities	2 (6)	2 (8)	-	-	-	1 (6)	5 (39)	3 (33)	7 (10)	6 (11)	13 (11)
Nearness	5 (15)	5 (19)	-	3 (100)	-	7 (39)	-	2 (22)	5 (7)	17 (29)	22 (18)
Availability of adequate loan	1 (3)	4 (15)	-	-	-	-	3 (22)	3 (33)	4 (6)	7 (13)	11 (9)
Friendliness of Employees	7 (21)	-	-	-	13 (59)	8 (44)	-	-	20 (30)	8 (14)	28 (23)
Total	33	26	-	3	22	18	13	9	68	56	124
No deposit	74	61	14	8	23	19	13	9	111	88	199
Total	107	87	14	11	45	37	13	9	179	144	323

Source: As in table 3.1

Note: As in table 3.1.

the interest rate charged on agricultural credit by the moneylenders was 36 percent, while it was 84 percent per annum in Hughy district near Calcutta. Due to the cumulative effect of the exorbitant rates of interest paid by the cultivators, low prices received from the sale of agricultural commodities, and the effect of various malpractices of the moneylenders who were also the dealers in agricultural produce, the debt once contracted kept on accumulating (F.A.O. 1957, p. 69).

The practice of money lending was dates back to *Manusmriti,* which had detailed illustration of the laws and regulations relating to money lending (Balwinder Singh: 2000, p. 2). The money lending business as an economic activity is not bad in itself but the malpractices, which add to the burden of rural indebtedness, constitute its antithesis. The following are some of the malpractices of moneylenders:

1) No receipt is given for the interest deducted in advance;
2) Getting thumb-impression or signature of borrowers on blank sheets of paper while lending money;
3) Manipulation of accounts and
4) Exploiting the illiterates and their emergency needs by entering large amounts as against the actually drawn.

The moneylenders are very particular to collect the interest. They encourage the postponement of principal repayment of the debtors. Even though the legislations do exist in the country for regulating their business (viz., Punjab Registration of Moneylender's Act 1938, Bihar Moneylenders Act 1938, Uttar Pradesh Moneylenders Act, 1939 and Bombay Moneylenders

Act, 1938), the increasing debt burden drags the poor farmers to commit suicides. Around 14833 farmers committed suicide during the year 1999. Of which 64 per cent took place in four states–Karnataka, Andhra Pradesh, Maharashtra and Madhyapradesh. In the States of Tamil Nadu, Gujarat, Orissa and Himachel Pradesh, the conditions of the farmers were more deplorable. During the year 2003, over 200 farmers in Karnataka committed suicides (*The Hindu*: 2003, p. 16). Apart from the reported number of farmers' suicides, the unreported cases were in large number (Sunil, M.: 2004, p. 1). The State Governments of Karnataka and Tamil Nadu had taken action over the exorbitant interest in money lending through the ordinance in 2003 and banned usury. Crisis in the agriculture sector due to crop failure, heavy droughts, and lack of irrigation facility, family problems together with harassment by moneylenders drove the farmers to suicide. But it was uniformly perceived that indebtedness was the common factor in the suicides by farmers (Sopan Joshi: 2004, p. 15).

Indebtedness dehumanized the people and immense them in reality leaving the least scope for the future; it alienates them from life and work. Indebtedness in rural India has placed the rural areas under perennial poverty and inhuman existence. The disinherited, poverty stricken labour-exhausted outcastes might sometimes resort to such an action that the whole community might lose its sense of security, peace and happiness and thus might put itself in the midst of threat and agitation (Mukesh Singh Rathore, 1994, p. 28). But such subaltern actions of the oppressed peasants have not brought for their emancipation in Indian history; besides, the 'wretched or condemned

Box 1: The Extent of Rural Indebtedness

Sl.No.	Name of the Commission/Expert	Year	Estimation
1.	Deccon Riots Commission	1875	• 1/3 of the occupants of Government land were in debt in 12 villages of Ahmed Nagar District, Bombay. • Average debt per occupant was Rs.371.
2.	Famine Commission	1880	• 1/3 landholding class was in debt • Another 1/3 in debt, but with power to repay the debt.
3.	Sir Fredrick Nicholson	1895	• The amount of rural debt was Rs.45 crores for Madras only.
4.	Famine Commission	1901	• ¼ of the cultivators lost their land in Bombay in debt • Less than ¼ of the cultivators free from debt.
5.	Sir Edward Maclagan	1911	• Total Agricultural debt of India stood Rs.300 crores based on the Nicholson's estimate for Madras.
6.	Mr.M.L.Darling	1925	• Estimated at Rs.600 crores based on the Punjab figure Rs.90 crores.

7.	Central Banking Enquiry Committee	1929	• Estimated total rural indebtedness at Rs.900 crores.
8.	The Agricultural Credit Department, RBI, 1937	1937	• Estimated total debt burden at Rs.1800 crores.
9.	Mr.P.J.Thomas	1939	• Total debt burden was Rs.900 crores in 1828-29. • Rural burden must be upto Rs.2200 crores during 1933.
10.	National Income Committee	1949	• Estimated the rural debt at Rs.915 crores • Of the debt, 83 percent was unproductive and only 5 percent was supplied by Cooperatives
11.	Rural Credit Survey Committee	1951-52	• The amount of debt owed to agriculturist and Professional Moneylenders was 14.2 percent and 44.8 percent respectively of total debts.
12.	All India Debt and Investment Survey	1961-62	• The average debt for an indebted household was Rs.647 crores in 1961-62, • Outstanding total debt stood Rs.2380 crores.

Source: 1. Pratap Mal (2001), Institutional financing for agriculture and Rural Development, Mohit Publications, New Delhi, pp. 4-7.

2. Bhagirath Singh (2001), Rural Finance, RBSA publishers, Jaipur, pp.22-25

Box 2: Illustrative Evidences for the Malpractices of Moneylenders

S.No	Profile of the affected party	Debt burden	Consequence
1.	Channamma, 68 years old, Karnataka	• 8000 from Cooperative Bank • 43000 from Moneylender	• Lands mortgaged with moneylenders • Heavy pressure to repay the irredeemable debt • Hanged herself on September, 7th, 2003.
2.	Puttasamy, 32 years old, Karnataka	• 70000 from Moneylenders	• Committed suicide on November 8th, 2003.
3.	Puttasamy Gowda, 40 years old, Karnataka	• Rs. 50000 from moneylenders	• The moneylenders used to come like elephants 10 to 15 of them together harassed him • Committed suicide on September 9th, 2003.
4.	Ramachandra Sivappa, 40 years old, Karnataka	• Rs. 2.5 lakh	• Sold the land and clear off loan arrears of 2.5 lakh and left with a loan of Rs.1 lakh • Pressure to repay the rest by creditor • Committed suicide in August 2003.

5.	Shekawa Hiremath	• Rs. 75000 bank loan • Rs. 85000 form private financiers	• The records of indebtedness were recovered form his body, his land mortgage papers, bank loan documents and his anguished jottings at the harassment, he faced from private financiers.
6.	Karasiddappa, Mahantayya Hiremath	• 55000 from PACS • Rs. 45000 form Nationalised Banks • Private Moneylenders for Rs. 50000	• Hanged himself as a way out of his desperate plight during August 2003.
7.	Ishwarappa Bhagoji, 40 years old farmer	• Loan from moneylender	• With his family, he committed suicide during August 2003.
8.	Krishna Gowda, 40 years old farmer	• Loan from Moneylender to drill a borewell	• Failed to yield water • Unable to repay • Moneylenders repeatedly abused him in the Channarayapatna Market • Unable to bear the humiliation, he committed suicide.

Source: 1.Hindu, Sep.14,

2.Hindu, Nov.9, 2003.

of the earth' who could not get the 'virgin soil upturned' had to undergo further deprivation, denial and dehumanization. Indebtedness thus causes a vicious circle, which prophesies no real hope inside (Desai A.R. (ed)., *Peasant Struggles in India,* 1979; Robin Jenkins, *Exploitation,* 1971; and Fanar F., *The Condemned of the Earth,* 1967).

Extent of Indebtedness

Attempts were made from time to time, even before independence, to assess the extent of rural indebtedness (Box-1).

According to the Debt and Investment Survey 1991 (NSS – 48th round which is latest), the total outstanding debt of rural households was Rs. 22211 crores, which was 60 percent of the total outstanding debt of all households in the country. The cultivator households owed Rs. 17,668 crores, which was about four fifths of the outstanding debt of rural households. The results of this survey further showed that in 1991, over 23 percent of the rural households were found to be indebted. One out of every six rural households was indebted to the IAs whereas only one out of 10 households was indebted to the non-institutional agencies. In states like Andhrapradesh, Rajasthan and Tamil Nadu, where the incidence of debt was found to be high an exceptionally high proportion of households were indebted to the NIA. As the debt of the individual households increases, their access to IAs is curtailed this further strengthens the role of NIAs in the RCM.

The illustrative cases proved (Box 2) that it was

common to find a small farmer with less than 2 acres of land owing to the moneylender between Rs. 5000 and Rs. 70000 as debt, whereas the debt to a bank or cooperative society was lesser than that with the former. A body of evidence suggests that while access to financial services is not a panacea, there are definite casual links between access and growth and poverty reduction. Given the massive scale of the failure of access within India it may even be possible to conjecture that this is indeed the missing link between the 6 to 8 percent growth rate that we have and the 8 to 10 percent that we need (Classens: 2005, p. 1122). With this background, the extent of indebtedness of the sample respondents is analyzed hereunder.

Table 3.31: Prevalence of Indebtedness

S.No	Particulars (Village Panchyati)	Dry (Land-akottai)	Wet (Athuri)	Total
1	Total Households as Per 2001 Census	673	989	1662
2	30 Percent of the households	202	310	512
3	No of Household who did not borrow from any sources	58	131	189
4	No of Households indebted to IAs (Total Sample Respondents)	144	179	323
5	No of Households who borrowed from NIAs out of Total Sample Respondents	130	149	279
6	Percentage of Non-borrowers to sample	29	42	37
7	Percentage of IAs borrowers to sample	71	58	63
8	Percentage of borrowing households of NIAs to sample	90	83	72

Source: As in table 3.1

Note : As in table 3.1.

This study found that 63 per cent of the households remained indebted in the study area. The incidence of indebtedness was high in the dry region compared to the wet region (Table 3.31). The source analysis found that more than 83 percent of the respondents in the dry and 90 percent in the wet remained indebted to NIAs (Table 3.32)

Friends, relatives, village traders, commission agents and the chit funds were the other NIAs accessible to rural borrowers. The agency wise and source wise analysis showed that more than 70 percent of the respondents remained to the moneylenders in the study area (Table 3.33). This showed that moneylenders were the main NIAs in rural Tamil Nadu. While analyzing the causes for the sustenance of the NIAs, it was found that more than 80 percent of the respondents have had access with these NIAs due to the increasing credit needs, inadequacy of formal loans, presence of bureaucratic hurdles, pressing consumption requirements etc., It showed that the main objective of institutionalization had failed and gradually the position of the NIAs in the RCM had been strengthened in due course. It was also found that though no respondent of the SHGs approached the moneylenders their friends and relatives were the sources for their additional credit needs, It showed that the interest burden of the respondents of the SHGs remained reduced but not the debt burden as such (Ravichandran, K. & Revathi Bala, M.: 2004, p. 12).

The relationship between the agency, borrower and his guarantor governs the rules and regulations of informal credit market. It was found that the majority of the respondents i.e., more than 70 in wet and 90 percent in dry region, approached more than one of the informal sources whereas sources in the formal system, a borrower could have access with only one source. About 82 percent of the respondents had access

Table 3.32: Indebtedness with Non-Institutional Agencies

(Figures in numbers)

Particulars	*PACB*		*PCARDB*		*CB*		*SHG*		*Total*		*Grand*
	Dry	*Wet*	*Dry*	*Wet*	*Dry*	*Wet*	*Dry*	*Wet*	*Dry*	*Wet*	*Total*
Indebted with IA	16 (15)	3 (3)	-	2 (18)	9 (20)	6 (16)	5 (38)	3 (33)	30 (17)	14 (10)	44 (14)
Indebted with NIA	91 (85)	84 (97)	-	9 (82)	36 (80)	31 (84)	8 (62)	6 (67)	149 (83)	130 (90)	279 (86)
Total	107	87	14	11	45	37	13	9	179	144	323

Source: As in table 3.1

Note: As in table 3.1.

Table 3.33: Types of Non–Institutional Agencies

(Figures in numbers)

Particulars	PACB		PCARDB		CB		SHG		Total		Grand
	Dry	Wet	Dry	Wet	Dry	Wet	Dry	Wet	Dry	Wet	Total
Money Lenders	70	58	8	6	30	26	-	-	108	90	198
	(77)	(69)	(57)	(74)	(83)	(84)			(73)	(69)	(71
Friends	9	10	-	1	-	1	5	4	14	16	30
	(10)	(12)		(13)		(3)	(62)	(57)	(9)	(12)	(11)
Relatives	3	10	-	-	-	1	3	3	6	14	20
	(3)	(12)				(3)	(38)	(43)	(4)	(11)	(6)
Village Trade:	2	-	-	1	-	1	-	-	2	1	3
	(2)			(13)		(3)			(1)	(1)	(1)
Commission Agents	2	4	6	-	6	2	-	-	14	7	21
	(2)	(5)	(43)		(17)	(7)			(9)	(5)	(8)
Chit Funds	5	2	-	-	-	-	-	-	5	2	7
	(6)	(2)							(4)	(2)	(3)
Total	91	84	14	8	36	31	8	7	149	130	279
Indebted with IA	16	3	-	2	9	6	5	3	30	14	144
Grand Total	107	87	14	11	45	37	13	9	179	144	323

Source: As in table 3.1

Note: As in table 3.1.

Table 3.34: Number of Sources to which Respondents were indebted

(Figures in numbers)

Particulars	*PACB*		*PCARDB*		*CB*		*SHG*		*Total*		*Grand Total*
	Dry	*Wet*	*Dry*	*Wet*	*Dry*	*Wet*	*Dry*	*Wet*	*Dry*	*Wet*	
Only one source	14 (15)	22 (26)	-	2 (22)	-	11 (36)	-	2 (33)	14 (9)	37 (29)	51 (18)
More than one informal sources	77 (85)	62 (74)	14 (100)	7 (78)	36 (100)	20 (64)	8 (100)	4 (67)	135 (91)	93 (71)	228 (82)
Total	91	84	14	9	36	31	8	6	149	130	279
Indebted with NIA	16	3	-	2	9	6	5	3	30	14	144
Grand Total	107	87	14	11	45	37	13	9	179	144	323

Source: As in table 3.1

Note: As in table 3.1.

to more than one informal source in order to retain the clientele of credit agencies (Table 3.34).

The study also found that the majority of the respondents who remained indebted with only one NIA had access to credit with the moneylenders. The access to several sources of informal credit, in a way, makes the rural households as debtors instead of generators, or productive investors.

For the purpose of analysis, the data regarding the extent of debt of the respondents before and after they became clientele with the IAs were also obtained. The mean debt of sample respondents before and after they had clientele with the IAs did not show much difference (Chart 3.2). Further, the share of NIAs in the total debt was high and the mean debt of the sample respondents in the wet region was higher than that for their counterparts in the dry region. Institution wise analysis also showed that the clientele with IAs has only increased the debt burden (Table 3.35 & 3.36).

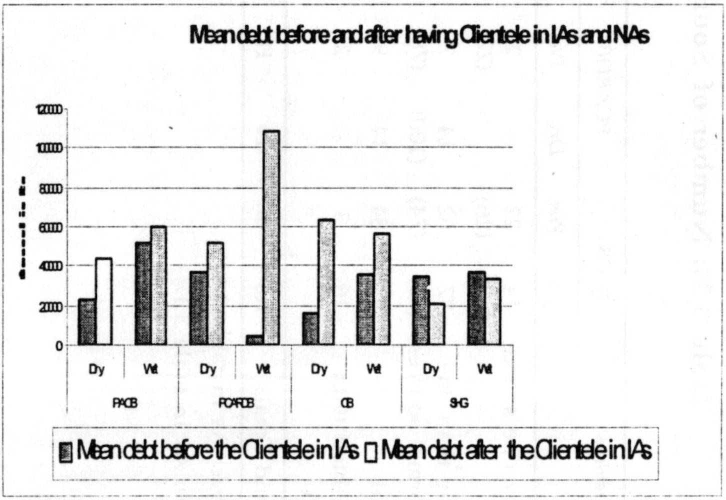

Chart 3.2

Table 3.35: Share of Non-institutional Agencies in Rural Credit before having clientele in IAs

(Figures in percentage)

Particulars	*PACB*		*PCARDB*		*CB*		*SHG*		*Total*		*Grand Total*
	Dry	*Wet*	*Dry*	*Wet*	*Dry*	*Wet*	*Dry*	*Wet*	*Dry*	*Wet*	
Money Lenders	81	45	52	36	90	75	74	70	78	51	61
Friends	3	3	-	-	2	2	6	4	3	3	3
Relatives	11	9	32	-	-	5	20	26	13	8	10
Village Trader	2	3	4	-	-	-	-	-	2	2	2
Commission Agents	2	39	11	62	7	16	-	-	3	35	23
Chit Funds	1	1	1	2	1	2	-	-	1	1	1
Mean debt with NIAs	23336	51859	36705	4866	15598	35392	34138	37188	23302	47034	70202

Source: As in table 3.1

Note: As in table 3.1 and 3.36

An estimation of the mean credit gap of the sample respondents revealed that the financial institutions have failed to meet the credit needs of the rural poor to the extent of Rs. 31253 and Rs. 44971 per borrower respectively in the dry and wet regions.

Nature of Indebtedness

The nature of indebtedness may either be the legacy of inheritance acquired or presently or both. Ancestral debt burden is a dangerous trap. It has led, in few cases, to bonded labour (Mishra, S.D: 2003, p. 20). Instead of accumulation of resources being pushed on to the next generation, the burden of debt was offered as a birth trap. To come to terms with this trap, some of the borrowers either continue to deal with that source or seek other credit mechanisms only to sink further in debt or even commit suicide.

The present study found that more than 60 percent of the respondents had current debt in both regions (Table 3.37). The ancestral burden was also carried by the respondents and its proportion was found to be high among the respondents in wet region (25 percent). The duration of indebtedness with the private parties of 40 percent of the borrowers in both regions was within 5 years (Table 3.38). Though a fourfold increase was found in the GLC delivered at the National. State and District levels in 2001-02, the extent of indebtedness of the borrowers had not been reduced. It proved the first hypothesis viz., the institutional credit was unable to mitigate the problem of indebtedness in the study area. The debt burden of most of the farming community remained as such with fluctuations but not with any property for redemption.

Table 3.36: Share of Institutional and Non-institutional Agencies in Rural Credit after having clientele in IAs

(Figures in percentage)

Particulars	*PACB*		*PCARDB*		*CB*		*SHG*		*Total*		*Grand*
	Dry	*Wet*	*Dry*	*Wet*	*Dry*	*Wet*	*Dry*	*Wet*	*Dry*	*Wet*	*Total*
Money Lenders	80	58	42	51	74	78	-	-	71	53	61
Friends	4	5	-	-	5	3	41	81	4	4	4
Relatives	9	12	22	12	-	8	59	19	10	12	11
Village Trader	1	17	15	24	21	8	-	-	8	13	11
Commission Agents	3	1	21	13	-	3	-	-	5	2	3
Chit Funds	3	7	-	-	-	-	-	3	2	16	11
Mean debt with	29553	40520	41438	44667	34001	37928	20418	33305	31253	44971	37645
NIAs - (1)	(68)	(68)	(80)	(41)	(54)	(67)	(100)	(100)	(65)	(67)	(67)
Mean debt with	14175	19464	10714	63333	29028	18968	-	-	16678	21485	18917
IAs - (2)	(32)	(32)	(20)	(59)	(46)	(33)			(35)	(33)	(33)
Total Mean debt (1)+(2)	43728	59984	52152	108000	63029	56896	20418	33305	47931.	66456	56562

Source: As in table 3.1

Note: As in table 3.1.

Table 3.37: Nature of Indebtedness

(Figures in numbers)

Particulars	PACB		PCARDB		CB		SHG		Total		Grand
	Dry	Wet	Dry	Wet	Dry	Wet	Dry	Wet	Dry	Wet	Total
Ancestral	14	24	-	4	-	4	-	-	14	32	46
	(15)	(29)		(44)		(12)			(9)	(25)	(17)
Present	73	51	11	4	36	25	8	6	128	86	214
	(80)	(61)	(79)	(44)	(100)	(81)	(100)	(100)	(86)	(66)	(77)
Both	4	9	3	1	-	2	-	-	7	12	19
	(5)	(10)	(21)	(12)		(7)			(5)	(9)	(7)
Total	91	84	14	9	36	31	8	6	149	130	279
Indebted with NIA	16	3	-	2	9	6	5	3	30	14	144
Grand Total	107	87	14	11	45	37	13	9	179	144	323

Source: As in table 3.1

Note: As in table 3.1.

Causes for Indebtedness

Various studies have been conducted unearthing the causes for indebtedness. Pramod Lata Jain (1990, p. 129 & 130) deserved that the ancestral debt, subdivision and fragmentation of holding, vagaries of climate conditions and other calamities, ignorance and illiteracy of the cultivator, failure to provide for deficiency, low income of the cultivator, extravagant spending and borrowings and absence of adequate marketing facilities were the causes. Desai S.S.M. (1990, p. 228) found out that the deficit profile of majority of the farmers' agricultural operations, unscrupulous methods and actions of the village moneylenders, total absence of past savings, recurrent social ceremonies, inter and intra family disputes and ancestral debts were the causes for indebtedness.

In this study, it was found out that the inevitable clearance of old debts of NIAs emerged as a major cause for the indebtedness in both regions (36 percent in dry and 30 percent in wet) which was followed by farm/business expenses (Chart 3.3).

All these causes were unproductive and repetitive. For about 11 percent of the respondents, the repayment of institutional debt was the cause for indebtedness (Table 3.39) and this was more so in the case of respondents belonging to PACB.

Borrowings from IAs

It was observed that the cooperatives remained as the mainstay of agricultural financing followed by the private agencies and CBs (Satya sai K.J.S et.al., 1987, p. 54). Despite several built-in organizational constraints,

Table 3.38: Duration of Indebtedness

(Figures in numbers)

Particulars	*PACB*		*PCARDB*		*CB*		*SHG*		*Total*		*Grand*
	Dry	*Wet*	*Dry*	*Wet*	*Dry*	*Wet*	*Dry*	*Wet*	*Dry*	*Wet*	*Total*
1-5 Years	39 (43)	29 (35)	8 (57)	2 (22)	9 (25)	18 (58)	8 (100)	6 (100)	64 (42)	55 (42)	119 (42)
6-10 Years	20 (22)	24 (29)	6 (43)	4 (44)	21 (58)	7 (23)	-	-	47 (32)	35 (27)	82 (28)
11-15 Years	26 (29)	19 (23)	-	3 (34)	6 (17)	4 (13)	-	-	32 (22)	26 (20)	68 (23)
16-20 Years	6 (6)	9 (11)	-	-	-	2 (6)	-	-	6 (4)	11 (9)	18 (6)
Above 20 Years	-	3 (4)	-	-	-	-	-	-	-	3 (2)	3 (1)
Total	91	84	14	9	36	31	8	6	149	130	279
Indebted with NIA	16	3	-	2	9	6	5	3	30	14	144
Grand Total	107	87	14	11	45	37	13	9	179	144	323

Source: As in table 3.1

Note: As in table 3.1.

Table 3.39: Causes for Indebtedness

(Figures in numbers)

Particulars	PACB		PCARDB		CB		SHG		Total		Grand
	Dry	Wet	Dry	Wet	Dry	Wet	Dry	Wet	Dry	Wet	Total
Farm Business Expenses	25 (27)	20 (23)	11 (80)	4 (36)	-	3 (7)	-	-	36 (24)	27 (20)	63 (22)
Family Expenses	16 (18)	22 (25)	3 (20)	3 (28)	12 (27)	10 (26)	-	3 (50)	31 (21)	38 (29)	69 (25)
Medical Expenses	8 (9)	3 (3)	-	-	3 (7)	3 (9)	-	-	11 (7)	6 (5)	17 (7)
Repayment of institutional debt	12 (13)	12 (14)	-	-	-	4 (12)	3 (20)	1 (9)	15 (10)	16 (12)	31 (11)
House/Renovation Expenses	1 (1)	1 (1)	-	-	-	2 (5)	-	-	1 (1)	3 (2)	4 (1)
Clearance of Old Debts with Private	27 (30)	26 (30)	-	2 (18)	21 (46)	9 (24)	5 (40)	3 (33)	53 (36)	40 (30)	93 (33)
Educational Expenses	2 (2)	-	-	-	-	-	-	-	2 (1)	-	2 (1)
Total	91	84	14	9	36	31	8	9	149	130	279
Indebted with NIA	16	3	-	2	9	6	5	3	30	14	144
Grand Total	107	87	14	11	45	37	13	9	179	144	323

Source: As in table 3.1.

Note: As in table 3.1.

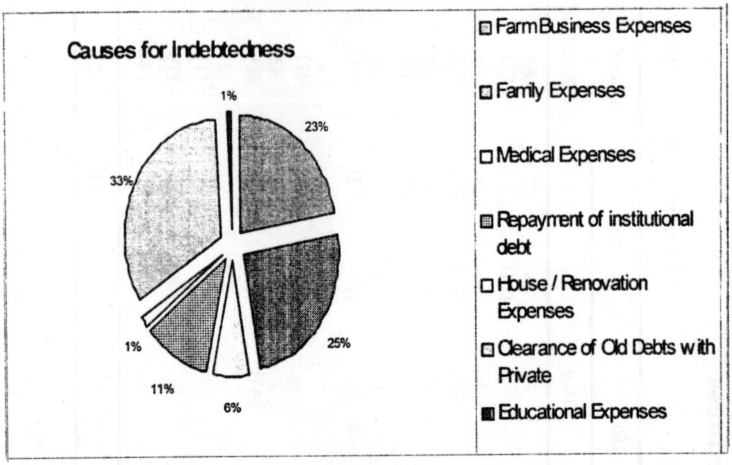

Chart 3.3

the Cooperative Banks still enjoy a unique position in the RCM due to their close association with the people and larger clientele base at the grassroots level (Mohanan N: 2004, p. 390). Contrary to this, few studies revealed that a larger number of loans were obtained from the CBs among the institutional sources whereas only 13 percent of the borrowers had taken from the PACS (Singh, A.K. et.al., 1993, p. 396). The landless artisans and women population remained completely neglected from the Cooperative Movement (Jugale, V.B: 1994, p. 61). The small and Marginal farmers were handicapped in the credit market and therefore their investment was constrained by credit (Ramachandra Reddy: 1995, p. 162). Increase in the credit disbursement is not accompanied by proportionate increase in the number of farmer borrowers i.e., more credit is provided to the same group of farmer borrowers (Shollapur M.R.: 1996, p. 25). As the size of the land holding increases the borrowing per household raises (Ramachandra Reddy, D. & Bagavan Reddy, B: 1994, p. 57). There is no significant difference in the performance of various financial agencies in Madurai District in lending to the agricultural and service sectors such as branches of SBI and its associates, Nationalized and Private Sector Banks and other agencies such as TIIC, Madurai District Central Cooperative Bank Ltd., etc., (Rengaswamy, V. & Ramnath, R.L: 2000, p. 82).

Table 3.40: Borrowings from Institutional Agencies

(Figures in numbers)

Particulars	*Dry*	*Wet*	*Grand Total*
PACB	107 (60)	87 (60)	194 (60)
PCARDB	14 (8)	11 (8)	25 (8)
CB	45 (25)	37 (26)	82 (25)
SHG	13 (7)	9 (6)	22 (7)
Total	179	144	323

Source: As in table 3.1.

Note: As in table 3.1.

The present study found that majority of the respondents (60 per cent) still approach PACB for their credit needs. The PACB has locality advantage and provides both cash and kind portion of credit such as seed, fertilizers and pesticides and needed support for the agriculturists. Small segment of sample respondents (8 per cent) had membership with PCARDB, which is located at District head quarters. As a result of SAA, the CBs have wide branch network at present. Thus, 25 percent of the sample respondents in both regions have access to credit from CBs (Table 3.40).

Purpose Wise Borrowing

As agriculture is the predominant occupation for the rural households, majority (59 per cent) of the respondents borrowed for cultivation expenses from the institutional agencies.

As the CBs concentrate on industrial development in rural areas, majority (60 per cent in dry and 52 per cent in wet) of the respondents, who borrowed from CBs invested in petty shops, idly shops, saloon shops, vegetable shops etc., Apart from these purposes, the sample respondents approached the IAs for the purpose of meeting the expenses on purchase of cattle/milch animals, land development, improved methods of irrigation, purchase of agricultural machineries, housing expenses etc., (Table 3.41).

Loan Amount Borrowed

IAs measures the demand for credit on the basis of need and its productivity and supply it on security. In other words, the IAs give more emphasis on purpose of borrowing and security that should be free from all encumbrances.

In the study, it was found that the loan amount borrowed differs from one institution to another and region to region. Majority of the PACB respondents borrowed between Rs. 5000 to Rs. 10000. In wet region, the extent of loan amount borrowed was higher than that in the dry region. The SHGs in the study area provide loans not exceeding Rs. 5000 per member (3.42).

Table 3.41: Purposes-wise Borrowing of the Respondents

(Figures in numbers)

Particulars	PACB		PCARDB		CB		SHG		Total		Grand
	Dry	Wet	Dry	Wet	Dry	Wet	Dry	Wet	Dry	Wet	Total
Cultivation Expenses	101 (94)	80 (92)	3 (20)	4 (41)	-	3 (7)	-	-	104 (59)	87 (60)	191 (59)
Purchase of Cattle/ Milch Animals	3 (3)	3 (4)	-	3 (25)	3 (7)	10 (26)	-	-	6 (3)	16 (11)	22 (7)
Land Development Purpose	-	2 (2)	-	6 (40)	-	-	-	-	4 (2)	4 (3)	8 (3)
Improved Methods of Irrigation	3 (3)	2 (2)	-	-	-	2 (5)	-	-	9 (5)	6 (4)	15 (5)
Marketing Purpose	-	-	-	1 (10)	6 (13)	1 (2)	-	-	6 (3)	1 (1)	7 (2)
Purchase of Machineries	-	-	-	-	3 (7)	2 (8)	-	-	4 (2)	2 (1)	6 (2)
To invest in other business	-	-	-	-	27 (60)	19 (52)	5 (40)	4 (44)	32 (18)	23 (16)	55 (16)
Family expenses	-	-	-	-	-	-	5 (40)	5 (56)	5 (3)	5 (4)	10 (3)
Housing Expenses	-	-	-	-	6 (3)	-	-		6 (3)	-	6 (2)
Social ceremonies	-	-	-	-	-	-	3 (20)	-	3 (2)	-	3 (1)
Total	107	87	14	11	45	37	13	9	179	144	323

Source: As in table 3.1. *Note:* As in table 3.1.

Expenses Incurred to Avail Loans

The scope for reducing non-interest costs especially the cost of obtaining loans may be significant than the reduction of interest rates (Pramod Lata Jain; 1990, p. 138). The twin problems of high transaction costs and poor repayment performance should be tackled first, if a vibrant credit delivery system specifically designed to meet the development imperatives is to be evolved (Majumdar N.A.: 1997, p. 73). The borrower transaction costs are the major constraints hindering credit access to the poor, which includes travel costs, opportunity costs of time taken to negotiate, documentation, and repay loans (Rama Mohana Rao: 2000, p. 32). The transaction cost of the borrowers, in this study, includes traveling expenses, cost of loan application and other incidental charges.

Most of the respondents (more than 50 per cent) in both regions incurred transaction cost above Rs.1000 per loan (Table 3.43). The considerable proportion of loan amount spent as transaction cost, made the respondent loose the amount for the desired purpose; he borrowed. The quantum of amount spent to obtain credit from the institutional agencies by the borrowers was saved in SHGs.

Reasons to Select the Agency to Borrow Money

Generally, the borrowers approach an institution to fulfill their credit needs. The respondents have stated several reasons to select the concerned agency to borrow money. The purpose of loan that mainly catered by the agency, distance factors and the quantum of loan

Table 3.42: Loan Amount Borrowed

(Figures in numbers)

Particulars	*PACB*		*PCARDB*		*CB*		*SHG*		*Total*		*Grand Total*
	Dry	*Wet*	*Dry*	*Wet*	*Dry*	*Wet*	*Dry*	*Wet*	*Dry*	*Wet*	
Below 2000	2 (2)	1 (1)	-	-	-	-	13 (100)	3 (36)	15 (8)	4 (3)	19 (6)
2001-5000	28 (26)	13 (15)	-	-	15 (33)	2 (6)	-	6 (64)	43 (24)	21 (14)	64 (20)
5001-10000	52 (48)	23 (26)	3 (21)	-	15 (33)	10 (27)	-	-	70 (39)	33 (23)	103 (32)
10001-15000	18 (18)	10 (12)	3 (21)	4 (36)	12 (27)	12 (32)	-	-	33 (18)	26 (18)	59 (18)
15000-20000	5 (5)	9 (10)	8 (58)	2 (18)	-	8 (21)	-	-	13 (8)	19 (13)	32 (10)
Above 20000	2 (2)	31 (36)	-	5 (46)	3 (7)	5 (14)	-	-	5 (3)	41 (29)	46 (14)
Total	107	87	14	11	45	37	13	9	179	144	323

Source: As in table 3.1.

Note: As in table 3.1.

amount required were the determinants to select the particular agency to borrow loan.

It was found that only 32 per cent of respondents have approached the institution with the only intention to get loan. Improving the economic status was the main concern for the respondents of CB in both regions and the respondents of Cooperative Banks in dry region, whereas getting loan in anticipation of waiver was the main reason for the respondents of the Cooperative Banks in the wet region. The rest had among reasons, i.e., to improve economic status (23 per cent), lesser rates of interest (10 per cent), nearness of institution (7 per cent), to have the attitude of 'our bank' or 'group' (7 per cent), to avail consumption credit (3 per cent), to invest in business (3 per cent) and to increase savings (2 per cent). Majority of the SHG borrowers have the attitude of 'our bank' or 'group' followed by the increase in savings, which was not deservable in other institutions (Table 3.44).

Easy Accessible Sources of Credit

Having access to both IAs and NIAs for credit, the rural households have experienced and are well known with the relative advantages and disadvantages.

When asked which source was easily accessible to them at present and the reasons underlying in it, majority of the respondents felt that the NIAs were easily accessible sources (Table 3.45). It reveals that the NIAs have a strong niche in the RCM.

Factors that Decide Access to Credit

In order to find the effect of the demographic variables,

Table 3.43: Expenses incurred to avail Loan

(Figures in numbers)

Particulars	PACB		PCARDB		CB		SHG		Total		Grand
	Dry	Wet	Dry	Wet	Dry	Wet	Dry	Wet	Dry	Wet	Total
No transaction cost	-	-	-	-	-	-	13 (100)	9 (100)	13 (7)	9 (7)	22 (7)
1-500	64 (60)	35 (40)	-	2 (18)	21 (47)	5 (14)	-	-	85 (47)	42 (29)	127 (39)
500-1000	40 (37)	25 (29)	8 (60)	3 (27)	12 (26)	7 (18)	-	-	60 (34)	35 (24)	95 (29)
1001-1500	3 (3)	12 (14)	6 (40)	2 (18)	6 (13)	5 (14)	-	-	15 (8)	19 (13)	34 (11)
1501-2000	-	10 (12)	-	1 (9)	3 (7)	13 (36)	-	-	3 (2)	24 (17)	27 (8)
2001-2500	-	3 (3)	-	3 (28)	1 (7)	5 (14)	-	-	3 (2)	11 (8)	14 (4)
2501-3000	-	1 (1)	-	-	-	1 (2)	-	-	-	2 (1)	2 (1)
3001-5000	-	1 (1)	-	-	-	1 (2)	-	-	-	2 (1)	2 (1)
Total	107	87	5	12	45	42	5	11	179	144	323

Source: As in table 3.1.

Note: As in table 3.1.

Table 3.44: Reasons to Select the Agency to Borrow Money

(Figures in numbers)

Particulars	PACB		PCARDB		CB		SHG		Total		Grand
	Dry	Wet	Dry	Wet	Dry	Wet	Dry	Wet	Dry	Wet	Total
To increase savings	-	2 (3)	-	-	-	-	5 (38)	-	5 (3)	2 (1)	7 (2)
To get loans	54 (50)	38 (44)	-	4 (36)	3 (7)	5 (14)	-	-	57 (32)	47 (33)	104 (32)
Improving economic status	20 (19)	6 (7)	6 (43)	2 (19)	24 (53)	9 (24)	3 (23)	3 (33)	53 (30)	20 (14)	73 (23)
To avail consu-mption credit	-	-	6 (43)	1 (9)	-	-	-	3 (33)	6 (3)	4 (4)	10 (3)
To get loan waiver	9 (8)	15 (17)	2 (14)	4 (36)	12 (27)	-	-	-	23 (12)	19 (13)	42 (13)
Lesser interest	8 (7)	18 (21)	-	-	-	5 (13)	-	-	8 (5)	23 (16)	31 (10)
Nearness	13 (13)	3 (3)	-	-	-	6 (17)	-	-	13 (7)	9 (6)	22 (7)
Our bank or group	3 (3)	5 (5)	-	-	-	7 (19)	5 (39)	3 (34)	8 (5)	15 (10)	23 (7)
To invest in business	-	-	-	-	6 (13)	5 (13)	-	-	6 (3)	5 (4)	11 (3)
Total	107	87	5	12	45	42	5	11	179	144	323

Source: As in table 3.1

Note: As in table 3.1.

Table 3.45: Easy Accessible Sources of Credit

(Figures in numbers)

Particulars	PACB		PCARDB		CB		SHG		Total		Grand Total
	Dry	Wet	Dry	Wet	Dry	Wet	Dry	Wet	Dry	Wet	
Formal	29 (27)	27 (32)	6 (40)	3 (25)	24 (53)	20 (53)	8 (60)	8 (91)	67 (37)	58 (40)	125 (39)
Informal	54 (50)	40 (46)	2 (20)	6 (58)	15 (33)	10 (26)	-	-	71 (40)	56 (39)	127 (39)
Both	24 (23)	20 (23)	6 (40)	2 (17)	6 (14)	7 (21)	5 (40)	1 (9)	41 (23)	30 (21)	71 (22)
Total	107	87	14	11	48	37	13	9	179	144	323

Source: As in table 3.1

Note: As in table 3.1.

social variables and economic variables on the access to credit, separate Regression Analyses were attempted for each type of variables for the dry and wet regions for each of the credit agencies. The Regression equations were arrived at and interpreted accordingly.

Institution-PACB

In the wet region, there were 87 borrowers in PACB. Firstly, access to credit (Y) was regressed linearly on Age (X_1) and Sex (X_2). The mathematical form of the estimated equation is:

$$Y = 0.875 + \underset{(0.912)}{1.235X_1^{NS}} - \underset{(0.013)}{0.284^{**}X_2}$$

$$R^2 = 0.48^{**} \qquad N=87$$

The R square is 0.48 which is significant at one percent level of probability indicating the fact that forty eight percent of the variations in the access to credit is being explained by the two choice variables Age and Sex. The regression co-efficient is negative and significant for Sex. Since male is given the score one and the female zero which indicates that the males have more accessibility to credit. The non-significant co-efficient for Age indicates the nil effect of the variable Age on credit accessibility. Same set of variables when regressed for the dry region resulted in the following equation.

$$Y = 0.923 + 0.975^{NS} x_1 - 0.113^{*} x_2$$
$$\qquad\qquad (1.17) \qquad (0.058)$$

$$R^2 = 0.38^{*} \qquad N = 107$$

The R square is 0.38 which is significant at 5 percent level of probability indicating that thirty eight percent of the variations in the accessibility to credit is being explained by the two variables Age and Sex. As in the case of wet region here also the regression coefficient for the variable Age is not significant and it is significant for the variable Sex impressing the fact that irrespective of the regions the males have higher accessibility to credit.

In the case of the effect of social variables on the access to credit, the included variables are the Community (X_1), Education (X_2), Type of Family (X_3), Exposure to Mass-Media (X_4), Contact with Change Agents (X_5) and Membership in Social Organizations (X_6). The estimated equation for the wet region is:

$$Y = 0.1856 - 0.052^{NS} X_1 + 0.837^{NS} X_2 + 1.104^{NS} X_3 + 0.517^{*} X_4 + 0.267^{*} X_5 + 0.372^{*} X_6$$
$$\qquad (0.173) \quad (0.786) \quad (1.563) \quad (0.203) \quad (0.118) \quad (0.163)$$

$$R^2 = 0.61^{**} \qquad N = 87$$

R square is 0.61, which is significant at one percent level of probability indicating the fact that sixty one percent of the variations in the access to credit is being explained by the variables Community, Education, Type of Family, Exposure to Mass Media, Contact With Change Agents and Membership in Social Organizations.

The significance of the co-efficient indicates that the variables viz., Community, Education, Type of Family have nothing to do with the access to credit. The effect is positive in the case of Exposure to Mass Media, Contact With Change Agents and Membership in Social Organizations. Probably Exposure to mass media creates awareness and the members could influence the banks through their frequent contact with change agents and Social Organizations.

Same set of variables when regressed on access to credit in the dry region resulted in the regression equation.

$$Y = 0.227 + 0.012^{NS}X_1 + 0.210^{**}X_2 - 0.117^{NS}X_3 + 0.218^{*}X_4 + 0.106^{*}X_5 + 0.003X_6$$
$$(0.137) \quad (0.042) \quad (0.663) \quad (0.093) \quad (0.042) \quad (0.013)$$
$$R^2 = 0.53^{**} \qquad N=107$$

Here, the R square is 0.53, which is significant at one percent level of probability indicating that fifty three percent of variations in the access to credit is being explained by the six independent variables used to estimate the equation.

The regression co-efficient is significant for Education, Exposure to Mass Media and Contact With Change Agents. This indicates that contrary to the wet region, in the dry region, education has a positive effect, which might probably be due to the fact that people with education in dry region could approach the officials easily and have access to credit. On the other hand, the Membership in Social Organization has no effect, which is contrary to that in the wet region. Thus irrespective of the region, the variables Exposure to Mass Media and Contact With Change Agents have positive effects on the access to credit. The non-significance of this variable might be due to the fact that irrespective of their membership, education has helped them to have access to credit.

In the case of the economic variables Occupation (X_1), Income (X_2), Alternative Sources of Income (X_3), Total Assets Holding (X_4), Total Farm Expenses (X_5), Extent of Old Debts (X_6), Purpose of Borrowing (X_7) and Extent of Borrowing (X_8) are taken as independent variables. The estimated regression equation for the wet region is:

$$Y = 0.028 + \underset{(0.004)}{0.013^{**}} X_1 + \underset{(0.046)}{0.118^{**}} X_2 + \underset{(0.033)}{0.086^{**}} X_3 + \underset{(0.021)}{0.053^{*}} X_4 + \underset{(0.015)}{0.044^{**}} X_5 - \underset{(0.128)}{0.304^{*}} X_6$$

$$- \underset{(0.12)}{0.010^{NS}} X_7 - \underset{(0.028)}{0.031^{NS}} X_8$$

$R^2 = 0.58^{**}$ N = 87

The R square is 0.58, which is significant at one percent level of probability. This indicates that fifty eight percent of the variations in the access to credit is being explained by the eight choice variables stated above. The regression coefficient is positive and significant for Occupation, Income, Alternative Sources of Income, Total Asset Holding and Total Farm Expenses indicating the positive effect of these variables on the credit accessibility. The negative significance of the co-efficient for the variable Old Debts indicated that the banks resisted issuing credits when the earlier debts remained uncleared. The other two variables viz., Purpose of Borrowing and Extent of Borrowing have no effect on the access to credit.

All the five positive significant variables constitute the economic factors. Among this the fifth variabe viz: Total Farm Expenses is a proxy for Farm Income. The increase in all the five variable is the implication of better economic position and the increase in old debts might be a wilful default or due to poor economic condition. Thus, the result indicates the carefulness of the banks in offering the loans in the wet region.

Same set of variables when regressed on access to credit in dry region resulted in the equation:

$$Y = 0.156 - 0.008^{*}X_1 - 0.201^{**}X_2 + 0.13^{*}X_3 + 0.004^{**}X_4 + 0.018^{**}X_5 - 0.003^{*}X_6 -$$
$$\quad (0.003) \quad (0.046) \quad (0.005) \quad (0.001) \quad (0.015) \quad (0.001)$$

$$+ 0.013^{**}X_7 + 0.006^{**}X_8$$
$$\quad (0.004) \quad (0.002)$$

$R^2 = 0.43^{**}$ N=107

R square is 0.43, which is significant at one percent level of probability indicating that forty three percent of variations in the access to credit is explained by the eight choice variables used. As in the case of the wet region, the variables Occupation (X_1), Income (X_2), Alternative Sources of Income (X_3), Total Assets Holding (X_4) and Total Farm Expenses (X_5), have positive effect on the access to credit and the Old Debts have negative effect. The only difference in the dry region is that the two variables Purpose of Borrowing and Extent of Borrowing also showed positive impact on the access to credit. This might probably be due to the problem of migration. Due to consecutive monsoon failure, the rural households in this region had migrated to urban centres especially to Tiruppur for employment. Hence, bankers were very much careful while issuing loans.

Comparison of the two results for the wet and dry regions showed that irrespective of the nature of the places the access to credit solely depended on the financial repayment capacity as assessed by the bank and in the case of the migrants they had taken extra care that there was no diversion of funds.

Institution-PCARDB

In the case of PCARDB, since the sample size was small viz., 11 for the wet region and 14 for the dry region, the functional analysis was not attempted due to the shortage in the degrees of freedom. Hence the researcher resorted to Correlation Analysis.

The Simple Correlation was worked out separately for the dry and wet regions for the variables Age, Occupation, Income, Alternative Sources of Income, Total Asset Holding, Total Farm Expenses, Extent of Old Debts, Extent of Borrowing, Education, Family Size, Exposure to Mass Media and Contact With Change Agents.

The computed value of the correlation and the level of significance for the dry and wet regions are presented below in Table 3.46.

Table 3.46 reveals that the variables Occupation, Income, Alternative Sources of Income, Total Assets, Mass Media, and Change Agents have positive association with the accessibility to credit irrespective of whether the region is dry or wet and indicating the same type of behavior with this sub sample group. The variable Extent of Old Debt has got negative association in both the regions as indicated in the functional analysis. The variables Education and Family Size have positive association with the credit accessibility only in the dry region. The reason might be the same as noted in the case of PACB. Thus irrespective of the cooperative banks, the general behavior of the loan issuing authorities was common towards all the respondents.

Institution-SHG

In the case of SHG also due to the limited size in the sample, the simple correlation analysis was applied. The result of the simple correlation analysis is presented in Table 3.47

Table 3.46: Simple Correlation for Access to Credit with regard to PCARDB

S.No	*Variables*	*Wet region*	*Dry region*
1	Age	0.227^{NS}	0.198^{NS}
2	Occupation	0.773*	0.682*
3	Income	0.786*	0.725*
4	Alternative sources of income	0.663*	0.645*
5	Total assets	0.641*	0.599*
6	Total farm expenses	0.203^{NS}	0.198^{NS}
7	Extent of old debts	-0.599*	-0.603*
8	Extent of borrowing	-0.112^{NS}	-0.162^{NS}
9	Education	0.223^{NS}	0.617*
10	Family size	0.301^{NS}	0.664*
11	Exposure to Mass Media	0.426^{NS}	0.371^{NS}
12	Change agents	0.325^{NS}	0.306^{NS}
		N=9	N=13

* *-Significant at five percent level of probability*

NS -Not significant.

The results presented in Table 3.47 showed that contrary to the earlier cases in this group, the two variables Exposure to Mass Media and Contact With Change Agents alone have positive association with the accessibility to credit irrespective of the regions. All other variables have expressed no association with credit accessibility. This might be due to the fact that these groups were nurtured by Change Agents and their higher Exposure to Mass Media might have helped them to have access to credit.

Table 3.47: Simple Correlation for Access to Credit with regard to SHG

S.No	*Independent Variables*	*Wet Region*	*Dry Region*
1	Age	0.132^{NS}	0.161^{NS}
2	Occupation	0.131 ^{NS}	0.187 ^{NS}
3	Income	0.248 ^{NS}	0.272 ^{NS}
4	Alternative sources of income	0.259 ^{NS}	0.151 ^{NS}
5	Total assets	0.137 ^{NS}	0.128 ^{NS}
6	Total farm expenses	0.113^{NS}	0.092^{NS}
7	Extent of old debts	-0.213 ^{NS}	-0.209 ^{NS}
8	Extent of borrowing	0.209^{NS}	-0.226^{NS}
9	Education	0.136^{NS}	0.113 ^{NS}
10	Family size	0.214^{NS}	0.199 ^{NS}
11	Mass media	0.627*	0.715*
12	Change agents	0.661*	0.709*
		N=11	N=14

**-Significant at five percent level of probability*
NS–Not significan.

Institution-Commercial Bank (CB)

Functional analysis similar to the one carried out for PACB is attempted for CB also. The estimated regression equation in the case of the demographic variables age and sex for wet region is:

$$Y = 1.135 + 0.516^{NS} X_1 - 0.472^{**} X_2$$
$$\qquad (0.463) \qquad (0.113)$$
$$R^2 = 0.52^{*}, \quad N = 37$$

and for the dry region is:

$$Y = 1.247 + 0.183^{NS} X_1 - 0.389^{**} X_2$$
$$\qquad (0.317) \qquad (0.105)$$
$$R^2 = 0.49^{*} \quad N = 45$$

In the wet region, the R square is 0.52 which is significant at 5 % level of probability indicating the fact that fifty two percent of the variations in the accessibility to credit is being explained by the variables Age (X_1) and Sex (X_2). In the dry region, forty nine percent of the variation in the credit accessibility is being explained by the variables Age and Sex. In both the regions, the two variables have behaved identically as in PACB. That is the variable Age has nothing to do with credit accessibility and the males have more accessibility in both regions. Thus the behavior of the Demographic variables does not vary between sources and between regions.

The same set of social variables viz.: Community (X_1), Education (X_2), Type of Family (X_3), Exposure to Mass Media (X_4), Contact With Change Agents (X_5), and Membership in Social Organizations (X_6) when regressed linearly on access to credit for both regions has yielded the following results for the two regions. For the wet region, the mathematical form of the estimated equation is:

$$Y = 0.517 - 0.0113NS\ X1 + 0.132^{*}X2\ -0.851\ NS\ X3 + 0.463\ NSX4 + 0.386^{**}X5$$

(0.156) (0.066) (0.956) (0.531) (0.125)

$$+0.264\ NSX6$$

$R2 = 0.63^{**}$ N=37

The R square is 0.63, which is significant at one per cent level of probability indicating the fact that sixty three percent of the variations in the access to credit is being explained by the variables Community, Education, Type of family, Exposure to Mass Media, Contact With Change Agents and Membership in Social Organizations.

The significance of the coefficient suggests that the variables Education and Contact with Change Agents alone have positive effect on the access to credit. None of the other variables have any effect on the credit in the wet regions. The above indirectly indicates that the higher perception through education and their frequent contact with change agents would have helped them to have access to credit with IAs. The estimated equation for the dry region is:

$$Y = 0.356 - 0.042^{NS} X_1 + 0.156^{**}X_2 + 0.276^{NS}X_3 + 0.314^{*}X_4 + 0.187^{**}X_5 - 0.056^{NS}X_6$$

(0.053) (0.047) (0.193) (0.116) (0.059) (0.043)

$R^2 = 0.59^{*}$ N=45

Here, the R Square is 0.59 which is significant at 5 per cent level of probability indicating the fact that fifty nine per cent of the variations in the access to credit is being explained by the six independent variables viz., Community (X_1), Education (X_2), Type of Family (X_3), Exposure to Mass Media (X_4), Contact With Change Agents (X_5) and Membership in Social Organizations (X_6) included in the study.

In the dry region apart from Education and Contact With Change Agents, the variable Exposure to Mass Media also has positive effect on the accessibility to credit.

In the case of CB also, as in PACB, the same set of economic variables viz., Occupation (X_1), Income (X_2), Alternative Sources of Income (X_3) Total Assets Holding (X_4) Total Farm Expenses (X_5) Extent of Old Debts (X_6) Purpose of Borrowing (X_7) and Extent of Borrowing (X_8) when regressed with the accessibility to credit has resulted in the following equations for the wet and dry regions. The estimated equation for the wet region is:

$$Y=\underset{(0.519)}{0.887+0.516^{**}}X_1+\underset{(0.110)}{0.342^{**}}X_2+\underset{(0.951)}{0.193^{*}}X_3+\underset{(0.314)}{0.252^{NS}}X_4+\underset{(0.189)}{0.246^{NS}}X_{5+}\underset{(0.154)}{0.173^{NS}}X_6$$

$$+\underset{(0.225)}{0.204^{NS}}X_7+\underset{(0.243)}{0.113}X_8$$

$R^2=0.63^{**}$ N=37

The R square is 0.63 which is significant at one percent level of probability indicating the fact that sixty percent of the variations in the access to credit is being explained by the variables Occupation, Income, Alternative Sources of Income, Total Assets Holding,

Total Farm Expenses, Extent of Old Debts, Purpose of Borrowing and Extent of Borrowing.

The regression coefficient is significant only for Occupation, Income and Alternative Source of Income. That is these variables alone have effects on the access to credit in Commercial Banks. Probably the Commercial Banks are more careful only in knowing the repaying capacity of their customers in order to issue loans.

For the same set of variables, the estimated equation in the case of dry region is given below:

$$Y=0.791 + \underset{(0.203)}{0.427^{*}X_1} + \underset{(0.311)}{0.617^{*}X_2} + \underset{(0.716)}{0.235^{**}X_3}$$
$$+ \underset{(0.179)}{0.264^{NS}X_5} + \underset{(0.289)}{0.346^{NS}X_6} + \underset{(0.327)}{0.448^{NS}X_7}$$
$$+ \underset{(0.175)}{0.102^{NS}X_8}$$
$$R^2=0.54^{**} \qquad N=45$$

The R square is 0.54 which is significant at one percent level of probability indicating the fact that fifty four percent of the variations in the accessibility to credit is being explained by the included variables viz., Occupation, Income, Alternative Sources of income, Total Assets Holding, Total Farm Expenses, Extent of old debts, Purpose of Borrowing and Extent of Borrowing. The regression coefficient is positive and significant for Occupation, Income and the Alternative Source of Income. This shows that only these variables have positive effect on the access to credit as in the case of the wet region, the reason being the same as above.

Advantages and Disadvantages of Availing Loan from NIAs and IAs

The PLP for Dindigul District evidences that the procedures and documentation were cumbersome and time consuming to the farmers of Dindigul District. The quantum of loan was felt to be inadequate by 20 per cent of the respondents. 30 per cent of the respondents felt that the banking facilities were inadequate as they had to go a long distance to reach their service area bank. Another indicator of insufficiency of bank credit was that 30 percent of the farmers had to borrow from moneylenders at interest rates of 36 per cent to 72 per cent per annum. Although the farmers felt that the interest rate charged by the institutional agencies was lower than that charged by the moneylenders, 40 per cent of the farmers felt that the interest rate was rather high compared to the interest rate offered for their deposits. Majority of the respondents (75 per cent) were in favour of subsidized credit for investment activities. The villagers' most important expectation was easy access to credit (NABARD: 2004-05, p. 97).

In order to understand the attitude of sample respondents with regard to IAs and NIAs, they were asked to state the advantages and disadvantages of these two agencies. The reasons were obtained and ranked and to know the consistency or otherwise of it, the Kendall's Coefficient of Concordance was worked out for each and the results are presented in the tables (3.48 & 3.50).

Advantages of Availing Credit from NIAs and IAs

The informal sources had provided several advantages. The respondents felt that the access to credit with the NIAs was confidential and convenient so long as the relationship was not abused by the NIAs through forgery or cheating or harassment. Because of this, the informal credit operates simultaneously and indeed more strongly alongside the formal credit (Sankar Bhowmick: 2002). The Marginal and Small Farmers have to depend on the NIAs, especially the moneylenders, because of their past dues (Balishter & Pankaj Kumar: 1995, p. 15).

The SAA, which is the functional approach for IAs, is the traditional approach of NIAs. Fulfillment of urgent needs, availability of credit at doorstep and time and confidentiality in transaction were the advantages felt by the respondents in availing credit from NIAs (Table 3.48).

Table 3.48: Advantages in availing Loan from NIAs (Kendall's Coefficient of Concordance)

Particulars	*PACB*	*PCARDB*	*CB*	*SHG*	*Total*
Fulfilment of urgent needs	45	2	10	-	29
Availability of credit at the door step	19	3	6	-	11
Availability of credit in time	24	3	21	-	68
Confidentiality in transaction	3	5	13	-	38
Others		1	-	16	30
Total	91	14	50	16	176

The Kendalls Coefficient of Concordance in these cases are:

W= 0.178 N = 5 K = 4 s = 28.5^{NS}

W is not significant; hence there is no agreement between the sample respondents and the reasons vary from bank to bank.

It was found out that a lesser rate of interest, Availing benefits under Government schemes and Simple formalities were the major advantages felt by the respondents in the study area with regard to loan from IAs (Table 3.49).

Disadvantages in Availing Loan from NIAs and IAs

The past studies showed that exorbitant rate of interest was the main disadvantage with the moneylenders. Apart from that, in this study, the respondents opined that unhealthy practices against delay in repayment, apathy towards unexpected losses and shorter duration of repayment were the main disadvantages (Table 3.50 and Chart 3.4).

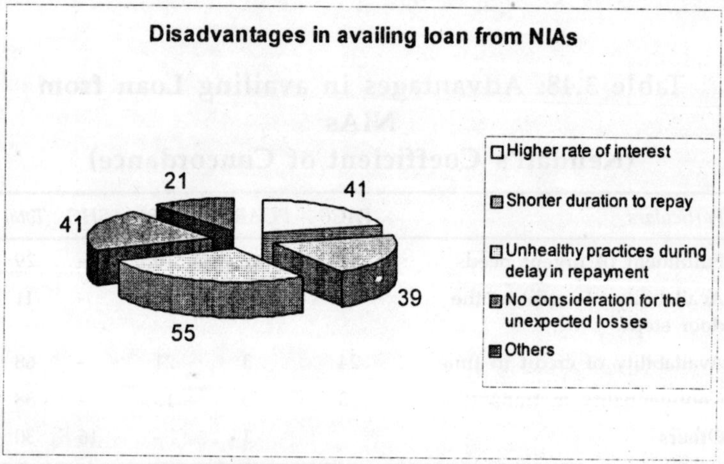

Chart 3

W is not significant; hence there is no agreement

Table 3.49: Advantages in availing Loans from IAs

(Figures in numbers)

Particulars	*PACB*		*PCARDB*		*CB*		*SHG*		*Total*		*Grand*
	Dry	*Wet*	*Dry*	*Wet*	*Dry*	*Wet*	*Dry*	*Wet*	*Dry*	*Wet*	*Total*
Lesser rate of interest	45 (42)	24 (27)	8 (60)	7 (60)	45 (100)	11 (29)	3 (20)	2 (22)	101 (56)	44 (30)	145 (45)
Simple formalities	5 (4)	13 (15)	-	-	-	8 (21)	3 (20)	5 (56)	8 (4)	26 (18)	34 (11)
Timely availability of loan	12 (11)	6 (7)	-	-	-	7 (19)	-	2 (22)	12 (7)	15 (10)	27 (8)
Loan for different purposes	2 (2)	-	3 (20)	2 (20)	-	6 (17)	7 (60)	-	12 (7)	8 (6)	20 (6)
Availing benefits under government schemes	31 (29)	22 (25)	-	-	-	2 (7)	-	-	31 (17)	24 (17)	55 (17)
Loans available in kind position	5 (5)	13 (15)	-	-	-	1 (2)	-	-	5 (3)	14 (10)	19 (6)
Announcement of waiver during drought	5 (5)	7 (8)	3 (20)	2 (20)	-	-	-	-	8 (5)	9 (6)	17 (5)
Others	2 (2)	2 (3)	-	-	-	2 (5)	-	-	2 (1)	4 (3)	6 (2)
Total	107	87	14	11	45	37	13	9	179	144	323

Source: As in table 3.1.

Note: As in table 3.1.

between the sample respondents and the reasons vary from bank to bank.

Table 3.50: Disadvantages in Availing loan from NIAs (Kendall's Coefficient of Concordance)

Particulars	*PACB*	*PCARDB*	*CB*	*SHG*	*Total*
Fulfilment of urgent needs	45	2	10	-	29
Higher rate of interest	23	2	13	3	41
Shorter duration to repay	22	2	12	3	39
Unhealthy practices during delay in repayment	44	5	6	-	55
No consideration for the unexpected losses	23	2	14	2	41
Others	12	4	2	3	21
Total	124	15	47	11	197

The Kendalls Coefficient of Concordance in this case is:

W = 0.053 N = 5 K = 4 s = 8. 5^{NS}

The sample respondents experienced disadvantages in availing loan from the formal agencies also. Non-availability of loan for consumption and in time followed by time consuming procedures were the major disadvantages in availing formal loans. High transaction cost, employees' unfriendliness and insufficiency of the loan amount were the other disadvantages stated by the respondents with regard to loan from IAs (Table 3.51).

Conclusion

Sir Frederick Nicholson in his famous report on the 'Possibility of Introducing Land and Agricultural Banks in Madras, 1895' stated that the lesson of universal history was that "an essential of agriculture is credit. Neither the condition of the country, nor the nature of the land tenure nor the position of agriculture will alter the one great fact that an agriculturist must borrow". From the above discussions, it is found that as high as 63 per cent of the rural households were indebted either to IAs or to the NIAs and the incidence of indebtedness was high in wet region as compared to the dry region. Hence, instead of old saying 'the Indian farmers is born in debt, live in debts and dies in debt', it is very opt to say that farmer may die to make his debt burden alive with his legal heirs. Contact with the change agents was the main social variable while Occupation, Income and Alternative sources of income were the main economic variables, which influenced the access to credit with the IAs. It only indicates that the resource poor who are in sizable number depending mainly on agriculture in the rural areas have had poor access to IAs. Hence, the NIAs still dominate in the RCM by contributing to more than sixty percent of the total credit needs of the borrowers, of which the share of moneylenders remained significant. It shows that institutional credit doesn't mitigate the problem of rural indebtedness in both the region; infact the extent of indebtedness of the rural borrowers had increased after they became the clientele of IAs. Similar findings were reported by Gautham Purkhayastha (2001, p. 4.)

Hence, debts with the NIAs were the major cause for indebtedness. Indebtedness blocks further access to institutional credit to the rural borrowers and again pushed them back in the trap of the moneylenders, increased their debt burden, spoiled the social

Table 3.51: Disadvantages in availing Loan from IAs

(Figures in numbers)

Particulars	PACB		PCARDB		CB		SHG		Total		Grand
	Dry	Wet	Dry	Wet	Dry	Wet	Dry	Wet	Dry	Wet	Total
Time consuming procedure	19 (18)	19 (22)	-	2 (18)	-	9 (24)	-	-	19 (11)	30 (21)	49 (15)
Employees are not friendly	-	3 (3)	-	3 (27)	12 (27)	2 (5)	-	-	12 (7)	8 (6)	20 (6)
Non-availability of loan for consumption	40 (38)	23 (27)	6 (40)	1 (9)	21 (46)	12 (33)	-	-	67 (37)	36 (25)	103 (32)
Non-availability of loan in time	25 (23)	18 (21)	2 (20)	2 (18)	-	6 (17)	-	-	27 (15)	26 (18)	53 (16)
High transaction cost	11 (10)	17 (19)	6 (40)	3 (28)	12 (27)	8 (21)	-	-	29 (16)	28 (19)	57 (18)
Insufficiency of the loan amount	12 (11)	7 (8)	-	-	-	-	13 (100)	9 (100)	25 (14)	16 (11)	41 (13)
Total	107	87	14	11	45	37	13	9	179	144	323

Source: As in table 3.1.

Note: As in table 3.1.

recognition in their neighborhood, made them resource poor, and finally drove them pathetically long for loan waiver schemes from Government. The dawn of the SHGs has relieved certain segment of the rural borrowers from the interest burden with the moneylenders though not from the total family debt burden. The SHG members' debt burden infact sandwiches their entrepreneurial qualities. Of course this seems to be a temporary phenomenon. If SHGs are allowed to grow naturally, they will find new solutions to address the age-old problem of rural indebtedness. Hence, it is inevitably concluded that the IAs have not mitigated the problem of rural indebtedness in the study area.

REFERENCES

1. Balwinder Singh (2000), *Agricultural Credit–Sources, Problems and Emerging Issues,* Deep & Deep Publications, New Delhi, p. 2.
2. Charles Malamoud (1983), *Debts and Debtors,* Vikas Publishing House Private Limited, New Delhi, p. 154.
3. Chidambaram, K. & Sankarasubramoniam, V. (1999), Factors Influencing Repayment of IRDP Loan—A Study, *Kurukshetra,* Vol. 47(6), March, p. 4 & 5.
4. Chinnappa Reddy, B.V., Venkataraman, J.V. and Keshava Reddy (1987), An Economic Analysis of Overdues among Farmers in Srinivaspur Taluk, Kolar District, *Land Bank Journal,* Vol. 26(2), December, p. 4
5. Classens, Stijin (2005), Universal Access to Financial Services: A Review of the Issues and

Public Policy Objectives' OECD–World Bank, Fifth Services Experts Meeting, February 3-4, OECD, Paris, quoted in: Nachiket Mor (2005), Expanding Access to Financial Services Where do we go from here?, *Economic and Political Weekly*, Vol.XL(12), March 19-25, p. 1122.

6. Dadhich, C.L. (1977), *Overdues in Farm Cooperative Credit*, Popular Prakashan Private Ltd., Bombay, p. 53 & 242.
7. Debabrata Das, (2002), Utilisation Pattern of Cooperative Credit: A Case Study, *Cooperative Perspective*, Vol. 36(4), Jan-march, p. 27.
8. Desai, B.M. (1996), Whither Rural Financial Institutions? *Economic and Political Weekly*, August, Quoted by Puhazhendhi V. and Jayaraman B. (1999), Rural Credit Delivery: Performance and Challenges before Banks, www.epw.com, p. 2.
9. Desai, S.S.M. (1990), *Agriculture and Rural Banking in India*, Himalaya Publishing House, Bombay, p. 228.
10. Dhimen Namhata and Broadway A.C. (1988), Profitable Utilisation of Cooperative Credit by Cultivators, *Indian Cooperative Review*, Vol. 25(3), p. 306.
11. F.A.O. (1957), *Credit Problems of Small Farmers in Asia and Far East* Quoted in Mamoria C.B. (1983), Kitab Mahal, Allahabad, p. 69.
12. GOI (1991-92), *All India Debt and Investment Survey*, NSS–48th Round, p. 17.
13. Grewal P. S. (1985), *Rural Banking in India*, Kalyani Publishers, New Delhi, p. 95.

14. Gautham Purkhayastha (2001), Rural Indebtedness in Assam, www.epw.org, p. 4

15. *Human Development in South Asia* (2002), Mahabub ul haq Human Development Centre, Oxford, p. 89, 114 & 115.

16. Joy Joseph Puthussery (1999), Socio-Economic Characteristics and Nature of Default—A Study of Primary Agricultural and Rural Development Banks in Kerala, *Land Bank Journal*, Vol.38(3), December, p. 9 & 10.

17. Jugale, V.B. (1992), *Cooperative Credit in Indian Agriculture—Its Socio-Economic and Technological Impact*, Mittal Publications, New Delhi, p. 86 & 87.

18. Jugale, V.B. (1994), Role of Cooperatives in Agricultural Finance, *Indian Cooperative Review*, Vol. 32(1), July, p. 61.

19. Karmakar, K.G. (1999), *Rural Credit and SHGs–Micro Finance Needs and Concepts in India*, Sage Publications, New Delhi, p. 211.

20. Krishna Naik, C.N. & Siddaiah, T. (1990), Behavioural Aspects of Cooperative Credit—A Survey, *Cooperative Perspective*, Vol. 25(2), July-September, p. 38.

21. Majumdar, N.A. (1997), Overhauling the Somnolent Rural Credit System, *Economic and Political Weekly*, Vol. 32 (43), October, p. 73.

22. Mamoria, C.B. and Badri Bishal Tripathi (2001), *Agricultural Problems of India*, Kitab Mahal Agencies, Allahabad, p. 397 & 400.

23. Maninder Kaur, Gill, S.S. & Sukhdev Singh (1997),

Rural Poverty in Punjab—A Case Study, *Indian Economic Panorama*, April–June, p. 31 & 32.

24. Mishra S.D. (2003), Poor in a Spider's Web of Debt, *IBA Bulletin*, April, Vol. 25 (4), p. 20.
25. Mohanan N. (2004), Sustainability of Credit Market in An Indian Village, *Journal of Rural Development*, Vol. 23(3), July-September p. 390
26. Mukesh Singh Rathore (1994), *Role of Institutional Finance in Development of Agriculture in India*, Mohit Publications, New Delhi, p. 28.
27. Namasivayam & Ramachandraiah G. (2000), End Use of Credit and Repayment Performance of the Institutional Borrowers: An Integrated Analysis, *Journal of Rural Development*, Vol. 19(3), p. 419.
28. Padmini C. (2004), Role of Linkages in the Development of Cooperatives, *The Indian Economic Journal*, Vol. 51, No. 3 & 4, p. 28.
29. Pattarnaraka K. (2003), Members' Participation in the Activities of a Production Credit Groups in Southern Thailand, *Journal of Rural Development*, Vol. 22 (2), p. 265.
30. Perumalsamy, P. (1996), *Economic Development of Tamil Nadu*, S. Chand & Co., Ltd., New Delhi, p. 382.
31. Pramod Lata Jain (1990), *Cooperative Credit in Rural India*, Mittal Publications, New Delhi, p. 129, 130 & 138.
32. Prasad, J.V.S, Naidu, M.R. & Venkateswaralu, U. (1987), Credit Overdues–Certain Factors for Default—A Micro Analysis, *Land Bank Journal*, Vol. 25(4), June, p. 5.

33. Priya Basu, Pradeep Srivastava (2005), Exploring Possibilities–Microfinance and Rural Credit Access for the Poor in India, *Economic and Political Weekly*, Vol. XL (17), p. 1747.

34. Rajput A.M and Verma A.R. (1993), 'Impact of Farm Loans on Farm Productivity—A Case Study of State Bank of India in Indore District of Madhya Pradesh, *Indian Cooperative Review*, Vol. 31(1), July p. 56.

35. Ramachandra Reddy (1995), An Evolution and Function of Cooperative Societies in Cuddapah District, *Indian Cooperative Review*, Vol. 33(2), October, p. 162.

36. Ramachandra Reddy D. & Bagavan Reddy B. (1994), Cooperative Credit in Delta and Non-Delta Regions of Cuddapah, *Cooperative Perspective*, Vol. 29(3), October–November, p. 57.

37. Ramamohana Rao (2000), *Banks, Borrowers and Barriers—Problems of Finance Against Poverty*, The University of Manchester, U.K. p. 32.

38. Ravichandran, K. & Revathi Bala, M. (2004), Role of SHGs and Cooperatives in Rural Credit Market, *CAB Calling*, RBI, p. 12.

39. RBI (1969), *All India Rural Credit Review Committee*, Bombay, p. 534.

40. Reddy, C.R. (1993), *Overdues Management in Cooperative Banks*, Himalaya Publishing House, Bombay, p. 33.

41. Rengasamy, V. & Ramnath, R.L. (2000), Performance of Financial Agencies in the Priority Sector Lending under the Service Area Approach

in Madurai District, *Prajnan*, Vol. 29 (1), April-June, p. 82.

42. Royal Commission Report on Agriculture (1966), Quoted by Mukesh Singh Rathore, *Role of Institutional Finance in the Development of Agriculture in India*, Mohit Publications, New Delhi, 1994, p. 280.

43. Satya Sai, K.J.S., Venkateswaralu, U., Seetharaman S. and Raghu Ram P. (1987), Structure of Rural Credit in West Godavari District, Andhra Pradesh, *Land Bank Journal*, Vol. 26(2), p. 54.

44. Savita Thakur Joshi (1999), *Women and Development–The Changing Scenario*, Mittal Publications, New Delhi, p. 8.

45. Shakuntala Devi (1996), *Rural Credit and Agricultural Development*, Sarup & Sons Publications, p. 8.

46. Sharma, K.C. (1998), *Advanced Rural Banking*, Indian Institute of Bankers, Mumbai, p. 126.

47. Shollapur, M.R. (1996), Appraisal of Effectiveness of Post-Sanction Follow-up of credit, *Indian Cooperative Review*, Vol. 33(4), April, p. 25.

48. Singh, A.K., Bajpai, D.K. and Gairia, P. S. (1993), Institutional Finance and the Rural Poor: Findings of a Field Study in a Backward Area, *Indian Cooperative Review*, Vol. 30(4), April, p. 396.

49. Sivaprakasam, P. (1993), Defaulters of the Agricultural Credit Cooperative: A Study with special reference to the Short-Term Agricultural Credit, In: *Cooperative Credit & Banking–Strategies for Development* (ed. by) Garg M.C. & Joshi, N.N., Deep & Deep Publications, 1997, p. 46.

50. Sopan Joshi (2004), Inevitable Tragedy, *Down to Earth*, Vol. 13(4), Society for Environmental Communication, New Delhi, p. 15.

51. Srivastava (1991), Cooperative Credit for Rural Development—A Regional Experience, *Indian Cooperative Review*, Vol. 29 (2), October, p. 189.

52. Subba Rao (2007), Financial Inclusion: An Introspection, www.epw.org.in/articles/2007/02/11039.pdf

53. Sunil, M. (2004), Growing Suicide Deaths: Chilling Depth of Agrarian Crisis, www.peoplesmarch/com/archives/2004/sept2k4/Growing.htm, p. 1.

54. Taimani, K.K. (1993), *Cooperative Development: The Next Phase, ICA* Domust Trust Publication, New Delhi, June p. 240.

55. *The Financial Express* (1996), March 2, p. 7.

56. *The Hindu* (2003), 14th September, Vol. 126 (37), p. 16.

4

Utilization Pattern and Repayment Behaviour of Borrowers

Introduction

Institutional credit aims at generating the sources for repayment through productive investments and makes the borrower self-reliant. Generally, there are three stages of credit extension viz., credit delivery, credit utilization and its repayment. The problem of institutional credit is not merely one of inadequate supply of finance; rather it is aggravated by its ineffective utilization. The IAs extended credit facilities to the rural poor for productive purposes. Credit serves as a productive input only when it is used for productive purposes in order to generate more income after paying the interest and capital. Thus, the IAs insist that credit should be utilized for the purpose for which it was given because proper utilization leads to proper repayment of credit. But in practice, the credit is availed by the borrowers for meeting their consumption or social needs under the alleged reason of borrowing for a productive purpose. Such diversion for unproductive purposes wou d affect the repaying capacity of the borrowers and create overdues at institutional level.

Overdue Syndrome

Loans provided to farmers are to be repaid out of the income generated from the investment for which the loan was given. If this cycling of funds is continuously realized without any trouble, the smooth functioning of the IAs and their financial soundness will not be questioned. But the syndrome of agricultural credit i.e., overdue has been increasing over the years and has eroded the financial soundness of the IAs thereby crippling the flow of institutional credit to agriculture. In fact, the contributing factors may vary but overdue is a pervasive phenomenon neutral to the type of credit institution (RBI: 1989, p. 538). The magnitude and causes for overdue have been studied at different levels by various Committees and Commissions and individual researchers.

The All India Rural Credit Survey Committee (1954, pp. 244-268) which made the first elaborate survey on Cooperative Credit found that about 20 percent of the total outstanding was overdue as on 30th June 1951 in 32 out of 75 selected districts. In ten districts more than 50 per cent of the loan outstanding was overdue at the society level. As far as Madras Presidency was concerned the proportion of overdues to outstanding was 18.8 percent for the same period.

The All India Rural Credit Review Committee (1969, p. 141), which reviewed the trend after Survey Committee's findings, found that, due to the increase in the volume of loans advanced by the cooperative credit societies, the average lending per member and per society also recorded an appreciable rise, despite the rise in the number of members and societies. Evidently at the end of 1967-68, the proportion of overdues to outstanding was still high at 30.2 per cent. While endorsing the same trend, the Fourth Plan document stated that out of the 344 CCBs functioning in the country in as many as 67 CCBs, the accumulated overdues exceeded 50 percent of the outstanding in 1967-68. At this level it was found that the increasing trend in overdues appeared to be a general phenomenon and not confined only to weak States or States susceptible to natural calamities. Among others, the unsound lending policies, unsatisfactory management and political factors were found to be the factors deciding the increasing trend in overdues. Further, The Review Committee seriously viewed this aspect since comparing of overdues with the outstanding loans would not reflect the true picture of the problem of overdues.

The Study Team on Overdues (1974, p. 10) went deep into this problem and revealed that the overdues exceeded the owned funds of almost 80 per cent of the CCBs and along with them the deposits of all the PACS. This had resulted in the crippling of the cooperative credit structure by making them unable to absorb the credit facility from the higher financing agencies and extend support to agricultural development programmes. Further, it concluded that the defaults were by and large willful besides being perpetrated by the lack of will and discipline among the cultivators to repay and the unhelpful attitude of the State Governments in creating a favourable climate for recovery.

The other important Committees, which made enquiry into this problem, were CRAFICARD (RBI: 1980, p. 55) and the Agricultural Credit Review Committee (1989). The CRAFICARD reviewed the magnitude of the problem of overdues against demand and found that the overdues increased from Rs.322.40 crores in 1970-71 to Rs.809.62 crores in 1977-78, constituting 43.3 per cent to demand in 1977-78 at the PACS level.

The Agricultural Credit Review Committee (RBI: 1989, p. 215), which reviewed the entire aspects of rural credit especially the Overdues Syndrome assessed that high delinquency rate in the recovery of loans was the key retarding factor in both widening and deepening of credit by the PACS. This review estimated that the overdues of PACS increased from Rs. 560.5 crores in 1975-76 to Rs. 1806 cores during 1985-86. While analyzing both the internal and external causes for overdues, the Committee viewed that the problem of overdues could not be studied in isolation. It came to the conclusion that overdues in agricultural loans were universal and neutral to the type of agency and the variations in the incidence of overdues, between different classes of borrowers were in most cases only marginal.

Even after the number of measures adopted based on the suggestions of the various Committees and Commissions still the problem of overdue is too serious and mounting year by year. At the all India level, the position of overdue in PACS level stood at Rs.6 crores during 1950-51; it mounted to Rs.1088 crores in 1979-80 (Pranab Kumar Chakrabarthy: 1983, p. 53) and to Rs. 11088.6 crores in 2001-02 (NCUI: 2004, p. 18). It has been raised upto Rs.16052 crores in 2005–06 (RBI: 2005–06, p. 131).

Non-Performing Assets

The banking sector reforms were initiated in the country since 1992. With the recommendations of Narasimham Committee, the RBI issued certain guidelines for treating a credit facility as Non-Performing Asset (NPA) instead of as overdue. It introduced norms for income recognition, classification of assets and provisioning for NPA as part of the Prudential Norms Framework for Banks during the year 1992-93. NPA was defined as a credit facility in respect of which the interest and /or installment of the principal has remained past due for a specified period of time.

The prudential norms not only tracked the defaulters for a specific loan amount, but even if they regularly repaid (RBI: 2004, p. 57). Due to the prudential norms, the public sector banks suffered losses of Rs.3293 crores in 1992-93 and Rs.4349 crores in 1993-94. During the year 2001-02, the NPA of Scheduled CBs stood at Rs.70905 crores as against Rs.45653 crores in 1997-98. It has been reduced to Rs.51947 crores in the year 2005–06. Among the total NPA position of all the IAs, the CBs have had more than 60 percent of the NPA between the years 1997-98 and 2005-06.

In order to bring transparency in the working of banks, the prudential norms on asset classification, income recognition and provisioning were made applicable to the SCBs/DCCBs from 1996-97 and to SCARDBs/PCARDBs from 1997-98. During the year 2001-02, the total NPA of the Cooperative Banks stood at Rs.21288 crores as against Rs.11402 crores during the year 1998-99. It has been increased upto Rs.29835.13 crores in the year 2005-06 (Table 4.1).

Table 4.1: Position of NPAs in IAs at all India level

(Rs. in crores)

Agency	*1997-98*	*1998-99*	*1999-00*	*2000-01*	*2001-02*	*2002-03*	*2003-04*	*2004-05*	*2005-06*
Cooperatives	8932	10240	10301	13260	15838	18436.4	22649.1	20591.2	19887.8
ARDBs	2470	2761	3674	4585	5450	6973.86	8352.23	9493.29	9947.23
CBs	45653	51710	60408	63883	70905	68780	64898	59161	51947
RRBs	3238	3168	3049	2978	3066	3508.15	13943.3	2804.35	2619.2

Source: 1. NABARD (1997-98), Best Performance Awards to Cooperative Banks for 1997-98, p. 16.

2. NABARD (2001-02), Annual Report, p. 128 & 135.

3. NABARD (2002-03), Annual Report, p. 107 & 115.

4. IBA (2004), Management of NPA by Indian Banks, IBA Bulletin, Vol. 26 (1), p. 63.

5. NABARD (2005–06), Annual Report, pp. 84–99.

Though the agricultural and non-agricultural advances of the RRBs under priority sector taken together increased from Rs.6226 crore in 1995 to Rs.10571 crores during 2002, the share of the RRBs in the total agricultural credit at the national level has remained low right from their inception at 8 to 9 percent (RBI: 2004, p. 71). During the year 2005-06, the NPA position of the RRBs at all India level stood at Rs. 2619.2 crores as against Rs.3066 crores in the year 2001–02 (Table 4.1).

Table 4.2: Percentage of Recoveries to Demand in IAs at State and District level

(Figures in percentages)

	District level			*State level*		
Particulars	*CCB*	*PCARDB*	*CB*	*CCB*	*PCARDB*	*CB*
1997-98	78.92	50.7	66.53	70	33	64
1998-99	77.4	52	65	50	35	70
1999-2000	76.7	47	65.31	58	38	63
2000-01	78.3	42.8	63.17	50	27	70
2001-02	79.6	43.5	69	70	35	74
2002 -03	71.3	23.4	72	79.6	36.5	76
2003-04	62	17	74	62.47	44	74
2004-05	83	11	79	81	36.5	76
2005-06	79	9	76	83	32	78

Source: Compiled from the NABARD State Focus Paper, Tamil Nadu and Potential Linked Credit Plan for Dindigul District for various years.

The figures given in table 4.2 have shown the percentage of recoveries to demand in the IAs at State as well as at District level. It seems that compared to the Cocperative Banks, the CBs were in an advantageous position. Among the Cooperative Banks, the percentage of recovery to demand was very poor in PCARDBs both at State and District level. The real picture is still worse in all institutions because in majority of the cases, book adjustments were in practice i.e., fresh loan applications were obtained from borrowers to clear off the old dues with the bank. In these cases, the transaction cost might be high at borrowers level, but the borrowers escaped from the burden of repaying debt for the time being. These adjustments may not be available to all classes of the borrowers, but common practice. among the banks. The postponing of recoveries through loan conversion and reschedulments makes it difficult to understand the real magnitude of the problem of indebtedness and overdue.

4.3 Causes for NPAs

The efficiency of IAs as a financial intermediary depends to a great extent on the timely recovery of the loans. The abnormal delay in recovering the loans is the root cause for overdue, which affects the IAs adversely with respect to liquidity. The blocked funds in the NPAs increase the cost of the financial intermediation as the IAs resort to raising deposits and borrowings at a higher cost to minimize the imbalance between cash outflow and cash inflow arising out of the NPAs. The factors affecting the recovery of the loans by the IAs may broadly be grouped into two, the external and the internal. Among the internal factors, some are related to the borrowers and some are related to the IAs. A few important factors responsible for the poor recovery of loans and consequent build up of the NPAs in the IAs are illustrated in Box 1. The external factors such as natural calamities, political interferences, policy changes and legal procedures are outside the control of IAs but are critical for creating conducive recovery climate.

Box 1: Reasons for Poor recovery of Loans in RFIs

A. External	*B. Internal*
• Natural calamities	I. RFI related
• Political interference	• Improper identification of borrowers
• Loan waiver, write off etc	
• Geographical factors	• Lack of appraisal skills
• Changes in policy environment	• Delay in loan sanction
• Changes in technology	• Under or over financing
• Changes in economic conditions	• Insufficient gestation or repayment period
• Target approach under Goverer-nment sponsored programmes	• Lack of post disbursement follow up
• Legal process	
• Inadequate market linkages	• Lack of borrower contact and poor understanding of rural clientele
	• No thrust on recovery
	• Laxity in internal control systems
	• Poor management information system
	• Failure to ensure adequate rapport with Government agencies
	• Low motivation and involvement of staff
	• Perception of bank as a charity institution
	• Poor industrial relations climate
C. Exclusive reasons for poor recovery of loans in cooperatives	*II Borrower Related*
	• Misutilisation of loan
• Lack of professional management	• Diversion of funds
• Imbalance among tiers	• Lack of technical and management skills
• Lack of transparency	

• Inadequacy of non-official and member education	• Poor maintenance of assets • Wilful default • Personal accident, death etc., • Shifting of place of residence or business

Source: BIRD (2000), NABARD's Best Performance Awards to Cooperative Banks for 1997-98 & 1998-99, p. XXII.

Several studies conducted in various parts of the country reported the causes like defective lending policies (RBI: 1954, p. 62 & RBI: 1974, p. 76), failure to tie-up lending with development programmes (RBI: 1980, p. 167), increasing politicization of agricultural credit (RBI: 1989, p. 83), member's desire to harass the management (Dadhich, C.L.: 1977, p. 65), dominance of moneylenders (Satyasai, K.J.S. et.al: 1987, p. 54) lack of cooperative education (Arul Anandam, et.al: 1988, p. 300), inadequate flow of cooperative credit (Indira Devi, P. et.al: 1992, p. 336), lack of adequate knowledge about direct and supporting farm activites (Loganathan P. et.al: 1992, p. 389), lesser investment in production process (Goyal, S.K. et.al: 1993, p. 296), lack of cooperative consciousness (Reddy, C.R.: 1993, p. 29), diversion of credit to unproductive purposes (Balishter & Pankaj Kumar: 1995, p. 18), misutilisation of loans (Mazumdar, D.K. & Baruah, H.K.: 1999, p. 2), willful default (Ravichandran, K.: 2000, p. 164), low agricultural productivity (Sidhu, et.al: 2002, p. 137), adverse effects of Debt Relief Schemes (Ravichandran, K.: 2000, p. 139 and Joshi, G.V.: 2002, p. 25) were the reasons attributed to the increase of overdue in Cooperatives. The cumulative result is that the members, who are mostly borrowers, have little or no sense on their stake in the cooperatives or any accountability in ensuring prudent management of funds. On the contrary, the Government policies (loan and interest waivers, delaying recoveries, the loans carrying State Guarantees) have, in a way, led the borrowers to presume that they could with impunity, delay or even fail to meet, their repayment obligations (GOI: 2004, p. 53).

The study conducted by Anil Suryawanshi (2003, p. 19) identified that misutilisation of the loans by beneficiaries, low income generation from the activity undertaken, natural calamities, intentional non-repayment of dues, non-adherence to lending norms/ sanctioned norms/conditions were the reasons at the borrower level in the selected RRBs. Selection of unsuitable scheme, political interference and wilful default were the reasons for the poor recovery in RRBs (Ranjit Kumar Das: 2002, p. 10).

Poor planning, delay in communication, ignorance of credit risk and commercial risks, overlooking of operational irregularities are the causes for the creation of the NPAs apart from the abrupt changes in Government policies, cost and time overruns, natural calamities which tend to mount them at the CBs level (Malyadri, P. & Sirisha, S. :2003, p. 7).

Implications of NPAs at the Institutional level

Implications of the NPAs at the institutional level would vary depending upon the size of the institution (both in terms of the number of loan accounts and area covered); business they perform for their clients and area in which they are (agriculturally developed or under developed) functioning. However due to increasing NPAs, all the IAs have to face certain difficulties which are outlined below:

1. The growth of the NPAs questioned the financial viability of the IAs, which resulted in the closure of loss making banks or their branches.
2. The PACS, which are performing only credit functions are adversely affected due to the growth of the NPAs and consequent erosion in owned funds; and
3. Under the situation, the IAs are forced to deny credit even for the new and genuine borrowers.

The efficiency of the banks is not always reflected only by the size of its balance sheet but by the level of return on its assets. The NPAs do not generate interest income for the banks but at the same time, the banks are required to make provisions for such NPAs from their current profits. The NPAs have a deleterious effect on the return on assets in several ways-viz.,

- NPAs erode current profits through the provisioning requirement;
- Which resulted in reduced interest income;
- NPAs require higher provisioning requirements affecting profits.
- NPAs limit recycling of funds, set in asset liability mismatches etc.

Implications of Debt at the Borrowers Level

Increasing debt has specific implications on the borrowers:

1. Due to non-availability of the loans from the IAs, the borrowers try to borrow from other NIAs, which is a high-cost credit. This burden affects their repaying capacity;

2. The borrowers will be put into the 'Vicious Circle' of borrower cum defaulter continuously even during the good harvest/cropping seasons;
3. Even after establishing a comprehensive institutional network for agricultural credit, the farmers are not entirely relieved from the burden of debt;
4. If defaults occur due to genuine reasons like natural calamities, drought and floods, the facilities of conversion, rephasement and rescheduling will not be available during all times and to all farmers. This will create an additional burden in repayment;
5. The big farmers continuously borrowing from IAs will divert the low cost loans to profitable avenues like relending;
6. Penal interest, which would be charged on overdues, loan will increase the burden of debt in the case of small farmers; and
7. Consequent to these factors, the IAs may not be in a position to provide fresh finance for the genuine and new members.

All these factors are responsible for the reduction in the number of borrowing members in the IAs and the non-recovery of loan from the existing borrowers.

These trends pose great challenge before the bankers and jeopardize the financial system.

To conclude:

1. Indian Banking System has not been able to internalize rural lending as a viable financial activity but only as a social obligation because the policy makers wanted it;

2. Institutional lending to rural areas were considered as a part of social sector lending and not commercial lending. All those who have availed loans were treated as only beneficiaries, not borrowers or customers;
3. This trend has developed an attitude that rural sector lendings are not bankable, i.e., that means the commercial principles could not be applied to rural lending.

In this context, the utilization of loan for the purpose for which it was given acquires greater importance. Proper utilization will lead to proper repayment. The loan utilization pattern and repayment ethics of the rural borrowers would become the area of study in the following paras.

Utilization of Credit

Proper utilization of the loans has a favourable influence on the ability of the borrower to generate additional income from the investment. Productive utilization of the borrowed funds generally increases the loan repaying capacity of the borrowers. This improves the chances of timely recovery of loans by the IAs. Higher the productive utilization of loans higher will be the loan repayment. Higher the loan repayment in time; better will be the recycling of scarce loanable funds with the IAs. The health of the IAs depends on this formula. The usefulness of institutional finance is to be judged not merely on the quantum of credit pumped into the sector, but on how far it is utilized properly by the borrowers. The extent to which it is utilized for productive purpose and the extent of its deviation from the stipulated purpose deserve the attention of all those concerned (Anandateerth Kittur: 1990, p. 774).

The financing institutions are to be more concerned with the creditworthy purpose rather than credit worthy person; feasibility of the project than the availability or adequacy of security; the end use of the credit apart from the end result of it (Muniraj: 1987, p. 38). The use of credit for productive and unproductive purposes depends upon the nature of utilization of the credit. If loan amount utilized for the productive purposes, it may generate its own means of repayment. But diversion creates problems and ultimately restricts the repayment (Patnaik et.al., 1999, p. 43).

Extent of Utilization of Loan

With the increasing reliance of rural households on credit for their agriculture and consequent expansion of the IAs network, the attention of the planners and the researchers have been diverted towards the exploration of certain questions regarding credit utilization. The RFIs in the study area mainly gives production-oriented credit, which facilitate the agricultural operations. Keeping in view, the necessity of the efforts for improving the credit utilization pattern of loans, the present study endeavors to examine the utilization pattern among the sample respondents.

It was found that irrespective of all institutional agencies, less than 50 percent of the respondents utilized the loan amount for the purpose for which it was given. The extent of utilisation was found very low among PCARDB borrowers (20 percent in dry and 27 percent in wet) indicating the fact that the medium and large farmers have misutilized more loan amount

Table 4.3: Extent of Utilization of Loan Amount

(Figures in numbers)

Particulars	*PACB*		*PCARDB*		*CB*		*SHG*		*Total*		*Grand*
	Dry	*Wet*	*Dry*	*Wet*	*Dry*	*Wet*	*Dry*	*Wet*	*Dry*	*Wet*	*Total*
Full utilization	50 (47)	39 (45)	3 (20)	3 (27)	24 (53)	19 (50)	13 (100)	9 (100)	90 (50)	70 (49)	160 (49)
Diversion	57 (53)	48 (55)	11 (80)	8 (73)	21 (47)	18 (50)	-	-	89 (50)	74 (51)	163 (51)
Grand Total	107	87	14	11	45	37	13	9	179	144	323

Source: Compiled from respondents schedule

Note: Figures in parenthesis indicates percentage to column total.

(Table 4.3). Further, the percentage of credit utilized to credit obtained is calculated by using the following formula: Mean credit utilized/Mean credit availed x 100

Table 4.4: Region Wise Classification of Utilization of Loan Amount

Region	*No. of borrowers*	*Mean credit availed*	*Mean credit utilized*	*Mean credit misutilised*	*Percentage of loan amount utilized*	*Percentage of loan amount mistualised*
Dry	179	16678	10507	6171	63	37
Wet	144	21485	11817	9668	55	45
Total	323	18917	10972	7945	58	42

Source: Compiled from respondents schedule

Table 4.5: Institution wise classification of Utilization of Loan Amount

Particulars	*PACB*	*PCARDB*	*CB*	*SHG*	*Total*
No.of borrowers	194	25	82	22	323
Mean credit availea	4918	6053	6810	1136	18917
Mean credit utilized	2633	2633	4499	1206	10972
Mean credit misutilised	2707	4061	2990	-	9668
Percentage of loan utilized	55	45	26	100	-
Percentage of loan misutilised	45	55	74	-	-

Source: Compiled from respondents schedule

The mean credit disbursed was Rs. 18917 and the mean credit utilized properly by the borrowers worked out to Rs. 10972 indicating that 58 percent of the loan amount was utilized for the purposes for which the loan was issued by the IAs (Table 4.4). Further, the incidence of misutilisation was higher in wet region as compared to the other regions.

Reasons for the Full Utilization of Loans

Earlier experiences show that the loan amount availed have been fully utilized for cultivation expenses rather than for consumption due to higher production and productivity of the crops (Indira Devi: 1992, p. 337). But, Dindigul, being drought prone where agriculture has been much affected, most of the respondents of this study were not able to secure expected income from the amount invested on agriculture.

It was found that 49 percent of the respondents fully utilized the loan amount with the expectation of good yield from investment. Next to this, the availability of loan in time (29 per cent), lesser-unexpected expenses (12 per cent), awareness on the consequences of diversion (6 per cent) and proper supervision (4 per cent) were the factors that led to the full utilization of the loans. The SHG members observed that the availability of credit in time (60 per cent in dry and 78 per cent in wet) was the reason to fully utilize the loan amount (Table 4.6 and Chart 4.1). Misutilisation was among the respondents belonging to the Cooperatives and CBs. As the SHGs provide loans for consumption purposes also, the utilization was cent percent.

Table 4.6: Reasons for the Full Utilisation of Loan

(Figures in numbers)

Particulars	*PACB*		*PCARDB*		*CB*		*SHG*		*Total*		*Grand*
	Dry	*Wet*	*Dry*	*Wet*	*Dry*	*Wet*	*Dry*	*Wet*	*Dry*	*Wet*	*Total*
Expecting good yield from investment	34 (68)	27 (69)	3 (100)	2 (67)	6 (25)	7 (37)	-	-	43 (48)	36 (51)	79 (49)
Lesser unexpected expenses	8 (16)	7 (18)	-	-	-	3 (16)	-	1 (11)	8 (9)	11 (16)	19 (12)
Availability of loan in time	5 (10)	2 (5)	-	-	18 (75)	7 (37)	7 (60)	7 (78)	30 (33)	16 (23)	46 (29)
Proper supervision	-	-	-	1 (33)	-	2 (10)	3 (20)	-	3 (3)	3 (4)	6 (4)
Awareness on the consequences of diversion	3 (6)	3 (8)	-	-	-	-	3 (20)	1 (11)	6 (7)	4 (6)	10 (6)
Total	50	39	3	3	24	19	13	9	90	70	160
Diversion	57	48	11	8	21	18	-	-	89	74	163
Grand Total	107	87	14	11	45	37	13	9	179	144	323

Source: As in table 4.2.

Note: As in table 4.2.

Effort Made by the Organization to Utilize Loans

Institutional credit is distinguished from non-institutional credit on the ground of supervision and for this the former is designated as supervised credit. The credit agencies have to play a more dynamic or catalytic role by stressing the supervision and guidance aspects of credit more than credit deployment.

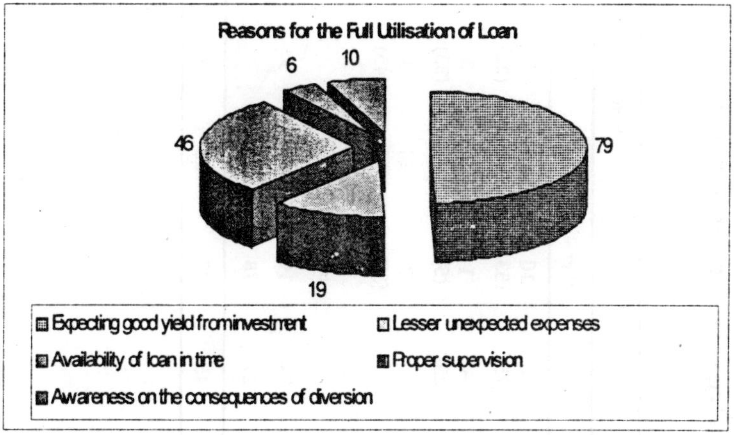

Chart 4.1

The institutional initiatives such as proper supervision (28 per cent), loan in time (22 per cent), adequate quantum of loan (26 per cent), loan with kind portion (24 per cent) facilitated the respondents to properly utilize the loan amount (Table 4.7). Institution wise analysis shows that proper supervision was the prime effort made by the CBs whereas the provision of loan with kind portion making the respondents of PACBs to fully utilize the loan. Provision of adequate loan and in time followed by proper supervision were the efforts made by the SHGs for the full utilization of the loans.

Table 4.7: Effort made by the Organization for the Full Utilization of Loan

(Figures in numbers)

Particulars	PACB		PCARDB		CB		SHG		Total		Grand Total
	Dry	Wet	Dry	Wet	Dry	Wet	Dry	Wet	Dry	Wet	
Proper supervision	3 (6)	12 (31)	-	-	18 (75)	10 (53)	-	2 (22)	21 (23)	24 (34)	45 (28)
Providing loan in time	17 (34)	5 (13)	-	-	6 (25)	1 (5)	3 (23)	3 (33)	26 (29)	9 (13)	35 (22)
Providing adequate loan	11 (22)	7 (18)	-	3 (100)	-	7 (37)	10 (77)	4 (45)	21 (23)	21 (30)	42 (26)
Providing loan with kind portion	19 (38)	15 (38)	3 (100)	-	-	1 (5)	-	-	22 (25)	16 (23)	38 (24)
Total	50	39	3	3	24	19	13	9	90	70	160
Misutilisation	57	48	11	8	21	18	-	-	89	74	163
Grand Total	107	87	14	11	45	37	13	9	179	144	323

Source: As in table 4.2.

Note: As in table 4.2.

Misutilisation of Loan Amount

One of the defects of the supervised credit is the misutilisation of loans for the purposes other than the noted ones which become the main reason for the non-repayment of loan by most of the defaulters (Balishter, et.al: 1994, p. 382), (Reddy, B.R. et.al: 1996, p. 19), (Balishter et.al: 1991, p. 39).

Usually short term productive finance is misutilised for consumption purposes. This practice of misutilisation is minimized in the case of the medium and long-term loans because of the nature of the utility of the loans. But in the case of short-term loans, such practice is inevitable. It could be minimized but not completely avoided. It was proved that there is negative relationship between the diversion of loan and size group of the farmers i.e., to the medium and big farmers, the misutilisation of loan is due to their productive expenses (Arunachalam R. et.al: 1991, p. 182), (Kulwant Pathania, et.al: 1992, p. 49), (Makadia, J.J. et.al: 1992, p. 59), (Modi, M.K. et.al: 1993, p. 254), (Tiwari, S.N. et.al: 1986, p. 27). Misutilisation is less among higher income group farmers than low income group farmers (Kulwant Pathania et al: 1992, p. 49). The diversion of loans was negatively related to the amount of borrowers (Debabrata Das: 2002, p. 27). Cooperative education (Arul Anandam, et.al: 1988, p. 300), inadequate flow of cooperative credit (Indira Devi, P. et.al: 1992, p. 336), lack of adequate knowledge about direct and supporting farm activites (Loganathan, P. et.al: 1992, p. 389), lesser investment in production process (Goyal, S.K. et.al: 1993, p. 296), lack of cooperative consciousness (Reddy, C.R.: 1993, p. 29),

Table 4.8: Misutilisation of Loan Amount

(Figures in numbers)

Particulars	PACB		PCARDB		CB		SHG		Total		Grand
	Dry	Wet	Dry	Wet	Dry	Wet	Dry	Wet	Dry	Wet	Total
2001-5000	19 (38)	9 (22)	-	-	-	3 (16)	-	-	19 (25)	12 (20)	31 (23)
5001-10000	31 (62)	19 (49)	3 (100)	-	10 (42)	5 (26)	-	-	44 (57)	24 (39)	68 (49)
10001-15000	-	3 (8)	-	3 (100)	12 (50)	7 (37)	-	-	12 (15)	13 (21)	25 (18)
15001-20000	-	8 (21)	-	-	2 (8)	4 (21)	-	-	2 (3)	12 (20)	14 (10)
Total	50	39	3	3	24	19	-	-	77	61	138
Diversion	57	48	11	8	21	18	-	-	89	74	163
Grand Total	107	87	14	11	45	37	13	9	179	144	323

Source: As in table 4.2.

Note: As in table 4.2.

In this study, it was found that majority of the respondents of the cooperatives misutilised the loan amount between Rs. 5000 to Rs. 10000. The respondents of the CBs misutilised the loan amount ranging between Rs. 10000 to Rs. 20000. Absentee land lordship, lack of involvement in agricultural operations and seeking profitable avenues were the reasons found for the misutilisation of the loan by borrowers of CB (Table 4.8).

Reasons to Misutilise the Loan

The peculiar feature of Indian farming is that the farmers combine farm with home operations and the expenses of both are inseparable with each other. When provision is made for the loans only for the productive purposes of agriculture naturally it is misutilised. Under the existing loan policy, there is no provision for the disbursement of loans for consumption purposes as a part of production loans. In certain circumstances, consumption needs like medical or ceremonial expenses will be so pressing that will make an individual to misutilise the productive loans for consumption purposes.

The three main reasons for the misutilisation of short term loans as pointed out by the P. E.O's Report are as follows: 1. Economic exigencies 2. Concealment 3. Credit System. (Nakkiran, S. et.al: 1988, p. 119). The Economic exigencies arise for unavoidable or urgent needs for which the expenditure is considered necessary such as household needs or those relating to agriculture or purchase of livestock or other business purposes.

The small farmers use the loan to meet the consumption expenditure and for the redemption of old debts, etc., whereas the well-to-do ones borrow from the bank and use it for fictitious ends (Subbi Reddy, T. et.al: 1980, p. 32). The main reason for improper utilization of the borrowed money was short-period repayment and non-availability of the crop loan in time (Sharma, D.K. et.al: 1991, p. 18). Two-third of the total diverters used the loan for unproductive purposes like consumption purposes, other household needs, payment of old debts, miscellaneous expenditure etc. (Makadia, J.J. et.al: 1992, p. 59). The proportion of misutilisation mostly related to the expenditure on domestic affairs, social ceremonies, litigation, medical care etc. On the other hand, productive utilization was made for the purchase of animals and birds, foods and medicines, insurance, construction of sheds, purchase of equipments etc., (Mazumdar, D.K. et.al: 1999, p. 2). The increasing consumption and household expenses are the main reason for the misutilisation of loan (Modi, M.K. et.al: 1993, p. 254 and Debabrata Das: 2002, p. 27).

Social, Economic and Cultural Factors affecting the Misutilisation of Credit

Both inadequacy and abundancy in size of the loan are equally dangerous. As Fredrick Nicholson wrote 90 years ago, 'use of too little credit hampers production while borrowing too much leads to bankruptcy'. There are numerous factors affecting the utilization of credit by the borrowers. Generally, these factors can be classified into two: a. Borrower related factors and b. Lender related factors.

At the borrowers level, several socio-economic, political and psychological factors influence the utilization and repayment behaviour of the borrowers. Some of the important social factors are the level of literacy of the borrowers, size of family, proportion of dependent members of the family, caste, and contact with change agents. The economic factors include the income of the borrower from agriculture and other sources, farm and family expenditures, cropping pattern, irrigation facility and size of holdings. The political and psychological factors lead to the use of production loans to non-productive purposes, which in turn leads to overdues (Ravichandran, K.: 2000, p. 113). The lender related factors are nature of loan, loaning procedures, experience of the agency in rural credit, organizational structure and the network system.

Since use is conceptualized as a binary variable in order to study the effect of the political, organizational, social and economic variables, the Logit Form of Regression Equation is proposed. In the logit form the dependent variable being binary its probability is taken for constructing the dependent variable. We denote by pa, the probability that the borrower will utilize the amount properly, and then the dependent variable is:

$$\text{Log (pa / 1- pa)} = Y$$

Now, this is linearly regressed on membership in Political Parties (X_1), Age of the Membership (X_2), Motivation (X_3), Supervision (X_4), Education (X_5). Mass-Media Exposure (X_6), Contact With Change Agents (X_7), Occupation (X_8), Income (X_9), Alternative Sources of Income (X_{10}), Total Farm Expenses (X_{11}), Total Family Expenses (X_{13}), Extent of Old Debts (X_{14}), and Extent of Borrowing (X_{15}). The estimated equation according to Ordinary Least Squares is:

$$
\begin{aligned}
Y = 14.632 &+ \underset{(0.604)}{0.516^{NS}} X_1 + \underset{(0.113)}{0.283^{*}} X_2 + \underset{(0.149)}{0.344^{*}} X_3 + \underset{(0.140)}{0.271^{*}} X_4 + \underset{(0.099)}{0.193^{*}} X_5 + \underset{(0.058)}{0.114^{*}} X_6 \\
&+ \underset{(0.151)}{0.321^{*}} X_7 + \underset{(0.110)}{0.213^{*}} X_8 + \underset{(0.113)}{0.215^{*}} X_9 + \underset{(0.148)}{0.403^{**}} X_{10} + \underset{(0.055)}{0.115^{*}} X_{11} + \underset{(0.271)}{0.569^{*}} X_{12} \\
&- \underset{(0.341)}{0.653^{*}} X_{13} + \underset{(0.211)}{0.415^{*}} X_{14} - \underset{(0.059)}{0.118^{*}} X_{15}
\end{aligned}
$$

$R^2 = 0.48^{**}$ $N=301$

The R square is 0.48, which is significant at one percent level of probability. This indicates that 15 variables together could explain 48 percent of the variations in the utilization of the credit. Since, the form of equation is logit the coefficients of the different variables indicates only the proportionate changes. The sign of the coefficients indicate that Age of Membership (X_2), Motivation (X_3), Supervision (X_4), Education (X_5), Mass Media Exposure (X_6), Contact With Change Agents (X_7), Occupation (X_8), Income (X_9), Alternative Sources of Income (X_{10}), Total Assets (X_{11}), Total Farm Expenses (X_{12}) have direct positive influence on the utilization, whereas the variable membership in political parties (X_{13}), extent of old debts (X_{14}) and extent of borrowings (X_{15}) have direct negative effects on the use.

The regression analysis showed that the borrowers' contact with the political parties, old debt and current borrowings divert the purpose of loan, and led to misutilisation of loan and which in turn arrested the borrowers' repayment behaviour.

Other Factors Affecting the Misutilisation of Loan

Though there were various reasons to misutilise the loan, drought (10 per cent), higher rate of inputs (6 per cent), unexpected expenses (29 per cent), increase in consumption expenses (34 per cent) and delay in getting loans (18 per cent) were the main reasons to misutilize the loan amount among the cooperative and commercial bank borrowers in the study area (Table 4.9 and Chart 4.2).

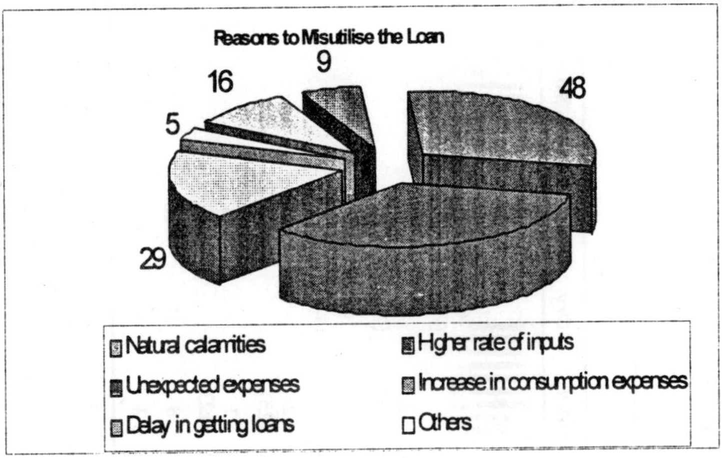

Chart 4.2

Pattern of Misutilisation

Diversion of loan amount can be termed as misutilisation. Diversion may either be productive or unproductive. Productive diversion means the misutilisation of the loan amount by the borrower but which generates income. To illustrate, the borrower who borrowed the loan for cultivation expenses spend such money for irrigation expenses.

Table 4.9: Reasons to Misutilise the Loan

(Figures in numbers)

Particulars	PACB		PCARDB		CB		SHG		Total		Grand
	Dry	Wet	Dry	Wet	Dry	Wet	Dry	Wet	Dry	Wet	Total
Drought	5 (8)	4 (8)	3 (27)	3 (38)	-	1 (6)	-	-	8 (9)	8 (11)	16 (10)
Higher rate of inputs	2 (4)	1 (2)	-	-	6 (29)	-	-	-	8 (9)	1 (1)	9 (6)
Unexpected expenses	20 (35)	10 (21)	5 (46)	2 (25)	6 (29)	5 (28)	-	-	31 (35)	17 (23)	48 (29)
Increase in consumption expenses	20 (35)	17 (35)	3 (27)	-	9 (42)	7 (38)	-	-	32 (36)	24 (32)	56 (34)
Delay in getting loans	10 (18)	16 (31)	-	2 (25)	-	1 (6)	-	-	10 (11)	19 (26)	29 (18)
Others (social ceremonies)	-	-	-	1 (12)	-	4 (22)	-	-	-	5 (7)	5 (3)
Total	57	48	11	8	21	18	-	-	89	74	163
Full utilization	50	39	3	3	24	19	13	9	90	70	160
Grand Total	107	87	14	11	45	37	13	9	179	144	323

Source: As in table 4.2.

Note: As in table 4.2.

Table 4.10: Productive Diversion of Loan Amount

(Figures in numbers)

Particulars	PACB		PCARDB		CB		SHG		Total		Grand
	Dry	Wet	Dry	Wet	Dry	Wet	Dry	Wet	Dry	Wet	Total
Purchase of milch animals	2 (5)	8 (50)	-	-	-	4 (44)	-	-	2 (5)	12 (43)	14 (21)
Investment in business	7 (19)	-	-	1 (33)	-	4 (44)	-	-	7 (18)	5 (18)	12 (18)
Construction of cowsheds	3 (8)	3 (19)	-	-	-	-	-	-	3 (7)	3 (11)	6 (9)
Construction of Farm Houses	3 (8)	1 (6)	-	-	-	-	-	-	3 (7)	1 (4)	4 (6)
Digging/desilting of wells	5 (14)	-	-	-	-	1 (12)	-	-	5 (13)	1 (4)	6 (8)
Reclamation of land	11 (30)	1 (6)	-	2 (67)	-	-	-	-	11 (28)	3 (10)	14 (21)
Irrigation arrangements	6 (16)	3 (19)	3 (100)	-	-	-	-	-	9 (22)	3 (10)	12 (17)
Total	37	16	3	3	-	9	-	-	40	28	68
Unproductive diversion	20	32	8	5	21	9	-	-	49	46	95
Utilisation	50	39	3	3	24	19	13	9	90	70	160
Grand Total	107	87	14	11	45	37	13	9	179	144	323

Source: As in table 4.2
Note: As in table 4.2.

The present study found that the causes for productive diversion of loan such as purchase of milch animals (21 per cent), investment in business (18 per cent), construction of cowsheds (9 per cent), construction of farm houses (6 per cent), digging and desilting of wells (8 per cent), reclamation of land (21 per cent) and irrigation arrangements (17 per cent) (Table 4.10).

Unproductive diversion denotes the misutilisation of the loan amount by the borrowers, which do not generally generate any income. In the study area, the respondents unproductively diverted the money for celebrating social ceremonies (34 per cent) and for the clearance of old debts (25 per cent). Family expenses, Medical expenses, Educational expenses and others also led the respondents to unproductively divert the loan amount borrowed (Table 4.11 and Chart 4.3).

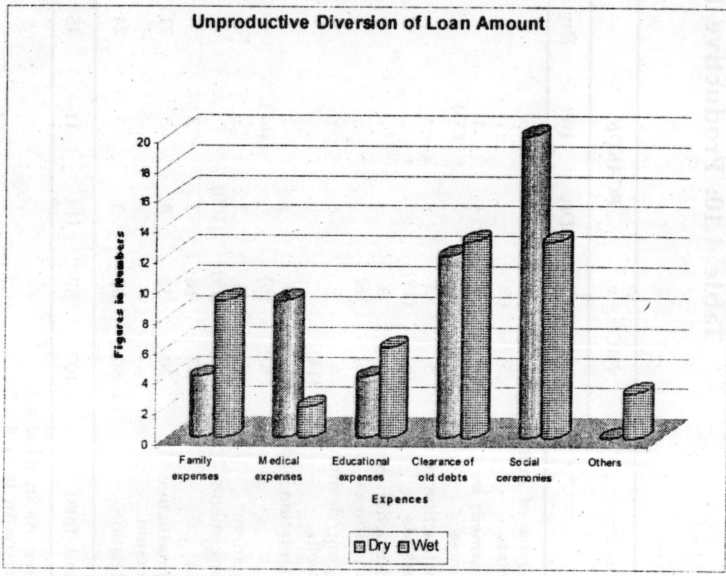

Chart 4.3

Table 4.11: Unproductive Diversion of Loan Amount

(Figures in numbers)

Particulars	*PACB*		*PCARDB*		*CB*		*SHG*		*Total*		*Grand*
	Dry	*Wet*	*Dry*	*Wet*	*Dry*	*Wet*	*Dry*	*Wet*	*Dry*	*Wet*	*Total*
Family expenses	-	6 (19)	4 (50)	-	-	3 (33)	-	-	4 (8)	9 (20)	13 (14)
Medical expenses	-	2 (6)	3 (38)	-	6 (29)	-	-	-	9 (18)	2 (4)	11 (12)
Educational expenses	3 (15)	5 (16)	1 (12)	1 (20)	-	-	-	-	4 (8)	6 (13)	10 (11)
Clearance of old debts	12 (60)	8 (25)	-	3 (60)	-	2 (22)	-	-	12 (25)	13 (28)	25 (25)
Social ceremonies	5 (25)	9 (28)	-	1 (20)	15 (71)	3 (33)	-	-	20 (41)	13 (28)	33 (35)
Others	-	2 (6)	-	-	-	1 (12)	-	-	-	3 (7)	3 (3)
Total	20	32	8	5	21	9	-	-	49	46	95
Uitlisation	50	39	3	3	24	19	13	9	90	70	160
Grand Total	107	87	14	11	45	37	13	9	179	144	323

Source: As in table 4.2

Note: As in table 4.2.

Repayment

The success of rural financing does not merely depend on the provision of financial assistance, but equally important is to make the borrowers capable enough to clear their dues completely so as to enable the banks to further recycle the funds. At the same time, the borrowers also should realize the responsibility to settle their dues in order to retain their clientele.

Repayment Ethics

Repayment Ethics means the moral responsibility of the borrowers to repay the loans in time. But the wilful defaulters lack such responsibility. Wilful defaulters are in general, socially and politically important people whose example to others is likely to emulate. In the present milieu, the bureaucracy in the credit agency is reluctant to touch the influential rural elite who wield a lot of formal and informal influence and considerable power (Nakkiran S: 1992, p. 119). That means these defaulters have the capacity to repay but not the interest to do. It implies that:

a. They might prefer indifference to repay since they could repay it at any time in future if warranted;

b. Sheer inertia to repay the dues in time;

c. They can foresee the interventions of the real sufferers/getting postponement of repayment or partial waiver of the entire loans or a portion of it or the interest; and

d. Their ultimate aim would be either to make it a practice of not repaying the loan in time or

Table 4.12: Loan Amount to be Repaid

(Figures in numbers)

Particulars	PACB		PCARDB		CB		SHG		Total		Grand
	Dry	Wet	Dry	Wet	Dry	Wet	Dry	Wet	Dry	Wet	Total
5000-10000	5 (6)	3 (4)	3 (33)	-	-	3 (10)	-	-	8 (7)	6 (5)	14 (6)
10001-15000	47 (57)	33 (41)	-	2 (20)	15 (46)	13 (43)	-	-	52 (41)	48 (40)	102 (24)
15001-20000	28 (34)	20 (25)	3 (33)	4 (60)	-	3 (10)	-	-	31 (25)	27 (23)	58 (24)
20001-30000	2 (3)	7 (9)	3 (34)	2 (20)	6 (18)	7 (23)	-	-	21 (17)	16 (13)	37 (14)
30001-40000	-	9 (11)	-	2 (20)	6 (18)	2 (7)	-	-	6 (5)	13 (11)	19 (7)
40001-50000	-	7 (9)	-	-	3 (9)	-	-	-	3 (2)	7 (6)	10 (4)
50001-60000	-	1 (1)	-	-	3 (9)	2 (7)	-	-	3 (2)	3 (2)	6 (3)
Total	82	80	9	10	33	30	-	-	124	120	244
Fully paid	25	7	5	1	12	7	13	9	55	24	79
Grand Total	107	87	14	11	45	37	13	9	179	144	323

Source: As in table 4.2

Note: As in table 4.2.

to cripple the financial agency from furthering its financial operations.

Loan Amount to be Repaid

In this study, it was found that majority of the borrowers i.e., 70 percent have to repay more than Rs. 15000. These borrowers have principal and interest dues to repay. The due amount accumulated and finally the borrowers have had to pay the same as one big lump sum. When majority of the rural borrowers have borrowed between Rs. 5000 to Rs. 10000, they had dues of more than Rs. 15000 (Table 4.12).

Extent of Repayment by the Respondents

Repayment behaviour serves as the yardstick to measure the performance of the particular organization and its sustainability. If the repayment by the borrowers is satisfactory, the institution withstands in the RCM as strong and viable.

Majority of the respondents (55 per cent in wet and 43 per cent in dry) have not yet paid the loans. The non-repayment of loan was found more among the respondents of the cooperatives whereas partial repayment was found among the respondents of CBs. All SHG members have fully paid their loans till the date (Table 4.13).

4.17 Debt at Borrowers Level

The data on principle and interest repaid and remaining unpaid were collected during field survey by pursuing the loan passbook and with the help of discussions

Table 4.13: Extent of Repayment by the Respondents

(Figures in numbers)

Particulars	*PACB*		*PCARDB*		*CB*		*SHG*		*Total*		*Grand*
	Dry	*Wet*	*Dry*	*Wet*	*Dry*	*Wet*	*Dry*	*Wet*	*Dry*	*Wet*	*Total*
Fully paid	25 (23)	7 (8)	5 (36)	1 (8)	12 (27)	7 (19)	13 (100)	9 (100)	55 (31)	24 (16)	79 (25)
Partially paid	25 (23)	20 (23)	3 (21)	2 (17)	18 (40)	19 (50)	-	-	46 (26)	41 (29)	87 (26)
Not yet paid	57 (54)	60 (69)	6 (43)	8 (75)	15 (33)	11 (31)	-	-	78 (43)	79 (55)	157 (49)
Grand Total	107	87	14	11	45	37	13	9	179	144	323

Source: As in table 4.2

Note: As in table 4.2.

with the borrowers. The principal and interest repaid and remaining unpaid in the case of each borrower was also verified with the bank records so as to ensure their accuracy. In this way, the total loans outstanding, loans repaid and overdues position of each borrower was determined. The overdues percentage was calculated by using the following formula:

=Average loan due remaining unpaid/Average loan outstandingx100

Here, loans outstanding, loans repaid and overdues of each borrower include principal and interest.

Table 4.14: Region-wise Classification of Repayment Performance and Overdue Position

Region	*Number of borrowers*	*Mean Loans Outstanding*	*Mean Loans Repaid*	*Mean Loans Overdue*	*Loans rapid as percentage of loan outstanding*	*Overdue as percentage of loan outstanding*
Dry	166	15051	7483	7568	49.71	50.28
Wet	135	19416	12726	6690	65.54	34.45
Total	301	34467	20209	14258	58.63	41.37

Source: Compiled from respondents schedule.

Region wise analysis of data revealed that in percentage terms, the repayment performance was better in wet region than in dry region (Table 4.14).

Institution wise data revealed that the repayment performance of the respondents of the CBs was quite satisfactory compared with the PACBs and PCARDBs. The percentage of overdues to loan outstanding among the respondents of the PACBs was 51.92 per cent and that relating to the PCARDB was 43.83 percent (Table 4.15).

Table 4.15: Institution–wise Classification of Repayment Performance

Region	*Number of borrowers*	*Mean Loans Outstanding*	*Mean Loans Repaid*	*Mean Loans Overdue*	*Loans rapid as percentage of loan outstanding*	*Overdue as percentage of loan outstanding*
PACB	194	14282	6867	7415	48.08	51.92
PCARDB	25	10465	5878	4587	56.17	43.83
CB	82	9720	7464	2256	76.79	23.21
Total	301	34467	20209	14258	58.63	41.37

Source: Compiled from respondents schedule

Reasons for Full Repayment

It was found that maintaining credibility and group pressure were the reasons for the full repayment of loan by the borrowers. Only 44 percent of SHG members have the reason to 'borrow another loan'. But in general, to borrow another loan and maintain credibility were the reasons for full repayment by the sample respondents in the study area (Table 4.16).

Persuasion to Full Repayment of Loan

Studies on the full repayment showed the higher price of products, self-consciousness, financial help by other members, pressure by the relatives, weekly instalment systems have influenced the timely loan repayment though these were less affecting factors (Moniruzzaman: 2002, p. 78).

It was found that the SHG members were persuaded to repay the loans by the animators. But the cooperative and commercial bank borrowers were persuaded by the bankers to repay the loans only to a limited extent

Table 4.16: Reasons for Full Repayment of Loan

(Figures in numbers)

Particulars	PACB		PCARDB		CB		SHG		Total		Grand
	Dry	Wet	Dry	Wet	Dry	Wet	Dry	Wet	Dry	Wet	Total
To borrow another loan	16 (64)	3 (43)	2 (40)	1 (100)	-	4 (57)	-	4 (44)	18 (33)	12 (50)	30 (38)
To maintain credibility	9 (36)	4 (57)	3 (60)	-	12 (100)	3 (43)	10 (77)	3 (33)	34 (62)	10 (42)	44 (56)
Group pressure	-	-	-	-	-	-	3 (23)	2 (23)	3 (5)	2 (8)	5 (6)
Total	25	7	5	1	12	7	13	9	55	24	79
Amount to be repaid	82	80	9	1	33	30	-	-	124	120	244
Grand Total	107	87	14	11	45	37	13	9	179	144	323

Source: As in table 4.2

Note: As in table 4.2.

Table 4.17: Persuasion for the Full Repayment of Loan

(Figures in numbers)

Particulars	*PACB*		*PCARDB*		*CB*		*SHG*		*Total*		*Grand*
	Dry	*Wet*	*Dry*	*Wet*	*Dry*	*Wet*	*Dry*	*Wet*	*Dry*	*Wet*	*Total*
Friends	3 (12)	-	-	-	-	1 (14)	-	2 (23)	3 (6)	3 (13)	6 (8)
Relatives	5 (20)	-	-	-	3 (25)	1 (14)	-	-	8 (14)	1 (3)	9 (11)
Family members	3 (12)	2 (29)	-	1 (100)	-	-	-	-	3 (6)	3 (13)	6 (8)
Bankers	8 (32)	2 (29)	-	-	3 (25)	1 (14)	-	-	11 (20)	3 (13)	14 (18)
Animator	-	-	-	-	-	-	10 (77)	7 (77)	10 (18)	7 (29)	17 (22)
Borrower himself	6 (24)	3 (42)	5 (100)	-	6 (50)	4 (58)	3 (23)	-	20 (36)	7 (29)	27 (33)
Total	25	7	5	1	12	7	13	9	55	24	79
Amount to be repaid	82	80	9	1	33	30	-	-	124	120	244
Grand Total	107	87	14	11	45	37	13	9	179	144	323

Source: As in table 4.2

Note: As in table 4.2.

but more by friends, relatives, family members, and by themselves (Table 4.17).

Repayment ethics should be taught by the RFIs to rural borrowers in order to arrest wilful defaulters. But that function is performed by other sources such as friends, relatives, family members etc., in the study area.

Sources for Repayment

Prompt repayment of loans is indispensable for the maintenance and expansion of rural credit. A loan should help to generate sufficient income to the borrower to meet his repayment obligations, besides leaving a surplus to improve his standard of living. Since the repayment of the debt without having sufficient income is an arduous task for the poor borrowers, it may carry adverse implication of their being debt trapped. In this study, the researcher has attempted to identify the sources, which are tapped by the sample borrowers to repay their loans. This enquiry might have opened up the possibility of studying how the rural people get sometimes entangled in the debt trap and how difficult it is for them to get out of it. Further, it may also help the policy makers to improve their lending operations.

It was found that most of the cooperatives and CB borrowers have got loans in order to fully repay the loans in the study area.

For instance, the PCARDB and CB borrowers in dry region fully repaid the loan amount by mobilizing money from moneylenders due to insufficient income from the investment, heavy interest burden, accumulation of dues etc., As a contrary, more than

Table 4.18: Sources for Full Repayment

(Figures in numbers)

Particulars	PACB		PCARDB		CB		SHG		Total		Grand
	Dry	Wet	Dry	Wet	Dry	Wet	Dry	Wet	Dry	Wet	Total
Income	11 (44)	2 (29)	-	-	-	6 (86)	8 (62)	7 (77)	19 (35)	15 (63)	34 (43)
New loan	14 (56)	5 (71)	5 (100)	1 (100)	12 (100)	1 (14)	5 (38)	2 (23)	36 (65)	9 (37)	45 (57)
Total	25	7	5	1	12	7	13	9	55	24	79
Amount to be repaid	82	80	9	1	33	30	-	-	124	120	244
Grand Total	107	87	14	11	45	37	13	9	179	144	323

Source: As in table 4.2

Note: As in table 4.2.

Table 4.19: Money Borrowed to Fully Repay the Loan

(Figures in numbers)

Particulars	*PACB*		*PCARDB*		*CB*		*SHG*		*Total*		*Grand*
	Dry	*Wet*	*Dry*	*Wet*	*Dry*	*Wet*	*Dry*	*Wet*	*Dry*	*Wet*	*Total*
Money Lenders	3 (21)	2 (40)	5 (100)	-	6 (50)	-	-	-	14 (38)	2 (22)	16 (36)
PACB	2 (14)	-	-	-	-	-	-	-	2 (6)	-	2 (4)
Friends	9 (65)	3 (60)	-	1 (100)	6 (50)	1 (100)	3 (60)	2 (100)	18 (50)	7 (78)	25 (56)
SHG	-	-	-	-	-	-	2 (40)	-	2 (6)	-	2 (4)
Total	14	5	5	1	12	1	5	2	36	9	45
Income	11	2	-	-	-	6	8	7	19	15	34
To be repaid	82	80	9	10	33	30	-	-	124	120	244
Grand Total	107	87	14	11	45	37	13	9	179	144	323

Source: As in table 4.2

Note: As in table 4.2.

60 percent of the SHG members repaid the loan out of the income earned from individual economic activities in the study area (GOI: 2002, p. 533) (Table 4.18).

The borrowers in both regions mobilize the money from friends, relatives, and loans from institutional agencies. The least percentage of the borrowers of the cooperatives and CBs and majority of the SHG members have not used the borrowed money to fully repay the loan (Table 4.19).

Reasons for Partial Repayment

While the insufficient income, non-remunerative price for the produces and heavy consumption expenses were the common reasons found among the respondents in the study area, the PACB borrowers had partially repaid the loan amount with the expectation of loan waiver (44 per cent in dry region and 25 in wet region).

Remaining of loan duration period, no continuous pressure from the agency are the other reasons stated by the borrowers in the study area for the partial repayment of the loan (Table 4.20).

Sources for Partial Repayment

Moneylenders were the main sources for the borrowers to partially repay the loan amount (above 60 per cent). Whenever the borrower was pressurized to settle the loan amount or intends to settle the same; he borrowed the money from the moneylenders or friends in the study area (Table 4.21).

Table 4.20: Reasons for Partial Repayment of Loan

(Figures in numbers)

Particulars	PACB		PCARDB		CB		SHG		Total		Grand
	Dry	Wet	Dry	Wet	Dry	Wet	Dry	Wet	Dry	Wet	Total
Insufficient income	6 (24)	10 (50)	3 (100)	-	9 (50)	4 (21)	-	-	18 (39)	14 (34)	32 (37)
Unexpected expenditure	-	-	-	-	3 (17)	3 (16)	-	-	3 (7)	3 (8)	6 (7)
Expecting loan waiver	11 (44)	5 (25)	-	-	-	-	-	-	11 (24)	5 (12)	16 (18)
Heavy consumption expenses	2 (8)	4 (20)	-	1 (50)	6 (33)	7 (37)	-	-	8 (17)	12 (29)	20 (23)
Non-remunerative price for the produce	2 (8)	1 (5)	-	-	-	1 (5)	-	-	2 (4)	2 (5)	4 (5)
Lack of continuous pressure	4 (16)	-	-	1 (50)	-	4 (21)	-	-	4 (9)	5 (12)	9 (10)
Total	25	20	3	2	18	19	-	-	46	41	87
Fully & Not yet paid	82	67	11	9	27	18	13	9	133	103	236
Grand Total	107	87	14	11	45	37	13	9	179	144	323

Source: As in table 4.2

Note: As in table 4.2.

Table 4.21: Sources for Partial Repayment

(Figures in numbers)

Particulars	*PACB*		*PCARDB*		*CB*		*SHG*		*Total*		*Grand*
	Dry	*Wet*	*Dry*	*Wet*	*Dry*	*Wet*	*Dry*	*Wet*	*Dry*	*Wet*	*Total*
Income	6 (24)	4 (20)	-	2 (100)	15 (83)	8 (42)	-	-	21 (46)	14 (34)	35 (40)
New loan	19 (76)	16 (80)	3 (100)	-	3 (17)	11 (58)	-	-	25 (54)	27 (66)	53 (60)
Total	25	20	3	2	18	19	-	-	46	41	87
Fully & Not yet paid	82	67	11	9	27	18	13	9	133	103	236
Grand Total	107	87	14	11	45	37	13	9	179	144	323

Source: As in table 4.2

Note: As in table 4.2.

Reasons for Default

Those who were irregular in repaying the loans, or not repaying at all, were asked to specify the reason for not repaying the loan. There were several reasons found in the study area for not repaying the loan amount by the borrowers. Drought, Irrigation expenses, Farm/business expenses, heavy consumption expenses, unexpected expenses, insufficient income, no additional income, expectation of loan waiver, no pressure from bankers/SHG, nobody asked to repay, other reasons such as loss in business and the attitude of not to repay were the reasons stated by the borrowers for not repaying the loan (Table 4.22).

Factors Affecting the Repayment Behaviour of Respondents

Repayment is conceptualized as a function of membership in Political Parties (X_1), Age of the Membership (X_2), Motivation (X_3), Supervision (X_4), Education (X_5), Exposure to Mass-Media (X_6), Contact With Change Agents (X_7), Occupation (X_8), Income (X_9), Alternative Sources of Income (X_{10}), Total Farm Expenses (X_{11}), Total Family Expenses (X_{13}), Extent of Old Debts (X_{14}), and Extent of Borrowing (X_{15}). Repayment, which takes the value one if the region takes, is wet and zero if it is dry (X_{16}).

Since the Linear Equation was found to be the most suitable as per the scattered diagram the Linear Multiple Regression Equation was fitted. The estimated equation is:

Table 4.22: Reasons for Default

(Figures in numbers)

Particulars	*PACB*		*PCARDB*		*CB*		*SHG*		*Total*		*Grand*
	Dry	*Wet*	*Dry*	*Wet*	*Dry*	*Wet*	*Dry*	*Wet*	*Dry*	*Wet*	*Total*
Flood/Drought	2 (4)	3 (5)	-	-	-	-	-	-	2 (3)	3 (4)	5 (3)
Irrigation expenses	8 (14)	-	-	-	-	-	-	-	8 (10)	-	8 (5)
Farm/business expenses	3 (5)	1 (2)	1 (7)	1 (9)	-	-	-	-	4 (5)	2 (3)	6 (4)
Heavy consumption expenses	11 (19)	13 (22)	6 (40)	6 (54)	-	-	1 (17)	3 (38)	18 (23)	22 (28)	40 (26)
Unexpected expenses	5 (8)	1 (2)	3 (20)	1 (9)	-	-	-	-	8 (10)	2 (3)	10 (6)
Insufficient income	20 (35)	19 (32)	3 (20)	1 (9)	-	-	3 (50)	-	26 (33)	20 (25)	46 (29)
No additional income	1 (2)	10 (16)	-	-	-	-	2 (33)	3 (38)	5 (6)	13 (16)	18 (12)

Expecting loan waiver	3 (5)	4 (6)	-	-	-	-	-	2 (24)	3 (4)	6 (7)	9 (6)
No pressure from bankers/SHG	2 (4)	6 (10)	-	-	-	-	-	-	2 (3)	6 (7)	8 (4)
No body asked to repay	2 (4)	2 (3)	-	-	-	-	-	-	2 (3)	2 (3)	4 (3)
Others	-	1 (2)	-	2 (19)	-	-	-	-	-	3 (4)	3 (2)
Total	57	60	15	11	-	-	6	8	78	79	157
Fully & partially paid	50	27	8	3	30	26	13	9	101	65	166
Total	107	87	14	11	45	37	13	9	179	144	323

Source: As in table 4.2

Note: As in table 4.2.

$$Y = 12.672 - 0.061^{*}X_1 + 0.0112^{*}X_2 + 0.0041^{*}X_3 - 0.121^{*}X_4 + 0.273^{*}X_5 - 0.212^{**}X_6$$
$$(0.029) \quad (0.058) \quad (0.0020) \quad (0.610) \quad (0.138) \quad (0.059)$$
$$-0.002^{*}X_7 + 0.114^{*}X_8 + 0.006^{*}X_9 - 0.217^{*}X_{10} - 0.143^{*}X_{11} - 0.121^{*}X_{12}$$
$$(0.001) \quad (0.054) \quad (0.0028) \quad (0.112) \quad (0.068) \quad (0.058)$$
$$-0.087^{*}X_{13} - 0.005^{*}X_{14} - 0.058^{*}X_{15} + 0.014^{NS}X_{16}$$
$$(0.044) \quad (0.002) \quad (0.030) \quad (0.123)$$
$$R^2 = 0.51^{**} \qquad N = 301$$

The R square is 0.51 which is significant at 1 per cent level of probability. This indicates that 15 variables together could explain 51 per cent of the variation in repayment of the credit. Since, the form of equation is logit the coefficients of the different variables indicates only the proportionate changes.

The sign of the coefficients indicates that the variables Age of Membership (X_2), Motivation (X_3), Education (X_5), Occupation (X_8), Income (X_9), have positive influence on repayment, whereas the variables Supervision (X_4), Exposure to Mass Media (X_6), Contact With Change Agents (X_7), Alternative Sources of Income (X_{10}), Total Assets (X_{11}), Total Farm Expenses (X_{12}), Total Family Expenses (X_{13}), Extent of Old Debts (X_{14}) and Extent of Borrowings (X_{15}) have negative effect on repayment.

The Hypotheses Get Tested

As stated in Chapter 3, the institutional credit was not able to mitigate the problem of rural indebtedness. Hence, the first hypothesis is proved. In order to test the Second Hypothesis viz., Accessibility to institutional credit has profound influence on the utilization and repayment practices and patterns; the Simple

Correlation was worked between accessibility and utilization. The correlation comes to 0.34, which is significant at 1 percent level of probability (N=301). This significant association indicated that more the accessibility, more the utilization. It might be that, when there is -accessibility, there will be inter relationship with the officials and their frequent visits might have induced to go for utilization.

In order to verify the Third Hypothesis viz., Productive utilization leads to proper repayment practices, the amount utilized is associated with the repayment. The correlation is 0.56**, which is significant at one percent level of probability indicating that there is association between utilization and repayment. This hypothesis indirectly proves the Fourth Hypothesis that diversion of loan arrests the repayment capacity of the borrowers.

The non-significant coefficient for the dummy variable X16 indicates that there is no regional difference in the repayment, which disproves the Fifth Hypothesis viz., Repayment practice is much better in wet areas than dry areas.

Expecting Loan Waiver: An Antithesis of Repayment

To perorate, one of the main problems, which had been plaguing the institutional rural credit system in India, is its politicization. Politically motivated schemes such as 'loan melas' and loan waivers have severely hampered the disciplined growth of the credit institutions (RBI: 1989, p. 572). The ARDRS (Agricultural Rural Debt and Relief Scheme) popularly known as 'loan waiver' scheme was the outcome of the promise made by the constituents of the National Front

Government during 1989 in General Election Campaign. The scheme was unprecedented by its sheer magnitude and coverage. The assurance by many political parties for loan waiver during 1989 and the announcement of the Scheme in February 1990 made almost all the borrowers to hold back the repayment of their dues. In fact, during the year 1990-91, according to the bank officials, there were practically very little cash recoveries directly from the farmers. Bulk of the recoveries was affected in the form of relief given by the Government towards loan waiver. As a result, a large number of PACS and PCARDBs became ineligible to borrow at the higher levels, which in turn brought down the loan disbursement from the cooperatives (Shylendra H.S. et.al: 1994, p. 155). The loan waiver scheme, whatever might be its genuine backdrop, is antithetical to the creation of a climate conducive for recovery (Mohan kanda: 1997, p. 34). In fact during this decade, the amount of loan waived exceeded the amount of loan given under short term, medium term and long term credit, but all these incentives have not created any real impact on agriculture since, as observed by officials, it saved only the big land lords from their debt burden (Ravichandran, K.: 1995, p. 133). Further, the Government of Tamil Nadu announced seven schemes regarding waiver of interest (penal interest of loans borrowed from cooperatives from 1999 to 2004). Of these, seven schemes a penal interest waiver scheme (2000) for Rs. 13.62 crores was fully borne by the banks. Further in 2004, MTC and MTR loans have been transferred to a blocked account involving a total of around Rs. 422.40 crores (GOI: 2004).

Table 4.23: Benefits Availed under Waiving Scheme

(Figures in numbers)

Particulars	*PACB*		*PCARDB*		*CB*		*SHG*		*Total*		*Grand*
	Dry	*Wet*	*Dry*	*Wet*	*Dry*	*Wet*	*Dry*	*Wet*	*Dry*	*Wet*	*Total*
Availed	31 (29)	37 (43)	8 (57)	7 (64)	-	-	-	-	39 (32)	44 (45)	83 (38)
Not availed	76 (71)	50 (57)	6 (43)	4 (36)	-	-	-	-	82 (68)	54 (55)	136 (62)
Total	107	87	14	11	-	-	-	-	121	98	219
Not Applicable	-	-	-	-	45	37	13	9	58	46	104
Total	107	87	14	11	45	37	13	9	179	144	323

Source: As in table 4.2

Note: As in table 4.2.

Table 4.24: Expecting Loan Waiver

(Figures in numbers)

Particulars	*PACB*		*PCARDB*		*CB*		*SHG*		*Total*		*Grand*
	Dry	*Wet*	*Dry*	*Wet*	*Dry*	*Wet*	*Dry*	*Wet*	*Dry*	*Wet*	*Total*
Expecting	107 (100)	87 (100)	14 (100)	11 (100)	-	-	-	-	121 (100)	98 (100)	219 (100)
Not Applicable	-	-	-	-	45	37	13	9	58	46	104
Total	107	87	14	11	45	37	13	9	179	144	322

Source: As in table 4.2.

Note: As in table 4.2.

Table 4.25: Reasons to Expect the Loan Waiver

(Figures in numbers)

Particulars	PACB		PCARDB		CB		SHG		Total		Grand
	Dry	Wet	Dry	Wet	Dry	Wet	Dry	Wet	Dry	Wet	Total
Drought	10 (9)	14 (16)	-	2 (18)	-	-	-	-	10 (8)	16 (16)	26 (12)
Employment opportunities	23 (21)	40 (46)	14 (100)	3 (27)	-	-	-	-	37 (31)	43 (44)	80 (37)
Increase in prices	11 (10)	13 (15)	-	1 (9)	-	-	-	-	11 (9)	14 (14)	25 (11)
Unremunarative price to the produce	5 (6)	13 (15)	-	-	-	-	-	-	5 (4)	13 (13)	18 (8)
Higher Interest	58 (54)	7 (8)	-	5 (46)	-	-	-	-	58 (48)	12 (13)	70 (32)
Total	107	87	14	11	-	-	-	-	121	98	219
Not Applicable	-	-	-	-	45	37	13	9	58	46	104
Total	107	87	14	11	45	37	13	9	179	144	323

Source: As in table 4.2.

Note: As in table 4.2.

In the study area, it was found that 68 percent of the respondents belonged to the Cooperatives in dry region and 55 percent of them in wet region have already availed the benefits under the loan waiver scheme and all of them reported that they intentionally delayed the repayment of loans with the expectation of loan waiver (Table 4.23 & 4.24). What was intended, as a blessing for the people had already turned into a curse?

The respondents were also inquired about the reasons for expecting loan waiver. Most of the respondents in both the regions (31 per cent in dry and 44 pre cent in wet) were of the view that unemployment and underemployment were the main reason. Next to this, Higher rate of interest (32 per cent), Increase in prices (12 per cent), drought (12 per cent) and unremunerative price for the produce (8 per cent) were the other reasons reported by the respondents of Cooperatives (Table – 4.25). All these causes do concern and all their plight real and empirical, but what is lost almost for ever is the repayment ethics, a political casuality.

Conclusion

From the above discussion, it is obvious that overdue is the serious problem of all IAs because of diversion and non-repayment of loan by borrowers. The credit utilisation and repayment behaviour of borrowers differ from one institution to another. More than 50 percent of the borrowers were found as loan divertees and defaulters. The non-repayment behaviour was found more among the borrowers of Cooperative Banks whereas partial repayment behaviour was found among the borrowers of CBs. All SHG members have fully repaid the loan due to group pressure and maintaining credibility. Loan in time, adequate quantum of loan as per the repayment capacity of the members and proper repayment ethics among them are the essence of SHGs, in which RFIs have failed so far.

REFERENCES

1. Anandateerth Kittur (1990), Diversion of Agricultural Loans of Formal Financial Institutions, *Journal of Rural Development,* Vol. 9(4), p. 774.
2. Anil Suryawanshi (2003), Non-Performing Assets- An Analysis of SGB, *Banking Finance,* Vol. 16 (9), September, p. 19
3. Arul Anandam B. (1988), Cooperative Overdues– The Influence of Socio–Economic Factors of Borrowers–A Case Study, *Indian Cooperative Review,* Vol. 25(3), January, p. 300.
4. Arunachalam, R. & Palanisamy A. (1991), Utilisation and Repayment of Cooperative Crop Loan, *Indian Cooperative Review,* Vol. 29(2), October, p. 182
5. Balishter and Pankaj Kumar (1995), A Study of Institutional Finance in Agriculture, *Land Bank Journal,* Vol. 34(1), September, p. 18.
6. Balishter, Roshan Singh & Singh A.K. (1991), Overdues of Loans in Land Development Banks in Agra District of Uttar Pradesh, *Cooperative Perspective,* Vol. 26(1), April-June, p. 39.
7. Balishter, Singh A.K. & Vishwajit (1994), A Study of Overdues of Loans in Agriculture, *Indian Cooperative Review,* Vol. 31(40), April, p. 382.

8. Dadhich, C.L. (1977), *Overdue in Farm Cooperative Credit*, Bombay, Popular Prakasam Private Limited, p. 65.

9. Debabrata Das (2002), Utilization Pattern of Cooperative Credit: A Study, *Cooperative Perspective*, Vol. 26(4), January-March, p. 27.

10. GOI (2004), *Report of the Advisory Committee on Flow of Credit to Agriculture and Related Activities*, Mumbai, June 2004, p. 53.

11. GOI (2002), The Role of Cooperative Credit in the Development of Different Size groups of Farmers in Gujarat, *Agro-Economic Research Centre, Ministry of Agriculture*, Gujarat, p. 533.

12. GOI (2004), *Draft Final Report of the Task Force on Revival of Cooperative Credit Institutions*, Annexure 4.

13. Goyal, S.K. Pandey, R.N. and Modi, M.K. (1993), Repayment Capacity of Defaulter and Non-Defaulater Borrowers of Cooperative Societies in Haryana, *Indian Cooperative Review*, Vol. 30(30), January, p. 296.

14. Indira Devi, P. (1992), Growth and Performance of Cooperative Agricultural Credit in Kerala, *Indian Cooperative Review*, Vol. 29(40), April, p. 336, 337.

15. Joshi, G.V. (2002), *Overdue in Cooperative Credit System*, Mohit Publications, New Delhi, p. 25

16. Kulwant Pathania & Yoginder Varma (1992), Impact of Size of Family Income and Value of Farm Assets on Cooperative Credit Utilization, *Indian Cooperative Review*, Vol. 30(1), July, p. 49.

17. Loganathan, P. (1992), Credit Information—A

Missing Link in Agriculture Credit—A Sample Survey, *Indian Cooperative Review,* Vol. 29(4), April, p. 389.

18. Makadia, J.J., Thumar B.L. & Shiyani, R.L. (1992), An Evaluation of Acquisition and Utilization of Cooperative Credit in Junagad District, *Indian Cooperative Review,* Vol. 30(1), July, p. 59.
19. Malyadri, P. & Sirisha, S. (2003), *NPAs in CBs–An Overview, Banking Finance,* January, Vol.16 (1), p. 7
20. Mazumdar, D.K. & Baruah, H.K. (1999), Repayment Performance of Institutional Finance on Allied Agricultural Acitivities—A Case Study, *Indian Cooperative Review,* Vol. 37 (1), July, p. 2.
21. Modi M.K & Rai K.N. (1993), Credit Utilization Pattern on Different Categories of Farms in District Kurukshetra, Haryana, *Indian Cooperative Review,* Vol. 30(3), January, p. 254
22. Mohan Kanda (1997), Agricultural Credit–Institutional Arrangements, Performance and Policy Issues, *Journal of Rural Development,* Vol. 16(1), January-March, p. 34.
23. Moniruzzaman (2002), Loan Utilisation Pattern of Bangaladesh Rural Development Board Women Cooperatives and Grameen Bank Groups: A Comparative Analysis, *Journal of Rural Development,* Vol. 21(1), January-March, p. 78.
24. Muniraj R. (1987), *Farm Finance for Development,* Oxford & IBH Publishing Company Private Limited, New Delhi, p. 38.
25. Nakkiran S. & John Winfred (1988), *Cooperative*

Banking in India, Rainbow Publishers, Coimbatore, p. 119.

26. NCUI (2004), *Cooperative Movement in India– A Statistical Profile,* p. 18.
27. Patnaik, U.C. & Mishra, R.N. (1999), *Rural Banking in India,* Anmol Publications, New Delhi, p. 43.
28. Pranab Kumar Charkravarthy (1983), *Problems of Cooperative Development in India,* S.Chand & Co. New Delhi, p. 53.
29. Ranjit Kumar Das (2002), Recovery and Overdues Problems of RRBs with Particular Reference to Uttar Banga Kshetrial Gramin Bank, *Banking Finance,* October, Vol. 37, p. 10
30. Ravichandran K.(2000), *Crop Loan System and Overdues,* Spell Bound publications, Rohtak, p. 113, 139, 164.
31. Ravichandran, K. (1995), Loan Waiver Schemes– The Menance of Cooperative Credit, *International Journal of Development Planning and Literature,* Vol.10 (1&2), Spell Bound Publications, Rohatak, p. 133.
32. RBI (1954), *All India Rural Credit Survey Committee,* Abridged Edition, p. 62.
33. RBI (2005-06), *Report on Trend and Progress of Banking in India,* p. 131.
34. RBI (1954), *Report of the All India Rural Credit Survey Committee,* Vol. 1, Part 2, pp. 264-268.
35. RBI (1969), *Report of the All India Rural Credit Review Committee,* p. 141.
36. RBI (1974), *Report of the Study Team on Overdues of Cooperative Credit Institutions,* p. 10 and 76.

37. RBI (1980), *Report of the Committee to Review the Arrangements For Institutional Credit For Agriculture and Rural Development*, 1980, p. 55, 167.

38. RBI (1989), *Report of the Agricultural Credit Review Committee*, p. 83, 215, 538, and 572.

39. RBI (2004), *Report of the Advisory Committee on Flow of Credit to Agriculture and Related Activities*, June, p. 57 and 71.

40. Reddy, B.R. & Laxminarayana (1996), *Overdues in Cooperatives: A case Study in Andhra Pradesh, Cooperative Perspective*, Vol. 31(3), p. 19.

41. Reddy, C.R. (1993), *Overdue Management in Cooperative Banks*, Bombay, Himalaya Publishing House, Bombay, p. 29.

42. Satyasai, K.J.S., (1987), Structure of Rural Credit in West Godavari District, A.P., *Land Bank Journal*, Vol. 26(2), December, p. 54.

43. Sharma, D.K., Koshta, A.K. & Jain, B.C. (1991), Availability and Utilization of Crop Loan in Central Madhyapradesh, *Land Bank Journal*, Vol. 30(1), September, p. 18.

44. Shylendra, H.S. & Katar Singh(1994), The Impact of the Loan Waiver Scheme in the Recent Performance of Credit Cooperatives in Karnataka In: *Agricultural Credit System in India* (ed. by) Mruthyanjaya V.C. Mathur, Praduman Kumar, *Agricultural Economic Research Association of India*, New Delhi, p. 155.

45. Sidhu, R.S. (2002), Extent and Pattern of Loan Overdues in Punjab, *Indian Cooperative Review*, Vol. 40 (1), July, p. 137.

46. Subbi Reddy, T. & Ramamuni Reddy, C.(1980), Utilisation of Loans, *Land Bank Journal,* Vol. 18(3), March, p. 32.

47. Tiwari, S.N. & Sharma, P.K. (1986), Farm Credit and Rural Savings, *Cooperative Perspective,* Vol. 21(1), April-June, p. 27.

5

Findings, Conclusions and Suggestions

Introduction

In India the RCM is a diversified and complex subject. As one of the players in the RCM, the NIAs is traditional and has no formal rules and regulations. The player IAs is a century old and institutional. Even then, the NIAs dominate in the RCM because more than 40 percent of the rural households are still away from the purview of the institutional sources. In this context, the present study unearthed several factors that decide the access to institutional credit, utilization pattern and repayment behaviour of the rural borrowers. The present chapter reports the salient findings of this study, conclusion, suggestions to overcome the problems associated with institutional credit and Scope for future research.

Findings of the Study

Nature of Rural Credit Market

1) *Institutional Agencies:* At present, in respect of

formal rural credit/institutional credit system, multi-agency system has been in vogue. The Cooperative Banks, CBs, RRBs and SHGs are the partners of this system. It was found that the multi-agency system in rural credit has increased the flow of credit considerably over the years. For example, the total credit provided at all India level during 1992-93 was Rs.15169 crores, which had increased over the years and stood at Rs.62045 crores during the year 2001-02. At the end of the year 2005–06, it stood Rs.180485 crores.

2) *Ground Level Credit Flow:* At Tamil Nadu level, the flow of institutional credit had increased from Rs.2319 crores during the year 1992-93 to Rs. 11432 crores during the year 2001-02 and Rs. 22036 crores in the year 2005-06. In Dindigul District, the GLC flow has increased from Rs. 66.91 crores to Rs. 364.60 crores and Rs. 822.10 crores during the same period. However, the share of the different agencies was uneven over the years at all levels.

3) *Non-Institutional Agencies:* It was found that the informal credit market was having strong base in the study area. Professional moneylenders were the market leaders. Village Traders, Commission Agents, Friends and Relatives were also partners of the informal credit market in the study area.

Indebtedness and Access to Credit

1) *Age:* The age wise distribution of respondents shows that in all RFIs, the participation of middle age group was high except in PACB in both regions. The respondents with above 50 years of age were high in PACB in both wet and dry regions. This may be due to the fact that this group of respondents had

high affinity with their cooperatives due to their long years of membership. However, though the impact of age of the respondent in their relationship with their institutions and repayment behaviour varied across the region and institution, the participation of the middle age group was high; this is the sign of development.

2) *Sex:* In this study, it was found that women constitute only around 15 percent to total sample population. Only 25 percent of women in wet and 6 percent of them in dry had access to institutional credit. This development is due to the emergence of SHGs.

3) *Community:* The community-wise analysis showed that in dry region, the scheduled caste people had relationship only with the PACB and in both the regions; they did not have any relationship with the SHGs. It was found that the SHGs formed especially for this community could not continue their operations. The continuous migration of the labour force due to drought and the inability of local NGOs to develop these SHGs as IGPs were found to be the reasons.

4) *Education:* The institution wise analysis showed that the number of respondents with formal education was high in PACB compared to other institutions. Most of the respondents belonging to the CBs were at the level of secondary school education. Interestingly, it could be found that the SHGs were targeting the people with no formal education or school dropouts.

5) *Marital Status:* The marital status of the respondents showed that those in the unmarried category were having access with all institutions except in SHGs though they were in small number. The SHGs target only the married and the widowed. Unmarried

women were not in SHGs as the chance of mobility was high after marriage.

6) *Type of Family:* In the study area, it was found that irrespective of the agency, to which the respondent belonged, majority of them in both region belonged to nuclear family system which reflected the growing tendency among the younger generation to live separately from their parents when they became economically independent. Whatever might be the adverse climate boosted by the nuclear family system, it has realiy boosted the dispensation of rural credit as every individual family became the borrowers of the IAs.

7) *Exposure to Mass Media and Contact with Change Agents:* Irrespective of age group and educational status, majority of the rural folks were having access to either print or electronic media or both. It was found that in both the regions, Newspapers were the major source of information whereas in the case of the TV and Radio, the majority of respondents in both the regions have had regular access to these electronic media. It was found that more than 50 percent of the respondents were having contacts with Government and Non-Government Organizations in the study area. Further, it was found that all the respondents belonging to the SHG were having regular contact with these change agents.

8) *Membership in Social Organizations:* The study found that there was relationship between the respondents and their social organization, which included caste organizations and political organizations. It was found that majority of the respondents belonging to PACB (80 per cent) and PCARDB (above 40 per cent) had membership with the political parties in both the regions.

The respondents of CB also had membership with political parties in both the regions (13 per cent in dry and 46 per cent in wet). But SHGs had no link with the political parties. It was also found that political intervention in the dispensation of rural credit and its management has become a necessary evil.

9) *Occupation:* Agriculture is the major economic activity of the sample respondents. In both regions, very high proportion of the respondents depended on dairy, self-employment and weaving as secondary occupation. Generally, animal husbandry was found as secondary occupation in the rural areas. But the mechanization of agriculture and continuance of drought severely hit this occupation too. On the other hand, the big farmers and landlords have developed dairy as a main occupation by having dairy farms. The institution wise analysis shows that the majority of the SHG respondents were agricultural and non-agricultural laborers.

10) *Land Holdings:* Majority of the respondents belonging to the CBs (40 percent in dry and 64 percent in wet) and all sample respondents of SHG did not poses any land holdings. Majority of the landowners approached and availed credit only from the Cooperative Banks. This shows the long standing relationship between the landowners and their cooperatives.

11) *Deposits in Institutions:* It is found that the expenditure pattern of the respondents have spoiled the habit of savings. 50 percent of the respondents belonging to the CB have had savings whereas it was cent percent in the SHGs. Majority of the respondents belonging to the Cooperative Banks and 50 percent of the respondents belonging to the CB did not have

any savings at all due to the hardships of interest burden, failure of agriculture, insufficient income and attitudes like 'the banks are functioning to provide loan only'.

12) *Marketing:* The farmers in the study area had access only to informal market linkages viz., village traders, and village trader cum moneylenders and traders at mondi centres. Most of the respondents approached the village traders for marketing their produces in order to avoid transport risks, to enjoy the privileges of immediate cash payments and also as the customary practice of courtesy.

13) *Income from Agriculture:* The present study found that the majority of the respondents (53 per cent) got income from agriculture below Rs.10000 in both regions. Majority of the respondents belonging to the Cooperative Banks, for whom the agriculture was the primary occupation, earned an annual income from land below Rs.20000 (more than 32 per cent in dry and 24 per cent in wet).

14) *Annual Income:* In the study area, it was found that a majority of the respondents (60 per cent) were having income between Rs.11000 to Rs.25000. Among the respondents having alternative sources of income, more than 50 per cent of the respondents in both regions earned an income below Rs.5000 from alternative sources.

15) *Indebtedness:* This study found that 63 per cent of households were indebted in the study area. The incidence of indebtedness was high in dry region compared to the wet region. The source wise analysis found that more than 83 percent of the respondents in dry and 90 percent of the respondents in wet were

indebted with NIAs. Friends, relatives, village traders, commission agents and chit funds were the other NIAs accessible to the rural borrowers. Agency wise and source wise analysis showed that more than 70 percent of the respondents were indebted with moneylenders in the study area.

16) *Causes for sustenance of NIAs:* While analyzing the causes for the sustenance of the NIAs, it was found that more than 80 percent of the respondents have had access with these NIAs due to the increasing credit needs, inadequacy of formal loans, easy accessibility of credit from NIAs, pressing consumption requirements etc. It was also found that though no respondent of the SHG approached the moneylenders, instead their friends and relatives were the sources for additional credit needs. This trend revealed the fact that the interest burden of the respondents of the SHG was reduced but not the debt burden as such. It was found that majority of the respondents i.e., more than 70 per cent in wet and 90 percent in dry region approached more than one source of the informal sources. In the formal system, a borrower could have access with only one source. But in informal source, a person can have access to several sources. About 82 percent of the respondents have had access to more than one informal source in order to retain the clientele of credit agencies. The study also found that majority of the respondents who remained indebted with only one NIAs had access to credit with the moneylenders. The access to several sources of informal credit fossilizes the rural households as debtors instead of income generators, or a productive investors.

17) *Credit Gap:* An estimation of the mean credit gap of the sample respondents revealed that the

financial institutions have failed to meet the credit needs of the rural poor to the extent of Rs.31253 in dry region and Rs.44971 in wet region per borrower.

18) *Nature of Indebtedness:* The present study found that more than 60 percent of the respondents had current debt in both regions. The ancestral burden was also carried by the respondents and its proportion was found high among the respondents in the wet region (25 percent). The age of indebtedness with private parties of 40 percent of the borrowers in both regions was within 5 years. Though the fourfold increase was found in GLC delivered at National, State and District levels in 2005-06, the extent of indebtedness of the borrowers had not been reduced. It showed that the institutional credit was unable to mitigate the problem of indebtedness in the study area and the debt burden of most of the farming community was the present one.

19) *Causes for Indebtedness:* It was found that the clearance of old debts of the NIA emerged as a major cause for the indebtedness in both regions (36 percent in dry and 30 percent in wet). An interesting outcome of this study was that for about 11 percent of the respondents, the repayment of institutional debt was the cause for indebtedness and this was more so in the case of respondents belong to the PACB. Drawing fresh loan for the clearance of the old loan by adjustment and having no credit resource to continue with the agricultural operations, they took refuge under the NIAs becoming indebted in the process. This was found to be a vicious circle.

20) *Borrowing from the IAs:* The present study found that majority of the respondents (60 per cent) still approached the PACBs for their credit needs. The PACB

had locality advantage and provides both cash and kind portion of credit such as seed, fertilizers and pesticides and needed support for the agriculturists.

21) *Purpose wise Borrowings:* As agriculture is the predominant occupation for the rural households, majority (59 per cent) of the respondents borrowed for cultivation expenses from the institutional agencies. As the CBs concentrate on industrial development in rural areas, majority (60 per cent in dry and 52 per cent in wet) of the respondents, who borrowed from the CBs invested in petty shops, idly shops, saloon shops, vegetable shops etc. Apart from these purposes, the sample respondents approached the IAs for the purpose of meeting the expenses on purchase of cattle/ milch animals, land development, improved methods of irrigation, purchase of agricultural machineries, housing expenses etc.,

22) *Loan Amount Borrowed:* In the study, it was found that the loan amount borrowed differs from one institution to another and region to region. Majority of the PACB respondents borrowed between Rs.5000 to Rs.10000. In wet region, the extent of loan amount borrowed was higher than that in the dry region.

23) *Expenses Incurred to Avail Loan:* Most of the respondents (more than 50 per cent) in both regions incurred transaction cost of above Rs.1000 per loan. The considerable proportion of loan amount spent as transaction cost, made the respondents loose the said amount for the purpose, they borrowed. But the quantum of amount spent to obtain credit from the institutional agencies by the borrowers was being saved in the SHGs.

24) *Reasons to Select the IAs to Borrow Money:* It was found that only 32 per cent of the respondents

have approached the institution with the only intention to get loan. Improving the economic status was the main reason for the respondents of the CBs in both regions and of the Cooperative Banks in dry region whereas getting loan waiver was the main reason for the respondents of the Cooperative Banks in the wet region. Majority of SHG borrowers have developed the attitude of "our bank or group" followed by increase in savings which stood neglected in other institutions.

25) *Easy Accessible Sources of Credit:* Majority of the respondents felt that NIAs were the easily accessible sources. It revealed that the NIAs have a strong niche in the RCM.

26) *Advantages of Availing Loans from NIAs and IAs:* Fulfillment of urgent needs, availability of credit at doorstep and time, confidentiality in transaction and others were the advantages felt by the respondents in availing credit from the NIAs. It was found out that lesser rate of interest and availing benefits under Government schemes were the major advantages felt by the respondents in the study area with regard to loan from the IAs.

27) *Disadvantages of Availing Loan from NIAs and IAs:* The past studies showed that exorbitant rate of interest were the main disadvantage with the moneylenders. Apart from that, in this study the respondents revealed the fact that unhealthy practices on delay in repayment, no consideration for the unexpected losses and shorter duration to repay were the other disadvantages. The sample respondents experienced disadvantages in availing loan from the formal agencies also. They are high, transaction cost, non-availability of loan in time, unfriendliness of the employees and insufficient loan amount.

Utilization Pattern and Repayment Behaviour of Borrowers

1) *Level of Loan Utilization:* It was found that irrespective of institutional agencies, less than 50 percent of the respondents utilized the loan amount for the purpose for which it was given. The extent of utilization was found very low among the PCARDB borrowers (20 percent in dry and 27 percent in wet) making it clear that the large farmers have misutilized more loan amount.

2) *Mean Credit Utilized:* The mean credit disbursed was Rs.18917 and the mean credit utilized properly by the borrowers worked out to Rs.10972 indicating utilization of 58 percent of the loan amount for the purposes for which it was issued by the IAs. Further, the incidence of misutilisation was high in wet region.

3) *Reasons for the Full Utilization of Loan:* It was found that 49 percent of respondents fully utilized the loan amount with the expectation of good yield from investment. Next to this, availability of loan in time (29 per cent), lesser-unexpected expenses (12 per cent), awareness on the consequences of diversion (6 per cent) and proper supervision (4 per cent) were the factors that led to the full utilization of loans. The SHG members stated that the availability of credit in time (60 per cent in dry and 78 per cent in wet) was the reason to fully utilize the loan amount. Misutilisation was high among the respondents belonging to the Cooperatives and CBs. As the SHGs provide loans for consumption purposes also, the utilization was cent percent.

4) *Efforts Made by the Organization to Utilize the Loan:* The institutional initiatives such as proper supervision (28 per cent), loan in time (22 per cent),

adequate quantum of loan (26 per cent) and loan with kind portion (24 per cent) facilitated the respondents to properly utilize the loan amount. Institution wise analysis showed that proper supervision was the prime effort made by the CBs whereas provision of loan with kind portion was the concern of the PACBs. Provision of adequate loan and in time followed by proper supervision was the efforts made by the SHGs for the full utilization of loans.

5) *Reasons to Misutilize the Loan:* The regression analysis showed that the borrowers' contact with political parties and consequent loss of repayment ethics, burden of old debts and insufficiency of the current borrowings to meet the expenses were the reasons for the misutilisation of the loan and consequent non-repayment behaviour. There were various other reasons to misutilise the loan such as drought (10 per cent), higher rate of inputs (6 per cent), unexpected expenses (29 per cent), increase in consumption expenses (34 per cent) and delay in getting loans (18 per cent). These were prevalent among the cooperative and commercial bank borrowers in the study area.

6) *Repayment Behaviour of Respondents:* In this study, it was found that majority of the borrowers i.e., 70 percent, have to repay more than Rs.15000. These borrowers have principal and interest dues to repay. When majority of the rural borrowers have borrowed between Rs. 5000 to Rs.10000, they had dues of more than Rs.15000.

7) *Extent of Repayment by the Respondents:* The non-repayment of loan was found more among the respondents of the cooperatives whereas partial repayment was found among the respondents of the CBs. All the SHG members have fully paid their loans till date.

8) *Debt at Borrowers Level:* Institution wise data revealed that the repayment performance of the respondents of the CB was quite satisfactory compared with the PACBs and PCARDBs. The percentage of overdues to loan outstanding among the respondents of PACBs was 51.92 per cent and that relating to PCARDB was 43.83 percent.

9) *Reasons for the Full Repayment:* It was found that maintaining credibility and group pressure were the reasons for the full repayment of the loan by the borrowers. Only 44 percent of the SHG members have the reason to 'borrow another loan'. But in general, to borrow another loan and maintain credibility were the reasons for full repayment by the sample respondents in the study area.

10) *Sources for Full Repayment:* It was found that most of the cooperative and commercial bank borrowers have got loans in order to fully repay the loans in the study area. For instance, The PCARDB and CB borrowers in dry region fully repaid the loan amount by mobilizing money from the moneylenders due to insufficient income from investment, heavy interest burden, accumulation of dues etc. As a contrary, more than 60 percent of the SHG members repaid the loan out of the income earned from individual economic activities in the study area.

11) *Reasons for Partial Repayment:* While the insufficient income, non-remunerative price for the produces and heavy consumption expenses were the common reasons found among the respondents in the study area, the PACB borrowers had partially repaid the loan amount with the expectation of loan waiver

12) *Sources for Partial Repayment:* Moneylenders were

the main sources for the borrowers to partially repay the loan amount (above 60 per cent). Whenever the borrower was pressurized to settle the loan amount or intended to settle the same; he borrowed the money from the moneylenders or friends in the study area

13) *Reasons for Default:* Drought, Irrigation expenses, Farm/business expenses, heavy consumption expenses, unexpected expenses, insufficient income, no additional income, expectation of loan waiver, no pressure from bankers/SHG, nobody asked to repay, other reasons such as loss in the business and the attitude of not to repay were the reasons stated by the borrowers for not repaying the loan

14) *Expecting Loan Waiver:* In the study area, it was found that 68 percent of the respondents belonging to the Cooperatives in dry region and 55 percent of them in wet region have already availed the benefits under the loan waiver scheme and all of them reported that they intentionally delayed the repayment of loans with the expectation of loan waiver.

The respondents were also inquired about the reasons for expecting loan waiver. Most of the respondents in both regions (31 per cent in dry and 44 pre cent in wet) expressed the view that problems like unemployment and under employment were the main reasons. Next to this, higher rate of interest (32 per cent), increase in prices (12 per cent), drought (12 per cent) and unremunerative price for the produce (8 per cent) were the other reasons reported by the respondents of the Cooperatives.

15) *Testing of Hypotheses:* As stated in Chapter 3, the institutional credit was not able to mitigate the problem of Rural Indebtedness. Hence, the first

hypothesis was proved. In order to test the second hypothesis viz., Accessibility to institutional credit has profound influence on the utilization and repayment practices; the Simple Correlation was worked between accessibility and utilization. The correlation comes to 0.34, which is significant at 1 percent level of probability. This significant association indicated that more the accessibility; more was the utilization. It might be that, when there is accessibility, there will be inter relationship with the officials and their frequent visits might induce them to go for utilization.

In order to verify the third hypothesis viz., Productive utilization leads to proper repayment practices, the amount utilized is associated with the repayment. The correlation is 0.56**, which is significant at one percent level of probability indicating that there is association between utilization and repayment. This hypothesis indirectly proves the fourth hypothesis that diversion of loan arrests the repayment capacity of the borrowers.

The non-significant coefficient for the dummy variable X_{16} indicates that there is no regional difference in the repayment, which disproves the fifth hypothesis viz., Repayment practice is much better in wet areas than in dry areas.

Conclusion

In the Indian Context, the RCM remains complex than it empirically appears to be, because of the characteristics of the suppliers of credit and the peculiar nature of demand for credit. The institutional framework for supervised credit has developed adequate infrastructure and that helped for both green revolution and white revolution. However, the demand for credit has not been fully realized and met by the IAs. There have been regional imbalances in GLC flow. The usurious practices of the NIAs leading to farmers' suicides perpetrate unchecked.

The Indian Banking System has not been able to internalize rural lending as a viable banking activity but only as a social obligation because the policy makers wanted it. Institutional lending to rural areas are considered as a part of social sector lending and not commercial lending. All those who have availed loans were treated (both demand and supply side) as only 'beneficiaries', not 'borrowers or customers' of the IAs. This trend has developed an attitude that rural sector lending is not bankable which means that the commercial principles can not be applied to rural lending at all.

In this background, this study found that 63 per cent of the rural households remained indebted either to the IAs or NIAs and the incidence of indebtedness was high in wet region compared to the dry region. Contact with the change agents was the main social variable while Occupation, Income and Alternative sources of income were the main economic variables, which influenced the access to credit with the IAs. It only indicated that the resource poor who are in sizable number depending mainly on agriculture in rural areas have poor access to credit with the IAs. It showed that institutional credit did not mitigate the problem of rural indebtedness in both the regions; infact the extent of indebtedness of rural borrowers had been increased after they become the clientele of the IAs. Indebtedness blocked further access to institutional credit for the rural borrowers and pushed them back in the trap of the moneylenders, increased their debt burden, spoiled the social recognition in their neighborhood, made them resource poor, and finally drove them pathetically long for the loan waiver schemes from Government for writing off of dues with the IAs. Paradoxically, the loan waiving schemes, instead of helping the farming community, have eroded the willingness of the borrowers to repay the loan; boosted wilful default culture; crippled the financial viability of banking institutions and emerged as popular ethos of election manifestos. The alternative seems evasive, but the observation remains valid.

On the other hand, the dawn of the SHGs has relieved certain segments of rural borrowers from the interest burden with the moneylenders though not from total family debt burden. The SHG members' debt burden infact sandwiches their entrepreneurial qualities. Of course this seems to be a temporary phenomenon. If the SHGs are allowed to grow 'naturally', they would find new solutions to address the age-old problem of rural indebtedness. Pure spontaneity does not exist and conscious action based on existing realities might be expected in political action. It is inevitably concluded that the IAs have not mitigated the problem of rural indebtedness in the study area. The proper way out could be making the IAs' infrastructure more borrower friendly than merely enhancing the quantum of credit.

Suggestions

1). Kissan Credit Card

The KCCs set a significant trend in the loan operations of banks by giving importance for individual than the activity. A similar product called the Swarozgar

Credit Card (SCC) also has been introduced by the banks to meet the credit demand of the non-cultivators engaged in non-farm activities. These two products must be made popular and available to all rural households. Similar arrangements exclusively for the members of SHG may be developed in the name of Micro Credit Card (MCC). This will help to institutionalize both the savings and lendings in rural areas, thereby put a check over the growth of the NIAs.

In Dindigul District, as on 31st March 2006, the total number of KCC issued was 57684. Compared to total cultivators of Dindigul District i.e., 216559, this number is only 26 percent. Hence, efforts are needed to issue the KCC to all the cultivators.

2) Encouragement for Contact Farming

Contact farming has been becoming popular and has the inherent advantages like lesser risks, lower transaction cost and assured payments (both supply and demand side). Government may draw a detailed plan for encouraging contract farming, for assuring regular employment to rural population and thereby reducing poverty. Further, there is a greater scope for dispensing credit for dry land farming. Proper link between contract farming and dry land farming may bring a way out to solve some of the problems in rural credit.

In Dindigul District around 1.37 lakh hectares are under dry land farming and mostly owned by the small farmers. A detailed people's plan is needed to tap the potentialities of dry land farming.

3) Business Partnership with CSOs

The role of the Civil Society Organization (CSOs) in the development process has been recognized world over. Some of the banks have already used the CSOs as financial conduits. The best examples are Oriental Bank of Commerce's Grameen Project and NABARD's SHG-Bank Linkage Programme. Tapping the potentialities of the linkage programme, a new model is suggested hereunder for the banks in Dindigul District. This model may be called as Business Partnership Model, which shares both risk and profits between the banks and CSOs. The Banks will provide financial services; the CSO's will offer their experience in community outreach. This shared model will provide financial viability to the transactions of the banks as well as provide financial incentives to the CSOs, thereby the risk factor becomes a negligible issue (See Chart – 5.1).

In Dindigul District, there are more than 3000 SHGs, 15 leading NGOs, 25 VVV Clubs of Farmers, more than 600 Youth Clubs affiliated with Nehru Yuva Kendras and above all stands the Gandhigram Rural University. Banks could chalk out a detailed plan for rural banking by using the Business Partnership Model.

Scope for Future Research

The findings of the present study offers scope for further research on the following topics:

1. A Study on the Role of SHGs as financial conduits for Cooperative Banks.
2. A Study on the role of CSOs in Mitigating the Problems of Rural Credit Market
3. A study on Participatory Models for Rural Credit.

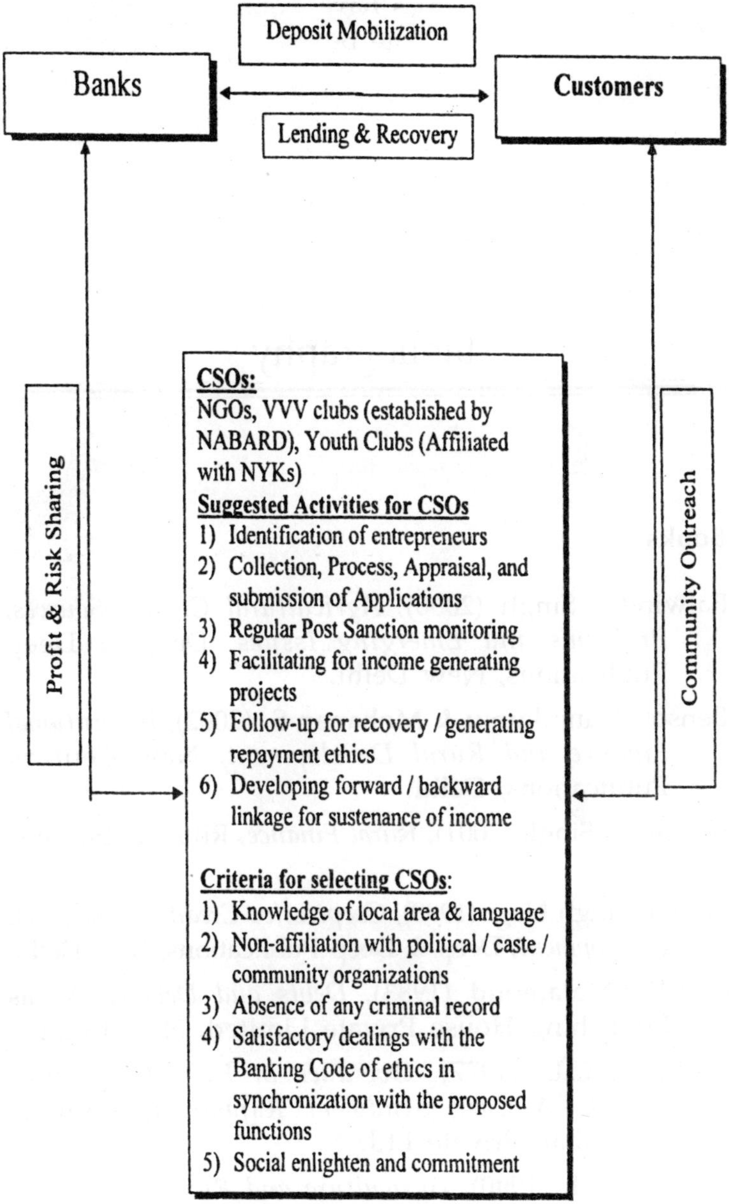

Chart 5.1: Business Partnership Model

Bibliography

Books

Balwinder Singh (2000), *Agricultural Credit—Sources, Problems and Emerging Issues*, Deep & Deep Publications, New Delhi.

Benson Kunjukunju & Mohanan S. (2002), *Institutional Finance and Rural Development*, New Century Publications, Delhi.

Bhagirath Singh (2001), *Rural Finance*, RBSA Publishers, Jaipur.

Bhupal Singh Negi (1990), *Cooperative Credit and Regional Development*, Deep & Deep Publications, New Delhi.

Charles Malamoud (1983), *Debts and Debtors*, Vikas Publishing House Private Limited, New Delhi.

Dadhich, C.L. (1977), *Overdues in Farm Cooperative Credit—A Case Study of Rajasthan*, Popular Prakashan Private Ltd.

Desai S.S.M. (1990), *Agriculture and Rural Banking in India*, Himalaya Publishing House, Bombay.

Frank Ratna Kumar, Savarimuthu, A & Ravichandran

K. (2003), *A New World Through Cooperatives, Rainbow Publications, Coimbatore.*

Garg, M.C. & Joshi, N.N., (1997), *Cooperative Credit and Banking—Strategies for Development,* Deep & Deep Publications, New Delhi.

Grewal, P.S. (1985), *Rural Banking in India,* Kalyani Publishers, New Delhi.

James Mathew, (2003), *Innovative Approaches and Challenges in Rural Credit,* Nirmala Academic Research & Publications, Nirmala College, Muvattupuzha,, Kerala.

Joshi, G.V. (2002), *Overdues in Cooperative Credit System,* Mohit Publications, New Delhi.

Jugale, V.B. (1992), *Cooperative Credit in Indian Agriculture—Its Socio-Economic and Technological Impact,* Mittal Publications, New Delhi.

Baidhyanath Misra (1997), *Cooperative Movement in India–A Case Study of Indian State,* A.P.H.Publishing House, New Delhi.

Kalyankar, S.P. (1983), *Crop Loan Overdues of Cooperative Finance,* Rainbow Publications, Coimbatore.

Karmakar, K.G. (1999), *Rural Credit and SHGs – Micro Finance Needs and Concepts in India,* Sage Publications, New Delhi.

Lakshmi Narasaiah, M. & Venkata Naidu, G. (1999), *Role of Banking in Rural Development,* Discovery Publishing House, New Delhi.

Lalitha, N. & Dayanandam, R. (2005), *NABARD and Rural Transformation,* Dominant Publishers and Distributors, New Delhi

Majumdar N.A. (2002), *Financial Sector Reforms and India's Economic Development,* Vol. 2, Academic Foundation, Ghaziabad, p. 255 & 264.

Mamoria, C.B. (1983), *Rural Credit and Agricultural Cooperation in India,* Kitab Mahal Agencies, Allahabad.

Mamoria, C.B. and Badri Bishal Tripathi (2001), *Agricultural Problems of India,* Kitab Mahal Agencies, Allahabad.

Martin, Patrick (1999), *Self-employment and Successful Entrepreneurship,* Kanishka Publishers, New Delhi.

Mruthyanjaya, V.C. Mathur, Praduman Kumar (1994), *Agricultural Credit System in India,* Agricultural Economic Research Association of India, New Delhi.

Mukesh Singh Rathore (1994), *Role of Institutional Finance in Development of Agriculture in India,* Mohit Publication, New Delhi.

Muniraj, R.(1987), *Farm Finance for Development,* Oxford & IBH Publishing Company Private Limited, New Delhi.

Nakkiran, S. & John Winfred (1988), *Cooperative Banking in India,* Rainbow Publishers, Coimbatore.

Pathania K.S. (1998) *Management of Cooperative Finance in India,* Anmol Publications Private Ltd., New Delhi.

Patnaik, U.C. & Mishra, R.N. (1999), *Rural Banking in India,* Anmol Publications, New Delhi.

Perumalsamy, P. (1996), *Economic Development of Tamil Nadu,* S. Chand & Co., Ltd., New Delhi, p.382.

Pramod Lata Jain (1990), *Cooperative Credit in Rural India,* Mittal Publications, New Delhi.

Pranab Kumar Charkravarthy (1983), *Problems of Cooperative Development in India,* S. Chand & Co. Ltd., New Delhi.

Pratap Mal (2001), *Institutional Financing for Agriculture and Rural Development,* Mohit Publications, New Delhi.

Ramamohana Rao (2000), *Banks, Borrowers and Barriers—Problems of Finance Against Poverty,* The University of Manchester, U.K.

Ramana Rao (2001), *Impact of Institutional Credit on the Socio-Economic Conditions of Rural Women in SHGs: A Case Study in Bidar District of Karnataka,* NIRD, Hyderabad.

Ravichandran, K. (2000), *Crop Loan System and Overdue,* Spell Bound Publications, Rohtak.

Reddy, C.R. (1993), *Overdues Management in Cooperative Banks,* Himalaya Publishing House, Bombay.

Reddy, C.R. (1988) *Cooperative Agricultural Finance,* Chugh Publications, Allahabad.

Renga Reddy, A. (1990), *Agricultural Development: Rural Credit and Problems of its Recovery,* Mittal Publications, New Delhi.

Satish, P. (1998), *Advanced Rural Banking – Rural Financial Institutions,* Module D., Indian Institute of Bankers, Mumbai.

Savita Thakur Joshi (1999), *Women and Development—The Changing Scenario,* Mittal Publications, New Delhi.

Shakuntala Devi (1996), *Rural Credit and Agricultural Development,* Sarup & Sons Publications.

Sharma, K.C. (1998), *Advanced Rural Banking,* Indian Institute of Bankers, Mumbai.

Shukla Mohanthy (1991), *Rural Credit in India,* Syndicate Publications, Patna.

Sinha, S.K. (1992), *Recovery of Loans from Farmers,* Deep & Deep Publications, New Delhi.

Taimani, K.K. (1993), *Cooperative Development: The Next*

Phase, ICA Domust Trust Publication, New Delhi.

Upendra Kunwar (1987), *Banking and Agricultural Growth—A Study of Land Development Bank,* Deep & Deep Publications, New Delhi.

Reports

GOI (1991-92), *All India Debt and Investment Survey,* NSS–48th Round.

Government of Tamil Nadu (1993-94, 1996-97, and 2001-02), *Tamil Nadu–An Economic Appraisal.*

GOI (2003-04), *Annual Report,* Department of Agriculture and Cooperation, Ministry of Agriculture.

Human Development in South Asia (2002), Mahabub ul haq Human Development Centre, Oxford.

NABARD (2001-02), *Annual Report.*

NABARD (2002), *Two Decades of Dedicated Service to the Nation (1992–2002).*

NABARD (2002-03), *Annual Report.*

NABARD (2005-06), *Annual Report.*

NABARD (1993-94 to 2007-08), *PLP for Dindigul District (with detailed projections).*

NABARD (1998-99 to 2006-07), *State Level Credit Seminar–State Focus Pape.*

NAFSCOB (1999-2000), *Performance of Primary Agricultural Credit Societies, Mumbai*

NAFSCOB (2005–06), National Conference on Rural Credit and Banking Institutions–Observations and Recommendations.

NCUI (2004), *Indian Cooperative Movement–A Profile.*

RBI (1954), *Report of the All India Rural Credit Survey Committee,* Bombay.

RBI (1969), *All India Rural Credit Review Committee*, Bombay.

RBI (1974), *Report of the Study Team on Overdues of Cooperative Credit Institutions, Bombay.*

RBI (1980), *Report of the Committee to Review the Arrangements For Institutional Credit For Agriculture and Rural Development.*

RBI (1989), *Report of the Agricultural Credit Review Committee—A review of the Agricultural Credit System in India*, Bombay.

RBI (2001), *Basic Statistical Returns of Scheduled Commercial Banks in India.*

RBI (2004), *Report of the Advisory Committee on Flow of Credit to Agriculture and Related Activities*, Mumbai, June.

RBI (2004), *Task Force on Revival of Cooperative Credit Institutions.*

RBI (2006), *Banking Statistics–Quarterly Hand out, Mumbai, March.*

RBI (2005-06), Report on Trend and Progress of Banking in India.

TNSCARDB (2005–06), *Annual Report.*

Journals and Newspapers

Anandateerth Kittur (1990), Diversion of Agricultural Loans of Formal Financial Institutions, *Journal of Rural Development,* Vol. 9(4), p. 774.

Anil Suryawanshi (2003), Non-Performing Assets—An Analysis of SGB, *Banking Finance,* Vol. 16 (9), September, p. 19

Arul Anandam, M.A. & Namasivayam, N. (1988), 'Cooperative Overdues–The Influence of Socio-Economic Factors of Borrowers—A Case Study,

Indian Cooperative Review, Vol. 25 (3), January, p.296 & 300.

Arunachalam, R. & Palanisamy, A. (1991), Utilisation and Repayment of Cooperative Crop Loan, *Indian Cooperative Review*, Vol. 29(2), October, p.182

Atibudhi, H.N. & Singh, J.P. (1995), Flow of Credit to Different Categories of Farmers–A Study in Cuttack District, Orissa, *Land Bank Journal*, Vol. 34(2), p.3.

Balasaheb Vikhe Patil (2005), Rural Banking—Problems of Localized Banking Institutions, *Economic and Political Weekly*, Vol. XL (12), March 19-25, p. 1225.

Balishter and Pankaj Kumar (1995), 'A Study of Institutional Finance in Agriculture', *Land Bank Journal*, Vol. 34(1), September, pp. 16 & 18.

Balishter, Roshan Singh & Singh A.K. (1991), Overdues of Loans in Land Development Banks in Agra District of Uttar Pradesh, *Cooperative Perspective*, Vol. 26(1), April-June, p. 38 & 39.

Balishter, Singh A.K. & Vishwajit (1994), A Study of Overdues of Loans in Agriculture, *Indian Cooperative Review*, Vol. 31(40), April, p. 382.

Basavaraj Banakar, Suryaprakash (1981) 'Borrowing and Utilization of Crop Production Credit in Karnataka: A Case Study, *Prajnan*, Vol. 16(1), January–March 1987, p. 78.

Chidambaram, K. & Sankarasubramoniam, V. (1999), Factors Influencing Repayment of IRDP Loan—A Study, *Kurukshetra*, Vol.47(6), March, p. 4 & 5.

Chinnappa Reddy, B.V., Venkataram, K.V. and Keshava Reddy, T.R. (1987), 'An Economic Analysis of Overdues Among Farmers in Srinivaspur Taluk, Kolar District', *Land Bank Journal*, Vol. 26(2), December, p. 4 & 5.

Daman Prakash (2001), Challenges and Development

Issues before the Agricultural Cooperatives and Farmer's Organizations in Asia, *Cooperative Perspective*, Vol. 35 (4), Jan-March, p. 5.

Debabrata Das (2002), Utilization Pattern of Cooperative Credit: A Study, *Cooperative Perspective*, Vol. 26(4), January-March, p. 27.

Dhimen Namhata and Broadway A.C. (1988), Profitable Utilisation of Cooperative Credit by Cultivators, *Indian Cooperative Review*, Vol. 25(3), p. 306.

Dinesh Singh Yadav (1999), 'Performance and Prospects of Agricultural Cooperative Credit Societies in Block Bilhapur District, Kanpur Dehat (U.P), *Indian Cooperative Review*, Vol. 37(2), October, p. 78.

Girija Srinivasan and Satish P. (2001), Networking for Micro Credit Delivery, *Journal of Rural Development*, Vol. 20(4), October-December, p. 636.

Goyal, S.K. Pandey, R.N. and Modi, M.K. (1993), Repayment Capacity of Defaulter and Non-Defaulater Borrowers of Cooperative Societies in Haryana, *Indian Cooperative Review*, Vol. 30(30), January, p. 296.

Goyel, G.B. (1997), Cooperative Research: Identification of Priority Gaps, *Indian Cooperative Review*, Vol. 34(5), p. 89.

Indira Devi, P. (1992), Growth and Performance of Cooperative Agricultural Credit in Kerala, *Indian Cooperative Review*, Vol. 29(40), April, p. 336,337.

Jaya S.Anand (1995), 'Utilisation of Long-Term Credit: A Case Study', *Land Bank Journal*, Vol. 34(2), December, p. 33.

Joy Joseph Puthussery (1999), Socio-Economic Characteristics and Nature of Default–A Study of Primary Agricultural and Rural Development Banks in Kerala, *Land Bank Journal*, Vol. 38(3), December, pp. 9 & 10.

Jugale, V.B. (1994), Role of Cooperatives in Agricultural Finance, *Indian Cooperative Review,* Vol. 32(1), July, p. 61.

Karmakar, K.G. (1997), 'Supplementary Rural Credit Delivery System–Some Asian Models', *Journal of Rural Development*, Vol. 16, July-September, p. 481.

Krishna Naik, C.N. & Siddaiah, T. (1990), Behavioural Aspects of Cooperative Credit—A Survey, *Cooperative Perspective,* Vol. 25(2), July-September, p. 38.

Kulwant Pathania & Yoginder Varma (1992), Impact of Size of Family Income and Value of Farm Assets on Cooperative Credit Utilization, *Indian Cooperative Review*, Vol. 30(1), July, p. 49.

Kulwant Pathania & Yoginder Verma (1991), Impact of Size of Loan and Types of Farmers on Cooperative Credit Utilisation, Indian Cooperative Review, Vol. 29(2), October, p. 155.

Loganathan, P. (1992), Credit Information—A Missing Link in Agriculture Credit—A Sample Survey, *Indian Cooperative Review,* Vol. 29(4), April, p. 389.

Lokanadhan, K. & Varadharajan, S. (1991), A Study on the Recovery of Crop Loans in Primary Cooperative Banks of North Arcot District, *Indian Cooperative Review,* Vol. 29(2), October, p. 111.

Majumdar, N.A. (1997), Overhauling the Somnolent Rural Credit System, *Economic and Political Weekly,* Vol. 32 (43), October, p. 73.

Makadia, J.J., Thumar, B.L. & Shiyani, R.L.(1992), An Evaluation of Acquisition and Utilization of Cooperative Credit in Junagad District, *Indian Cooperative Review,* Vol. 30(1), July, p. 59.

Malyadri, P. & Sirisha, S. (2003), NPAs in CBs—An Overview, *Banking Finance,* January, Vol. 16 (1), p. 7.

Maninder Kaur, Gill, S.S. & Sukhdev Singh (1997), Rural Poverty in Punjab—A Case Study, *Indian Economic Panorama*, April–June, p. 31 & 32.

Mazumdar, D.K. & Baruah, H.K. (1999), Repayment Performance of Institutional Finance for Allied Agricultural Activities—A Case Study, *Indian Cooperative Review*, Vol. 37 (1), July, p. 2 & 5.

Mishra, S.D. (2003), Poor in a Spider's Web of Debt, *IBA Bulletin*, April, Vol. 25 (4), p. 20.

Mishra, J.K. & Thani, R.K. (2004), Indian Banking System and Micro Finance, *Kurukshetra*, Vol. 52(4), p. 15.

Modi, M.K. & Rai, K.N. (1993), Credit Utilization Pattern on Different Categories of Farms in District Kurukshetra, Haryana, *Indian Cooperative Review*, Vol. 30(3), January, p. 252 & 254.

Mohan Kanda (1997), Agricultural Credit–Institutional Arrangements, Performance and Policy Issues, *Journal of Rural Development*, Vol. 16(1), January-March, p. 11 & 34.

Mohanan, N. (2004), Sustainability of Credit Market in an Indian Village, *Journal of Rural Development*, Vol. 23(3), July-September p. 390.

Moniruzzaman (2002), Loan Utilization Pattern of Bangaladesh Rural Development Board Women Cooperatives and Grammen Bank Groups: A Comparative Analysis, *Journal of Rural Development*, Vol. 21(1), Jan-March, p. 78.

Munikrishna Reddy, M., Ramesh Kumar Reddy and Reddy, G.P.V. (1987), 'Repayment Performance of Agricultural Credit Users', *Land Bank Journal*, Vol. 25(4), June, p. 23 & 26.

Nachiket Mor (2005), Expanding Access to Financial Services Where do we go from here?, *Economic and Political Weekly*, Vol. XL(12), March 19-25, p. 1122.

Namasivayam & Ramachandraiah, G. (2000), End Use of Credit and Repayment Performance of the Institutional Borrowers: An Integrated Analysis, *Journal of Rural Development*, Vol. 19(3), p. 419.

Namboodiri, N.V. (2001), 'Potential Role of SHGs in Rural Financing Deepening', *Indian Journal of Economics*, Vol. 56(3), July-September, p. 402.

Nirmala, V., Sham Bhat, K. & Bhuvaneswari, P. (2004), SHGs for Poverty Alleviation in Pondicherry, *Journal of Rural Development*, Vol. 23(2), April-June, p. 204.

Padmini, C. (2004), Role of Linkages in the Development of Cooperatives, *The Indian Economic Journal*, Vol. 51, No. 3 & 4, p. 28.

Pattaranarakha, K. (2003), Member's Participation in the Activities of a Production Credit Group in Southern Thailand, *Journal of Rural Development*, Vol. 22(2), April-June, p. 265.

Prasad, J.V.S., Naidu, M.R. and Venkateswaralu, U. (1987), 'Credit Overdues—Certain Factors for Default–A Micro Analysis, *Land Bank Journal*, Vol. 25(4), p. 5.

Pratap Singh (1988), Causes Underlying the Survival of the Money Lending Business in the Rural Economy of Punjab, *Indian Cooperative Review*, Vol. 25(3), New Delhi, p. 286.

Priya Basu, Pradeep Srivastava (2005), Exploring Possibilities–Microfinance and Rural Credit Access for the poor in India, *Economic and Political Weekly*, Vol. XL (17), p. 1747.

Raja Ram Gupta (2005), Micro finance in India–Empirical evidence, Alternative Models and Policy

Imperatives, *Economic and Political Weekly*, Vol. XL (12), March 19-25, p. 1229.

Rajput, A.M. and Verma, A.R. (1993), 'Impact of Farm Loans on Farm Productivity–A Case Study of State Bank of India in Indore District of Madhya Pradesh, *Indian Cooperative Review*, Vol. 31(1), July p. 55 & 56.

Ram Babu, P., Daivadeenam, P. & Eswara Prasad (1991), Repayment Pattern of Agricultural Credit—A Study of Andhra Bank in Guntur District, A.P., *Indian Cooperative Review*, Vol. 29(2), October, p. 160.

Ramachandra Reddy (1995), An Evolution and Function of Cooperative Societies in Cuddapah District, *Indian Cooperative Review*, Vol. 33(2), October, p. 162.

Ramachandra Reddy, D. (1995), Influence of Socio-economic Factors of Borrowers in Cooperative Overdues: A Case Study', *Cooperative Perspective*, Vol. 29(4), January–March p. 67.

Ramachandra Reddy, D. & Bagavan Reddy (1994), Cooperative Credit in Delta and Non-Delta Regions of Cuddapa, *Cooperative Perspective*, Vol. 29(3), October–December, p. 57 & 58.

Ramachandra Reddy, D. & Ramakrishna Reddy M. (1995), 'Cooperative Overdues: A Study of a set of PACS and Defaulters in Nellore Distirct: Andhra Pradesh, *Land Bank Journal*, Vol. 34(2), December, p. 10.

Ranjit Kumar Das (2002), Recovery and Overdues Problems of RRBs with particular reference to Uttar Banga Kshetria Gramin Bank, *Banking Finance*, October, p. 10

Ranjith Karmakar and Bholanath Ghosh (2002), Role of Women in SHGs: An Emerging Possibility to

Cooperativization at grass root, *Man in India*, Vol. 82(3&4), July–December, p. 449

Ravi Varma S. (1992), Utilisation and Overdues of Cooperative Loans in Andhrapradesh (A Case Study of Nagari Block of Chittoor District, *Indian Cooperative Review*, Vol. 29(3), January, p. 233 & p. 234.

Ravichandran, K. (1995), Loan Waiver Schemes—The Menace of Cooperative Credit, *International Journal of Development Planning and Literature*, Vol. 10 (1&2), Spell Bound Publications, Rohatak, p. 133.

Ravichandran, K. & Revathi Bala, M. (2004), Role of Cooperatives and SHGs in Rural Credit Market, *RBI-CAB Calling*, Vol. 28(1), January-March, p. 12 & 16.

Reddy, B.R. & Laxminarayana (1996), Overdues in Cooperatives: A Case Study in Andhra Pradesh, *Cooperative Perspective*, Vol. 31(3), p. 19 & 20.

Rengasamy, V. & Ramnath, R.L. (2000), Performance of Financial Agencies in the Priority Sector Lending under the Service Area Approach in Madurai District, *Prajnan*, Vol. 29 (1), April-June, p. 82.

Sarma, A.K. & Kharmowphlang, M.D. (1995), 'An Analysis of Overdues of Agricultural Credit in East Khasi Hill District of Meghalaya State', *Indian Cooperative Review*, Vol. 33(2), October, p. 123.

Sarthak Chowdury and Prabuddha Ray (2001), Cooperative Credit in Rural Sector–A Case Study, *Economic Affairs*, Vol. 46(3), September, p. 163.

Satya Sai, K.J.S., Venkateswaralu U., Seetharaman S. and Raghu Ram, P. (1987), Structure of Rural Credit in West Godavari District, Andhra Pradesh, *Land Bank Journal*, Vol. 26(2), p. 54.

Satyasai, K.J.S. & Viswanathan, K.U. (2003), Role of Moneylenders in Rural Credit Markets—A Temporal Comparison based on All-India Debt. Investment Survey, *National Bank News Review,* Vol. 19(4), October–December, p. 21.

Sharma, D.K., Koshta, A.K. & Jain, B.C.(1991), Availability and Utilization of Crop Loan in Central Madhyapradesh, *Land Bank Journal,* Vol. 30(1), September, p. 18.

Shollapur, M.R. (1996), Appraisal of Effectiveness of Post-Sanction Follow-up of Credit, *Indian Cooperative Review,* Vol. 33(4), April, p. 25.

Sidhu, R.S. (2002), Extent and Pattern of Loan Overdues in Punjab, *Indian Cooperative Review,* Vol. 40 (1), July, p. 137.

Singh, A.K., Bajpai, D.K. and Gairia, P.S. (1993), Institutional Finance and the Rural Poor: Findings of a Field Study in a Backward Area, *Indian Cooperative Review,* Vol. 30(4), April p. 396 & 401.

Somorendra Singh (2001), 'Trend in Recovery of Loan in PACS', *The Maharashtra Cooperative Quarterly,* Vol. 34(4), April-June, p. 14.

Sopan, Joshi (2004), Inevitable Tragedy, *Down to Earth,* Vol. 13(4), Society for Environmental Communication, New Delhi, p. 15.

Srivastava, A.P. (1991), Cooperative Credit for Rural Development–A Regional Experience, *Indian Cooperative Review,* Vol. 29 (2), October, p. 189 & 190.

Subbi Reddy, T. & Ramamuni Reddy, C.(1980), Utilisation of Loans, *Land Bank Journal,* Vol. 18(3), March, p. 32.

Subrahmanyam, B. (2003), Lending Agricultural Credit at Nine Percent: A view point of Agricultural

Cooperative Credit Institutions, *NAFSCOB Bulletin*, Vol. 20(3), NAFSCOB, July-September, p. 13.

Sudarshan Reddy, A. & Venkateshwar Rao (1999), Performance and Challenges of Cooperative Credit in the context of Sustainable Rural Development–An Experience of MCRB, *Indian Cooperative Review*, Vol. 37(2), October, p. 83.

Swain, B.K. (2004), Indian Banks in 2010: Emerging Scenario, *IBA Bulletin*, Vol. 26 (1), January, p. 165 & 166.

Tara S. Nair (2005), The Transforming World of Indian Micro Finance, *Economic and Political Weekly*, Vol.XL (17), April, p.1697.

The Financial Express (1996), March 2, p. 7.

The Hindu (2003), 14th September, p. 16.

The Hindu (2005), 23rd May, p. 11.

The Hindu (2003), 9th November, p. 3.

Tiwari, S.N. & Sharma. P.K. (1986), Farm Credit and Rural Savings, *Cooperative Perspective*, Vol.21(1), April-June, pp. 27 & 30.

Vaikunthe. L.D. (1991), Agricultural Cooperative Credit–Utilization and Recovery Performance', *Indian Cooperative Review*, Vol. 29(1), July, p. 42.

Venugopala Reddy and Rathakar (1996), 'Credit Utilization Pattern of Farmers, *Land Bank Journal*, Vol. 35 (1), September, p. 34.

Viswa Prasad. P. & Parthasarathy. P.B. (1993), Supply of Short-term Credit and Estimation of Credit Gaps in Medak District (A.P), *Indian Cooperative Review*, Vol. 30(4), April p. 336.

Viswanath. A.R. (2001), 'An Analysis of the Performance of Agricultural Credit Cooperatives and their

Overdues Problems in India, *Indian Cooperative Review,* Vol. 39(1), July, p. 58.

Sukhdev Singh, Sonia Goyal and Mandeep Mahal (2004), Debt of Peasants: Causes and consequences, *IASSI Quarterly,* Vol. 22940, p. 90.

Web Sites and e-Journals

www.epw.org

www.microcredit.com

www.indiapost.org

www.rbi.org

www.worldbank.org

www.peoplesmarch/com

www.indiabudget.nic.in

www.nabard.org

www.tn.gov.in

Research Articles

Malcolm Harper (2002), *Promotion of Self-Help Groups under the Bank SHG-Bank Linkage Programme in India,* paper presented at the seminar SHG-Bank Linkage Programme organized by NABARD in collaboration with the SDC, GTZ and IFAD at New Delhi, on 25th and 26th November, p.30.

Ravichandran, K. & Revathi Bala, M. (2004), *'Challenges faced by Entrepreneurs in Informal Sector Enterprises in Dindigul District–A Study',* the paper presented in UGC sponsored national seminar on Challenges before Indian Entrepreneurs in the 21st century held on 10th April 2004 organized by Adirampattinam Khadir Mohideen College, Adirampattinam, April 2004, p. 3.

Annexure – 1

PATTERN COOPERATIVE CREDIT STRUCTURE

SHORT TERM STRUCTURE

THREE TIER	TWO TIER	MIXED
1. Andhra Pradesh*	1. Andaman & Nicobar	1. Assam
2. Bihar	2. Arunachal Pradesh	2. Himachal Pradesh
3. Chhatisgarh	3. Chandigarh	3. Jammu & Kashmir
4. Gujarat	4. Delhi	
5. Haryana	5. Goa	
6. Karnataka	6. Manipur	
7. Kerala	7. Meghalaya	
8. Madhya Pradesh	8. Mizoram	
9. Maharashtra	9. Nagaland	
10. Orissa	10. Pondicherry	
11. Punjab	11. Sikkim	
12. Rajasthan	12. Tripura	
13. Tamil Nadu		
14. Uttar Pradesh		
15. West Bengal		
16. Jharkhand$		
17. Uttaranchal$		

* INTEGRATED (BOTH ST & LT) $ SCB not formed as on 31.03.2002

LONG TERM COOPERATIVE CREDIT STRUCTURE

THREE TIER	TWO TIER	MIXED
1. Assam	1. Chattisgarh	1. Himachal Pradesh
2. Bihar	2. Haryana	2. West Bengal
3. Gujarat	3. Karnataka	
4. Jammu & Kashmir	4. Kerala	
5. Manipur	5. Madhya Pradesh	
6. Pondicherry	6. Maharashtra	
7. Tripura	7. Orissa	
8. Uttar Pradesh	8. Punjab	
	9. Rajasthan	
	10. Tamil Nadu	

Annexure - 2

Coverage of Villages by PACS as on 31 March 2002			
State	*No. of Villages*	**No. of PACS**	**Ratio of villages to PACS**
Andaman and Nicobar	204	45	5:1
Andhra Pradesh	27592	4470	6:1
Arunachal Pradesh	3649	31	117:1
Assam	25590	714	36:1
Bihar	77694	7057	11:1
Chhatisgarh	20279	1333	15:1
Gujarat	155789	8250	19:1
Haryana	7077	2413	3:1
Himachal Pradesh	20118	2117	9:1
Karnataka	28569	5077	6:1
Kerala	1606	1988	1:1
Madhya Pradesh	76131	4475	17:1
Maharashtra	61676	20726	3:1
Meghalaya	5000	197	25:1
Mizoram	630	320	2:1
Nagaland	969	1719	1:1
Orissa	45208	3867	12:1
Pondicherry	264	53	5:1
Punjab	14584	4001	4:1
Rajasthan	40808	5153	8:1
Jharkhand	3611	208	17:1
Tamil Nadu	18515	4586	4:1
Tripura	962	270	3:1
Uttar Pradesh	112804	8929	13:1
West Bengal	41400	8968	5:1
ALL INDIA	**724374**	**98247**	**7:1**

Source: NAFSCOB

Annexure - 3
Kisan Credit Card Scheme

Kisan Credit Card Scheme was introduced in 1998-99 to facilitate access to credit from CBs and RRBs. The salient features of the scheme are as given below:

a. Farmers eligible for production credit of Rs.5000 or more are eligible for issue of KCC.

b. Eligible farmers to be provided with a KCC and pass book or card cum pass book.

c. Provision of revolving cash credit facility involving any number of drawals and repayments within the limit.

d. Entire production credit needs for full year plus ancillary activities related to crop production considered while fixing limit. In due course, all activities and non-farm credit needs may also be covered.

e. Limit to be fixed on the basis of operational land holding, cropping pattern and scale of finance.

f. Sub-limits may be fixed at discretion of banks

g. Card valid for 3 years subject to annual review.

h. Each drawal to be repaid within 12 months.

i. Conversion/rephasement of loans also permissible in case of damage to crops due to natural calamities.

j. As incentive for good performance, credit limits could be enhanced to take care fo increase in costs, change in cropping pattern etc.

k. Security, margin, rate of interest as per RBI norms.

l. Operations may be through issuing branch or at the discretion of bank, through other designated branches.

Withdrawals through slips/cheques accompanied by card and pass book.

Source: www.Indiabudget.nic.in

ACCESS, USE AND REPAYMENT OF INSTITUTIONAL CREDIT BY BORROWERS – A STUDY IN RURAL TAMILNADU

Interview Schedule for the Respondents

I. DEMOGRAPHY

1. Name of the Respondent

2. Address of the Respondent

3. Sex a. Male -1 b. Female - 2 ☐

4. Age ☐☐

II. SOCIAL

5. Community a. SC -1 b. MBC -2 d. BC - 3 ☐

6. Education

a. No formal education - 1 b. Primary - 2 c. Secondary - 3 ☐

d. Higher Secondary - 4 e. Degree - 5

7. Marital Status ☐

a.Unmarried - 1 b. Married - 2 c. Widowed - 3

8. Type of family a. Joint - 1 b. Nuclear – 0 ☐

9. Total number of members in the family

a. No. of dependents in the family ☐☐

b. No. of earning members in the family ☐☐

(The investigator use 1 for 'Yes' and 0 for 'No')

A. Exposure to Mass - Media

10. Do you read the following? Yes/No ☐

a. No - 0 a. News papers -1 b. Journals & Newspapers - 2

11. How often do you watch TV? ☐

a. Regularly - 3 b. Occasionally - 2 c. Rarely - 1 d. Never - 0

12. How often do you listen to radio? ☐

a. Regularly - 3 b. Occasionally - 2 c. Rarely - 1

B. Contact with Change Agents

13. Do Govt. officials come to your village to meet the public? ☐ 14.

Do Non-Govt. Officials come to your villages to meet the public? ☐

Yes/No

15. Have you met any of them any time? Yes/No ☐

16. In a month how many times you are meeting them? ☐☐

C. Membership

17. Are you a member of any institution? Yes/No ☐

18. If yes, in which institution? ☐

a. PACB -1 b. PARDB - 2 c. SHG - 3 d. PACB & PARDB - 4

e. PACB - 5 f. All three - 6
& SHG

19. How long you have been a member? (in years) ☐☐

20. Are you a member of any one of the following institution? Yes/No

a. Caste organisation ☐ c. Political parties ☐

d. Local clubs ☐

21. Is any any of your family member having membership in the following institution? ☐

a. No Membership b. PACB -2 c. PACB & PARDB - 3

III. ECONOMIC

A. Occupation

22. What is your Occupation?

Primary ☐

a. Agriculture - 1 b. Dairy - 2 c. Agri-Labour - 3

Secondary

d. Non-agri. labour - 4 e. Govt. employee- 5 f. Weaving - 6 ☐

g. Self - employed - 7 h. Others - 8

B. Assets

23. Do you own a house? Yes/No ☐

(In no skip to 26)

24. Type of your house ☐

a. Hut-1 b. Tiled- 2 c. Terraced- 3

25. Approximate value of your house ☐☐☐☐☐

26. Do you own any one of the following household items? Yes/No

a. Sewing machine ☐ b. Watch ☐ c. Sofa set ☐ d. Fan ☐

e. Radio ☐ f. Refrigerator ☐ g. Tape ☐ h.T.V ☐

i. VCR/VCP/VCD ☐ j. Bicycle ☐ k. Motorcycle ☐ l. Gas ☐

m. Telephone ☐☐ n. Others ☐

27. What is the total value of household assets? Rs. ☐☐☐☐☐☐☐

28. Do you own domestic animal? Yes/No ☐

29. Mention the value of your animal assets Rs. ☐☐☐☐☐☐☐
(To be inquired: Cow, Buffalo, Goat etc.,)

30. If you own agricultural machineries and equipments, what is the approximate value? Rs. ☐☐☐☐☐☐☐

(To be inquired: Tractor, Tiller, Pumpset, Lorry, Van, Bike, etc.,)

31. Do you own any agricultural land? Yes/No ☐

(If no, skip to 38) ☐

32. What is the type, size and extent of irrigation of land?

	Yes/No	Size of land Acres	Sources of Irrigation
a. Irrigated	☐	☐☐	☐
b. Un-irrigated	☐	☐☐	☐

(Under sources of irrigation, 1- canal, 2-well/bore well 3-River 4-lake)

33. What are the types of crops cultivated in your land? (Yes/No)

a. Paddy ☐ b. Sugarcane ☐ c. Maize ☐

d. Pulses ☐ f. Fruits ☐ e. Vegetables ☐

g. Flowers ☐ h. Millets ☐ i. Others (Specify) ☐

34. Do you practice organic farming? Yes/No ☐

35. What is the approximate value of own land ? (in Rs.)

Gasa ☐☐☐☐☐☐☐
Total ☐☐☐☐☐☐☐

36. What is the approximate income from Agriculture? Own ☐☐☐☐☐☐
(in Rs.) Total ☐☐☐☐☐☐

C. Marketing

37. Where do you market your agricultural products? Option1

a. Loss- 1 b. Village Trader – 2 c. Village trader cum moneylenders-☐

Option2

d. Trader at mondy center - 3 e. Market - 4 ☐

D. Income and Expenditure

38. What is your family Annual income? Rs. ☐☐☐☐☐☐

39. What is your average family expense? Rs.☐☐☐☐☐☐
Per Annum on:- (in Rs.)

a. Food b. Clothing c. Medical d. Travel

e. Education f. Interest g. Entertainment (Cable rent & other) h. Others (Specify)

40. How much do you additionally need to meet family expenses per annum? Rs. ☐☐☐☐☐☐

41. What is your average cultivation/ business expenses per Annum? (in Rs.)

a. Purchase of inputs b. Labour c. Processing ☐☐☐☐☐☐

d. Marketing e. Expansion f. Repair

g. Others (Specify)

42. How much do you additionally need to meet your business/ farm expenses per annum? (in Rs.) ☐☐☐☐☐☐

E. Savings Pattern

43. Do you have any deposits in any institution? ☐
Yes/No
(If no, skip to 48)

44. If yes in which of the following institution? Yes/No

a. Commercial bank (Specify) ☐ b. SHG ☐

c. Post Office ☐ d. Others (Specify) ☐

45. When did you open the account? (in years) □□

46. Mention the type of deposit and amount

S.No	Years	Type of deposit	Amount
1.	□□□□	□	□□□□□□□
2.	□□□□	□	□□□□□□□
3.	□□□□	□	□□□□□□□
4.	□□□□	□	□□□□□□□
5.	□□□□	□	□□□□□□□

Investment Plan

1. Savings 2. Current 3. Recurring 4. Fixed 5. Others

47. Why did you select this institution to save your money? Yes/No

	CB	Coop.	SHG	PO	Others
a. Safey & Security	□	□	□	□	□
b. Attractive rate of interest	□	□	□	□	□
c. Lesser formalities	□	□	□	□	□
d. Nearness	□	□	□	□	□
e. Availability of adequate loan	□	□	□	□	□
f. Friendliness of employees	□	□	□	□	□

IV. INDEBTEDNESS

48. Are you indebted to any private parties? Yes/No □

(If No, Skip to 58)

A. Informal source of credit

49. To which private parties you are indebted? □

a. Moneylenders - 1 b. Friends - 2 c. Relatives - 3

d. Village Trader - 4 h. Commission agents- 9 f. Chit funds - 5

50. What is the nature of your indebtedness? □

a. Ancestral - 1 b. Present - 2 c. Both - 3

51. How long are you indebted? (in Years) □□

52. To what extent you are indebted? a. Before membership b. After membership

		a. Before membership	b. After membership
a. Moneylenders	Rs.	☐☐☐☐☐☐☐	☐☐☐☐☐☐☐
b. Friends		☐☐☐☐☐☐☐	☐☐☐☐☐☐☐
c. Relatives		☐☐☐☐☐☐☐	☐☐☐☐☐☐☐
e. Village Trader		☐☐☐☐☐☐☐	☐☐☐☐☐☐☐
f. Commission Agent		☐☐☐☐☐☐☐	☐☐☐☐☐☐☐
h.Chit funds		☐☐☐☐☐☐☐	☐☐☐☐☐☐☐

53. Specify the rate of interest in percent a. Before membership ☐☐☐ b. After membership ☐☐☐

54. State the causes for indebtedness Yes/No

a. Farm/ business expenses ☐ b. Family expenses ☐

c. Medical Expenses ☐ d. Educational Expenses ☐

e. House Renovation/ construction ☐ f. Clearance of old debts with private ☐

g. Repayment of institutional loans ☐ h. Others (Specify) ☐

55. How the informal source was accessible to you? ☐

a. Relatives/ Friends-1 b. Personal credibility-2 c. Shorter distance -3

d. Loan available at the door step -4 e. No strict formalities-5 f. Economic status-6

56. List out the advantages in approaching the informal sources? ☐

a. Fulfillment of urgent needs -1 b. Availability of credit at the door step - 2

c. Availability of credit in time-3 d. Confidentiality in transaction - 4

e. Others (Specify) -5

57. What are the disadvantages with the informal sources? ☐

a. Higher rate of interest -1 b. Shorter duration to repay-2

c. Unhealthy practices during delay in repayment -3 d. No consideration for the unexpected losses -4

e. Others (Specify) -5

B. Formal Sources of Credit:

58 Did you borrow from any of the formal agency? Yes/No ☐

59. From which formal source, do you borrow normally? Yes/No

a. PACB ☐ b. Commercial Banks ☐ c. SHG ☐

d. PARDB ☐ d. Others (Specify) ☐

60. For what purpose did you borrow? Yes/No

a. Cultivation expenses ☐ b. Purchase of cattle / milch animals ☐

c. Land development purposes ☐ d. Improved methods of irrigation ☐

e. Marketing purpose ☐ f. Purchase of machineries ☐

g. To invest in other business ☐ h. Family expenses ☐

i. Housing Expenses ☐ j. Social ceremonies ☐

61. How much did you get as loan? Rs. ☐☐☐☐☐☐☐

62. Mention the details of loan availed by you?

S.No	Source	Type of Loans	Year	Amount in Rs.
1.	---	☐	----	☐☐☐☐☐☐☐
2.	---	☐	-----	☐☐☐☐☐☐☐
3	---	☐	----	☐☐☐☐☐☐☐
4	---	☐	-----	☐☐☐☐☐☐☐
5	---	☐	-----	☐☐☐☐☐☐☐

Use: 1-CB; 2-PACB; 3-SHG; 4-PARDB; 5-Others (Specify)

Type of loan: 1-ST; 2-MT; 3-LT

63. How much did you incur to avail loan? Rs. ☐☐☐☐☐☐☐☐

a. Document cost b. Transport cost c. Miscellaneous

64. Why did you select this agency?

	CB	PACB	SHG	PARDB	Others
a. To increase savings	☐	☐	☐	☐	☐
b. To get loans	☐	☐	☐	☐	☐
c. Improving economic status	☐	☐	☐	☐	☐
d. To avail consumption credit	☐	☐	☐	☐	☐
e. To get loan waiver	☐	☐	☐	☐	☐
	☐	☐	☐	☐	☐

	PACB	SHG	PARDB	Others	
f. Lesser Interest	☐	☐	☐	☐	☐
g. Nearness	☐	☐	☐	☐	☐
r Bank or Group	☐	☐	☐	☐	☐
i. To invest in business	☐	☐	☐	☐	☐

65. Who persuaded you to get loans from this agency?

CB PACB SHG PARDB Others CB PACB SHG PARDB Others

a. Friends ☐ ☐ ☐ ☐ ☐ e. Bank Employees ☐ ☐ ☐ ☐ ☐
b. Members ☐ ☐ ☐ ☐ ☐ f. NGO ☐ ☐ ☐ ☐ ☐
c. Relatives ☐ ☐ ☐ ☐ ☐ g. Animator of group ☐ ☐ ☐ ☐ ☐
d. Family ☐ ☐ ☐ ☐ ☐ h. Others (Specify) ☐ ☐ ☐ ☐ ☐

66. Which source of credit is easily accessible to you (Rank)

a. Formal ☐ b. Informal ☐ c. Both ☐

67. How was the formal source accessible to you? Yes/No ☐

a. Nearness ☐ b. Membership ☐ c. Friendliness of employee ☐
d. Support from other agencies ☐ e. My relatives/friends working in the bank ☐ f. Social status ☐
g. Economic status ☐

68. List out the advantage in availing loan form formal agencies? ☐

a. Lesser rate of interest - 1 b. Simple formalities - 2
c. Timely availability of loan - 3 d. Loans for different purposes - 4
e. Availing benefits under Govt. Schemes - 5 f. Loans available in kind portion - 6
g. Announcement of waiver during drought - 7 h. Others (Specify) - 8

69. What are the disadvantages with formal loan? ☐

a. Time consuming procedure -1 b. Employees are not friendly - 2
c. Non-availability of loan for consumption -3 d. Non-availability of loan in time - 4
e. Higher Transaction cost -5 f. Others (Specify) - 6

V. UTILISATION OF LOAN OF FORMAL SOURCES

70. What is the extent of utilization of loan amount? ☐

a. Full Utilization- 1 b. Diversion - 2

(If answer is 1, skip to 71) (If answer is 2, skip to 74)

71. What are the reasons for the full utilization of loan? Yes/No

a. Expecting good yield from investment ☐ b. Lesser unexpected expenses ☐
c. Availability of loan in time ☐ d. Proper Supervision ☐
g. Awareness on the consequences of diversion ☐

72. What is the effort made by the organization for the proper utilization of loan?

a. Proper supervision ☐ b. Providing loan in time ☐

c. Providing loan with kind portion ☐ d. Providing adequate loan ☐

(Skip to Repayment)

(If answer is 2)

B. Diversion

74. How much of the loan amount was diverted? Rs. ☐☐☐☐☐☐

75. What are the reasons for diversion?

a. Natural Calamities ☐ b. Higher rate of inputs ☐

c. Unexpected expenses ☐ d. Increase in consumption expenses ☐

e. Delay in getting loans ☐ f. Others (Specify) ☐

76. For what purpose, did you divert the loan? Yes/No

Productive

a. Purchase of milch animals ☐ b. Investment in business ☐

c. Construction of cow sheds ☐ d. Construction of farm houses ☐

e. Digging/Desilting of wells ☐ f. Reclamation of land ☐

g. Repair expenses h. Irrigation arrangements ☐

Unproductive

j. Family expenses ☐ k. Medical expenses ☐

l. Educational expenses ☐ m. Purchase of households, jewels etc., ☐

n. Clearance of old debts ☐ (Specify to whom) o. Others ☐

p. Social Ceremonies ☐

V. REPAYMENTS

77. What is the actual amount repaid ? Rs. ☐☐☐☐☐☐

78. What is the extent of the loan repaid?

a. Fully paid - 1 b. Partially paid - 2 c. Not yet paid - 3

(If answer is 1, skip to 79) (If answer is 2, skip to 83) (If answer is 3, skip to 87)

A. Full Repayment

79. State the reasons for the full repayment of the loan? Yes/No

a. To borrow another loan ☐ b. To maintain credibility ☐

c. Group pressure ☐

80. Who persuaded you to fully repay the loan? Yes/No

a. Friends ☐ b. Relatives ☐ c. Family members ☐

d. Bankers ☐ e. Animator ☐ f. Yourself ☐

81. How did you mobilize money to repay the loan?

a. Income-1 b. New loan-2 ☐

82. If answer is 2, from whom did you borrow?

	Amount in Rs.		Amount in Rs.
a. Moneylenders	☐☐☐☐☐☐☐	c. Friends	☐☐☐☐☐☐☐
b. PACB	☐☐☐☐☐☐☐	d.SHG	☐☐☐☐☐☐☐

B. Partial Repayment

83. State the reasons for the partial repayment of the loan amount? Yes/No

a. Insufficient income ☐ b. Unexpected expenditure ☐

c. Expecting loan waiver ☐ d. Heavy consumption expenses ☐

e. Non-remunerative price for the produce ☐ f. Others (specify) ☐

84. Whether any one motivated you to repay at least partially? Yes/No ☐

If yes, who are they? (put a mark)

a. Friends ☐ d. Family members ☐

b. Relatives ☐ e. One your own accord ☐

c. Bankers ☐

85. How did you mobilize money to partially repay the loan? ☐

a. Income -1 b. New Loan -2

(If answer is 2)

86. From whom did you borrow? ☐

a. Moneylenders - 1 b. Friends - 3 c. Income - 3

Non-Repayment

87. State the reason for not repaying the loan? ☐

a. Flood/drought f. Unexpected expenses

b. Irrigation expenses g. No additional income

c. Expecting loan waiver
d. Heavy consumption expenses
e. Insufficient income
h. No body asked to repay
i. No pressure from bankers/ SHG
j. Farm/business expenses

(If answer is I)

88. Who persuaded you for not repaying the loan? ☐

a. Friends -1 b. Relatives -2 c. Family members -3

d. Political leaders -4 e. Defaulted members -5

89. After getting the loan, how many times the bankers have visited you? ☐

a. One time-1 b. Two times-2 c. Three times - 3 d. Four times- 4

90. While repaying the loan, to which agency will you give preference? ☐

(Please rank on 6 point scale based on relative importance/ Preference)

a. Moneylenders ☐ b. Friends ☐ c. Relatives ☐
d. SHG ☐ e. Others (specify) ☐

91. State the basis for giving such preference? Yes/No

a. Higher interest ☐ d. Availability of next loan ☐

b. Strict supervision ☐ e. Others (specify) ☐

c. Maintaining discipline ☐

92. Do you know the scheme of waiver? Yes/No ☐

93. From whom did you get the announcement of loan waiver? Yes/No

a. TV ☐ b. Radio ☐ c. Newspaper ☐

d. Friends & Relatives ☐ e. Bankers ☐ f. Other members ☐

94. Have you availed benefits under waiving scheme already? Yes/No ☐

95. Do you expect that the Government has to waive your loans? Yes/No ☐

96. If yes, state the reason? Yes/No

a. Drought ☐ b. No employment opportunities ☐

c. Increase in prices ☐ d. Unremunarative price to the produce ☐

e. Higher interest ☐

97. Observation by the Researcher

Index